hellebore

THE ART OF MISSUPACEY

3dtotalPublishing

3dtotalPublishing

Correspondence: **publishing@3dtotal.com**
Website: **store.3dtotal.com**

Every effort has been made to ensure the credits and contact information listed are present and correct. In the case of any errors that have occurred, the publisher respectfully directs readers to **store.3dtotal. com/pages/information** for any updated information and corrections.

Thoughts and opinions expressed in this book belong to the author and not the publisher.

First published in the United Kingdom, 2025, by 3dtotal Publishing.

Address: 3dtotal.com Ltd,
29 Foregate Street, Worcester,
WR1 1DS, United Kingdom.

Hard cover ISBN: 978-1-915992-01-7

Printed and bound in China
by C&C Offset Printing Co., Ltd

Visit **store.3dtotal.com** for a complete list of available book titles.

Editorial Project Manager: Rhiannon Joseph
Lead Editor: Samantha Rigby
Lead Designer: Joseph Cartwright
Studio Manager: Simon Morse
Managing Director: Tom Greenway

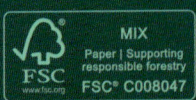

MIX
Paper | Supporting responsible forestry
FSC
www.fsc.org
FSC® C008047

50%
of net profits donated
TO CHARITY

In 2022, 3dtotal Publishing became successful enough to make a pledge to donate **50% of its net profits to charity**. This continues to be possible due to the incredible support from all our customers, employees, and partners. At the time of printing, we have donated over $1.62 million (USD) to charity.

We focus our giving on three charitable areas: **environmental**, **humanitarian**, and **animal welfare**. We use organizations such as Effective Altruism and Founders Pledge to guide who we help within these causes. Some ways of doing good are over 100 times more effective than others, so donating this way hugely increases the impact of our contributions.

See **3dtotal.com/charity**
for full details.

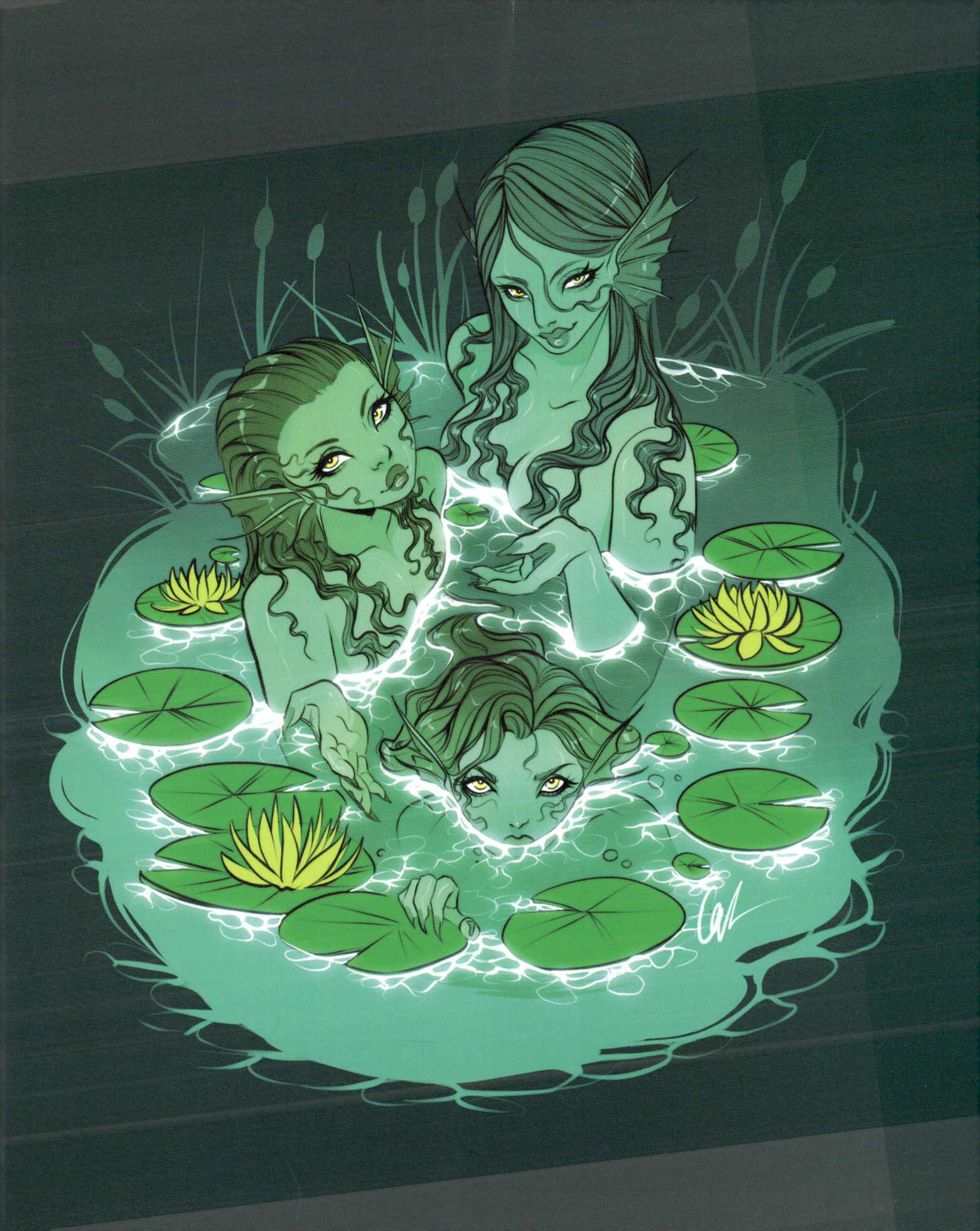

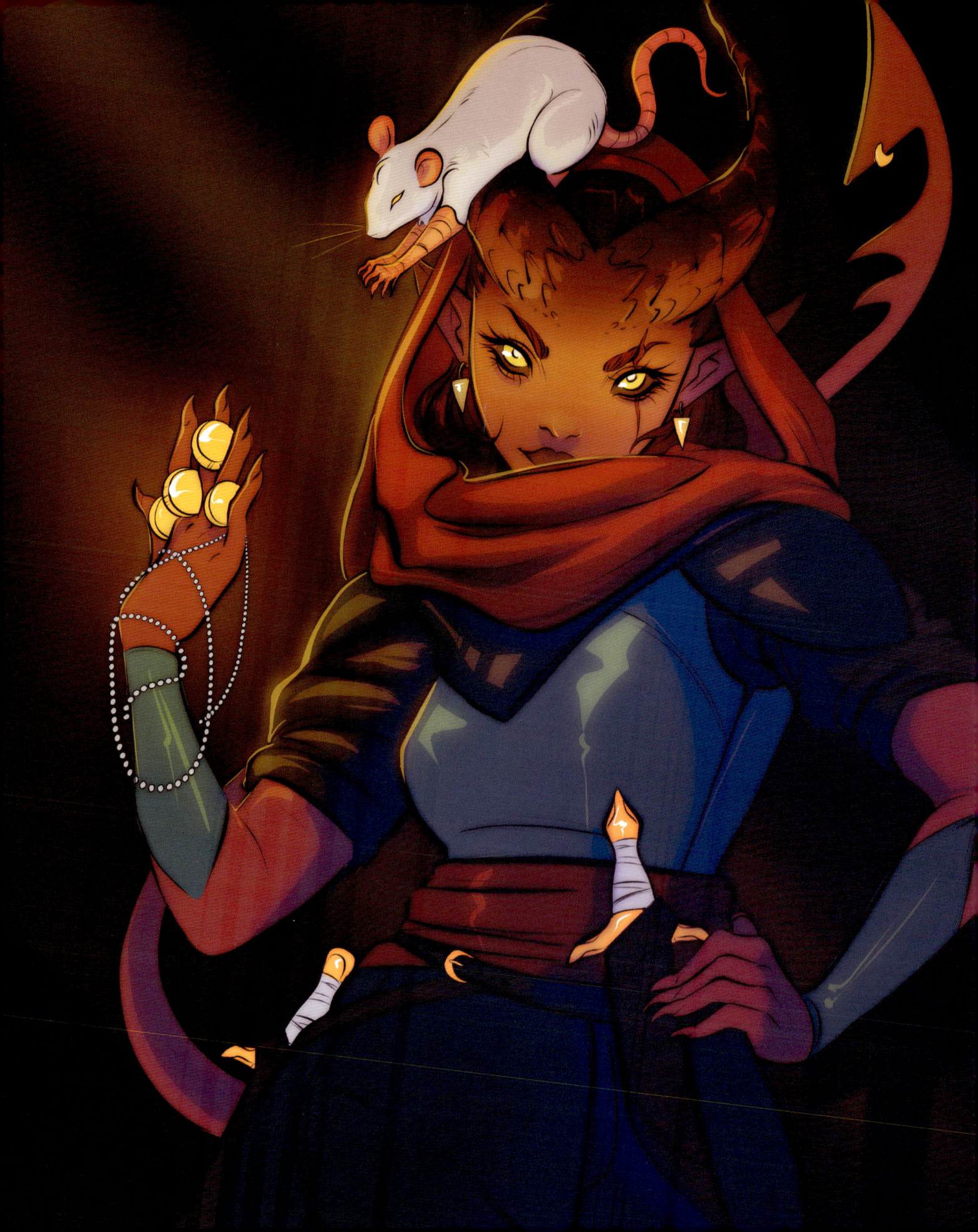

Contents

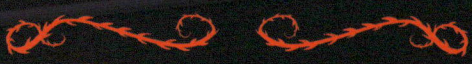

Foreword

I've loved and followed Missupacey's work for the past several years on Instagram, admiring her beautiful line work and unmatched work ethic from afar. In a serendipitous coincidence, we were seated next to each other at the New York Comic Con Artist Alley in 2023, where I met her for the first time (and finally learned how to pronounce her artist's name correctly: miss-you-pay-see). I was delighted to discover that she had been following my work for many years as well. I didn't know it at the time, but that was the start of our wonderful friendship.

Not long after NYCC, I was excited to travel all the way from Toronto to Pasadena for LightBox Expo, one of my favourite art conventions. Only a week before the trip, my accommodation plans suddenly collapsed and I was left panic-stricken since, at that point, all the hotels were already booked up and I didn't know anybody in the area. To my shock and delight, Missupacey happened to live nearby and was also attending LightBox – she graciously offered to host me for that trip. Having only met about a month prior, it was such an unexpected act of kindness and generosity! And what a coincidence as well. Missupacey is truly one of the sweetest and most caring people I have ever met. We had such an amazing time getting to know each other that weekend.

During our many conversations, I got to learn a lot about Missupacey's behind-the-scenes secrets and how she goes about running her art business, and even watched her work, too. Her art has such a stylish and elegant quality, and as a big fan of line work myself, it's an absolute pleasure to look at all the wonderful shapes she creates. I love Missupacey's limited colour palettes and explorations of monster girls and the macabre mixed with a touch of a dreamy, coquette pin-up aesthetic – subject matter that has always appealed to me. I love how fun and effortless she makes her work look. It always inspires me to want to make my own sticker designs and just draw more often for the pleasure of it, without overthinking. That being said, though it seems like Missupacey truly has fun while making her wonderful artwork, she is incredibly hard-working. I could definitely channel her drive for my own art endeavours.

As an artist of multiple mediums, I'm often torn about what kind of artwork I want to create. I've chosen to dedicate myself to an original comic-series project called *Gloamingvale*, but I often wish I could double my time and also make the kind of artwork Missupacey does. I've always loved turning my art into products and have a special place in my heart for stylish pin-ups with sharp digital lines and textures – quite different from what I typically end up drawing. Looking at Missupacey's work always inspires me to rekindle that aspect of my artwork.

Several years ago, I was thinking about making a self-published art book and using Kickstarter as the platform to launch the project. I was super nervous because it had been so many years since I'd done a Kickstarter campaign, and with changes to the platform, I didn't really know where to start. Coincidentally, Missupacey was running a campaign for one of her books at that time, and seeing her immense success really inspired me and gave me the motivation to go through with my own.

Missupacey's unique art style has grown and evolved over the years, and I can't wait to see where it goes in the future! It's always a pleasure to see what fun concepts, poses, shapes, and colour schemes she comes up with.

Hellebore is a vault of inspiration that will be an excellent resource for any art-book enthusiast or aspiring artist. Getting to learn the business side of art from such a prolific and successful creator is incredibly valuable, not to mention all the secrets behind her process. Missupacey's artwork is so energetic and full of vitality; I just know I will look at this book frequently for a zap of inspiration and motivation. And I'm sure you will too!

Cosmic Spectrum

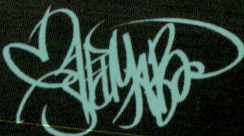

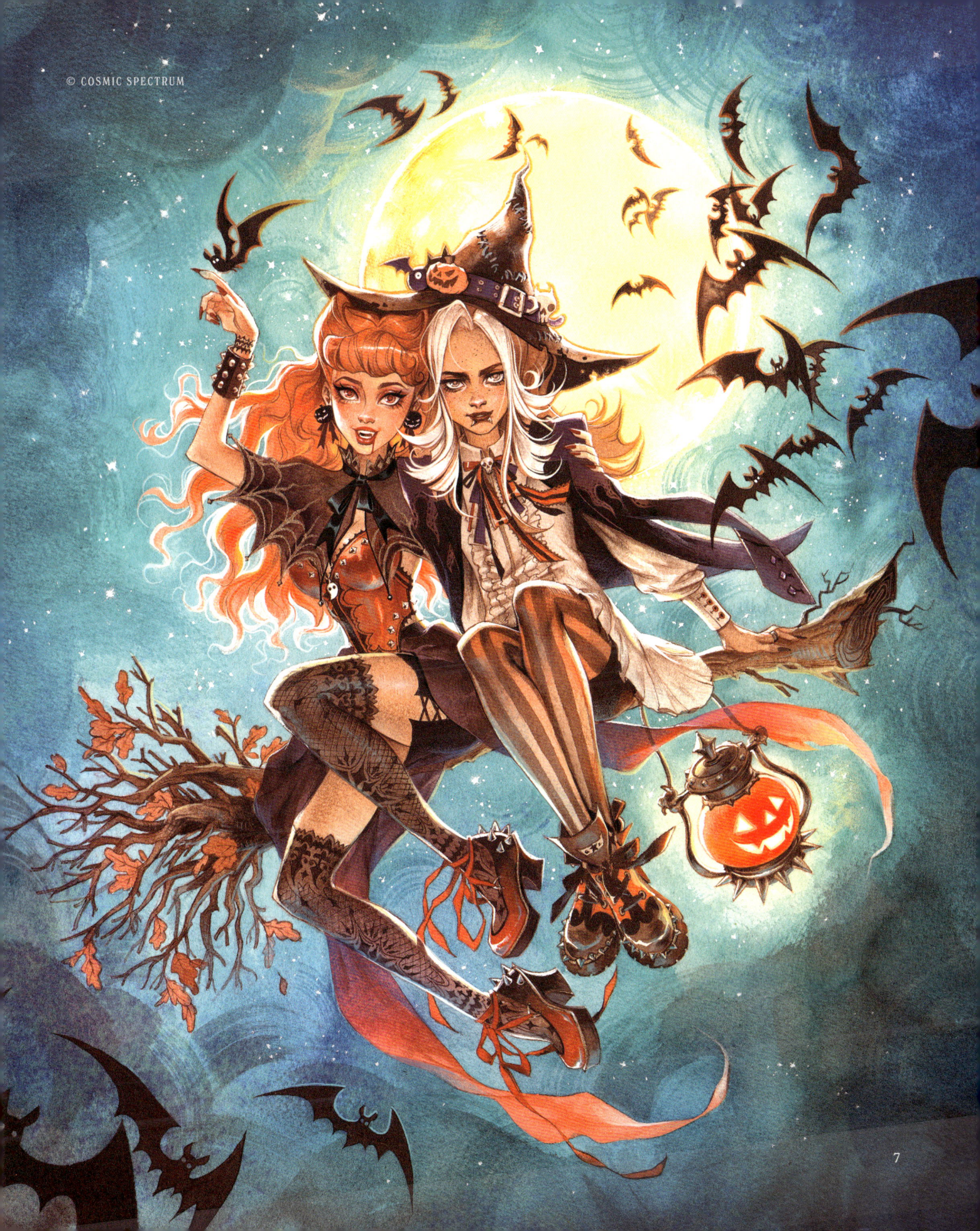

hellebore:
[hel-uh-bawr,-bohr]

noun
1. A poisonous flower that blooms at the very
   end of winter, right before spring. Though
   poisonous, it was used throughout history to
   treat various ailments such as madness, and
   was oftentimes associated with witchcraft.

My previous, self-published art book was named *Nightshade* to represent something dark yet beautiful. For *Hellebore*, I thought it would be fitting to continue that trend. This is the first time I am putting all my history down in one place. As such, this book symbolizes new beginnings. A fresh start. The shedding of winter into spring.

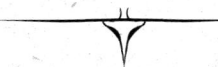

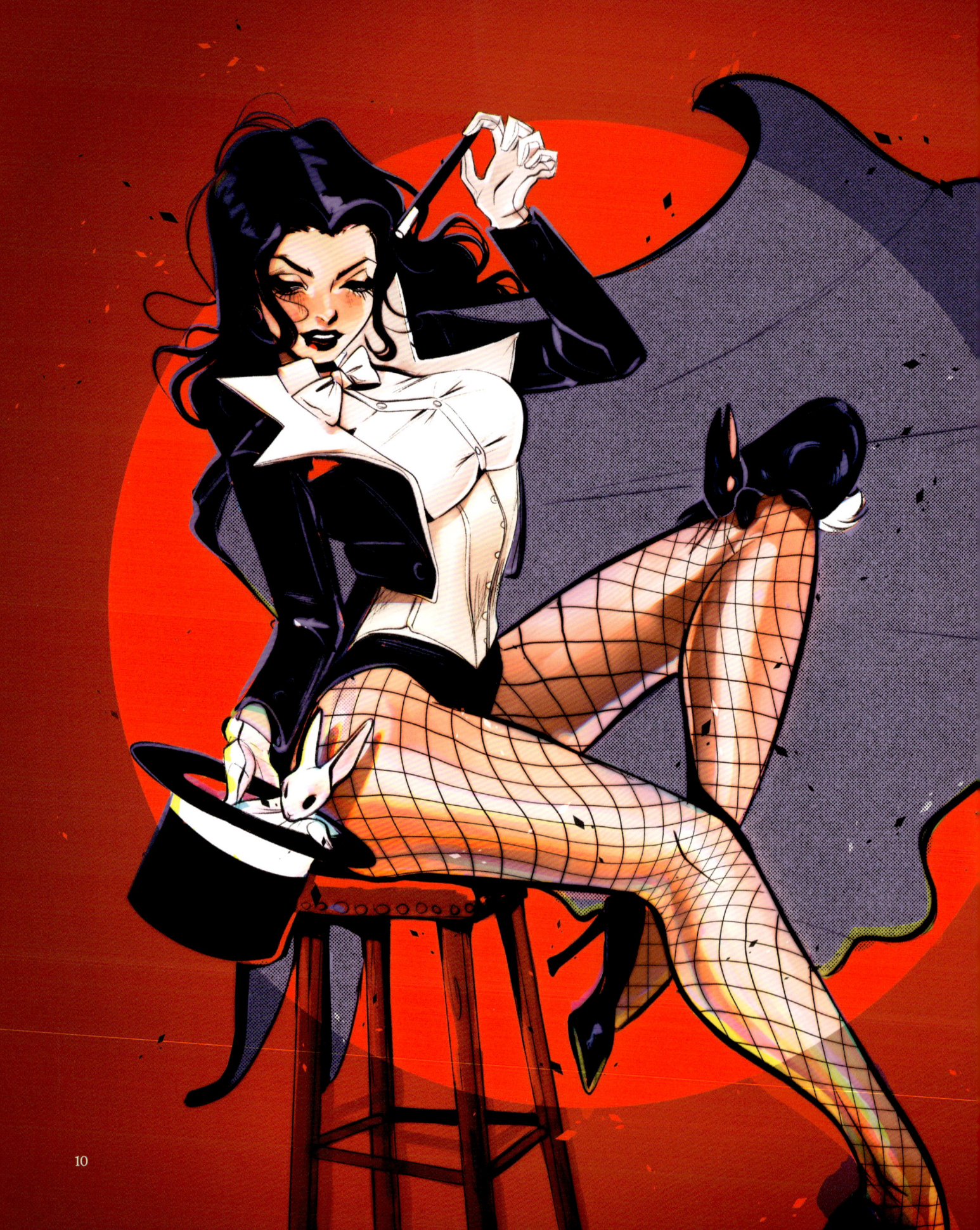

Introduction

It's crazy to think I'm writing an introduction for my first professionally published art book. I remember sitting in my college library, looking at all the amazing art books around me, hoping to one day be on those same shelves, and here I am. Most of the books that I self-published didn't go into too much detail about me as an artist. They were just collections of my art, little galleries you could hold in your hands. Honestly, I made those books for me, just so I could have all the pieces I created together in one place. *Hellebore* is different. It's my story through my own eyes, finally put down on paper. It's more than just a little gallery; it's a look into my art process, my sketch work, and more importantly, who I am as an artist. Essentially, this book is an extension of me.

Being an artist is one of the most important things about me. I've been one since I could pick up a pencil. It's been the thing that has kept me sane during the worst parts of my life, and the thing that has brought me joy in the best times. I need to draw, I need to create, just like everyone needs air to breathe and food to eat. I have always been that way. I guess it's just how I was born.

What I've drawn and how I've created art has changed plenty over the years, but it's something that I could never give up. I'm blessed to have a family who has always supported my passion. I've never had to convince or prove anything to anyone in my inner circles, which fostered a safe place for me to grow early on. Of course, I never thought that I would make art my profession – I never wanted my art to put food on the table. That wasn't my goal. However, once I started sharing my art, others started connecting to it. Instead of it being something just for me, it turned into something more: it became my purpose. It brought me so much joy to see others loving and supporting my art. I also loved turning other people's ideas into illustrations and seeing their excitement when it was brought to life. Now, my art truly is my whole world and I'm extremely grateful for that.

So, what I really want to say with this little introduction is thank you. Thank you to all those who have supported me in the past, who support me in the present, and who will continue to support me in the future. It means the world to me for you to connect with my art so much that you've picked up this book. I hope it brings you joy and inspiration. And I hope you're able to find what I found in art – a reason for being.

Creative journey

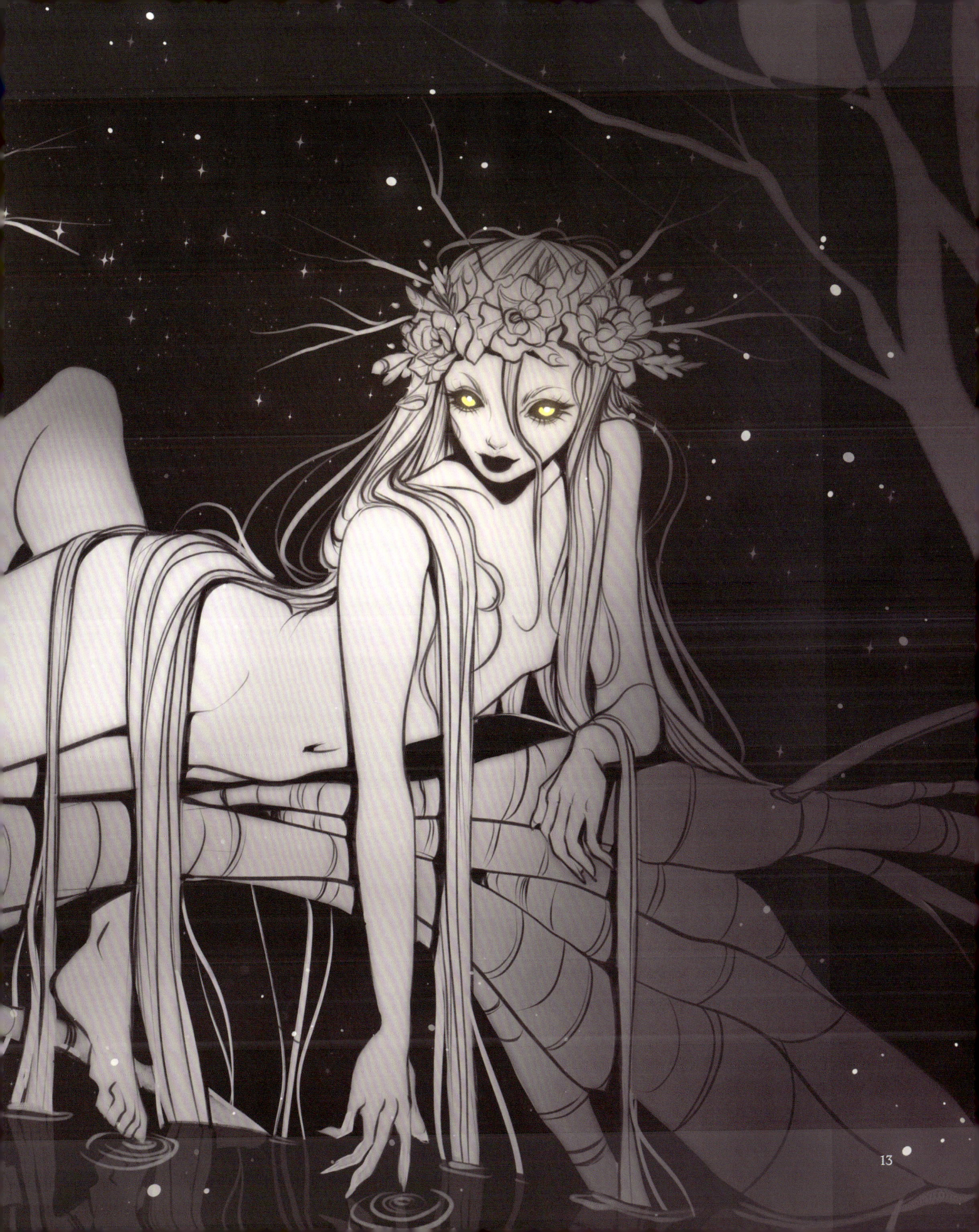

The beginning

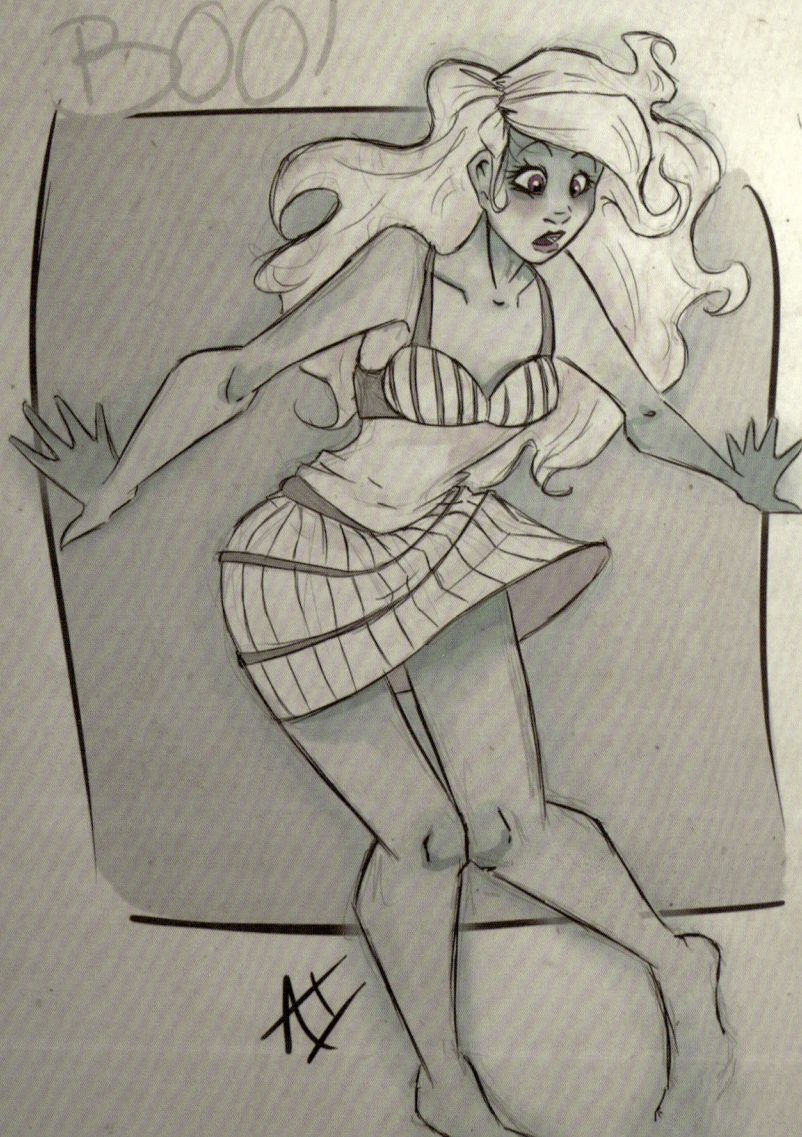

I grew up in a small town on the western side of Colorado called Grand Junction. It was just me, my parents, and my grandparents living together in a little farmhouse with all our animals. We had dogs, cats, chickens, and even horses.

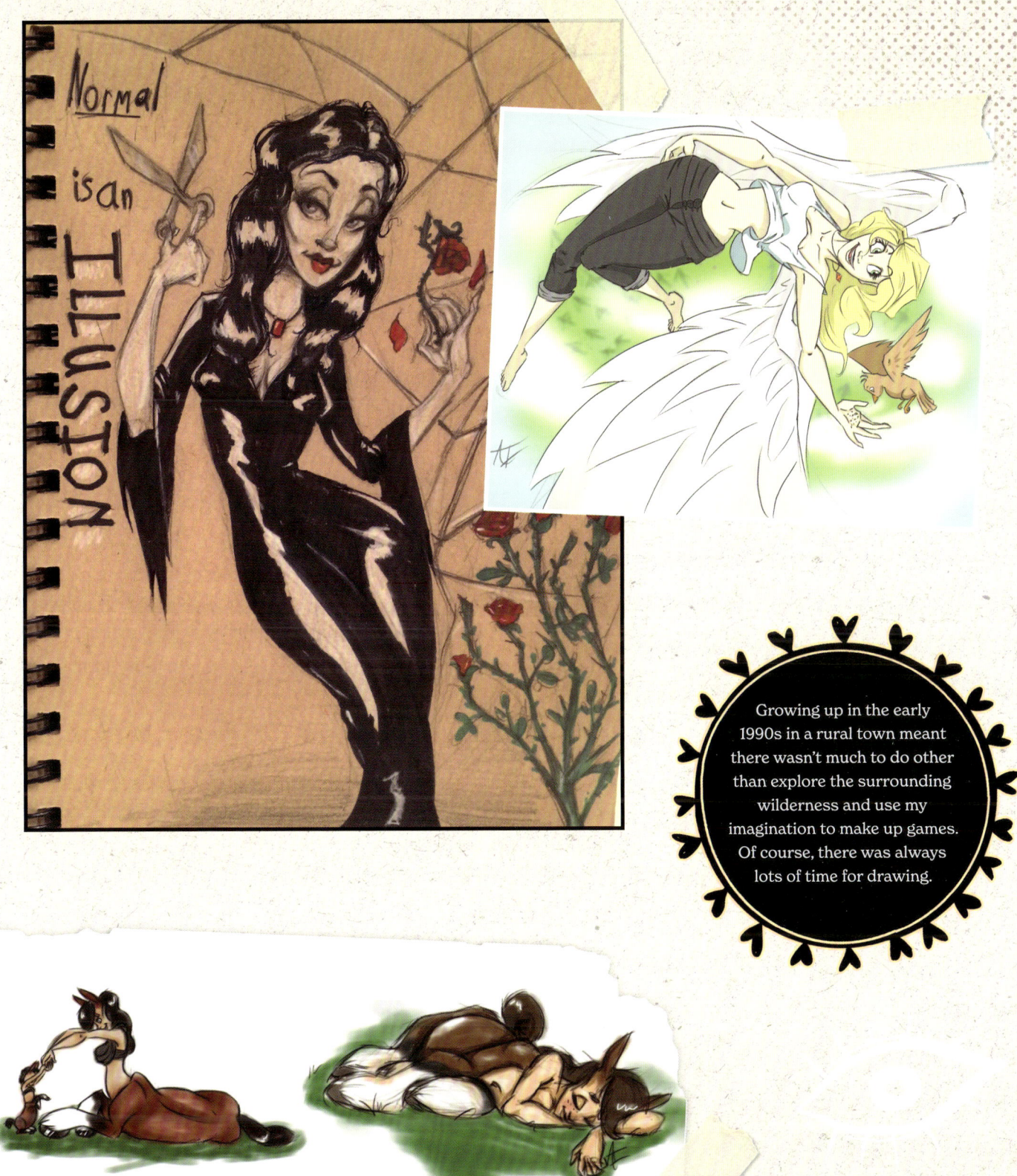

Normal is an ILLUSION

Growing up in the early 1990s in a rural town meant there wasn't much to do other than explore the surrounding wilderness and use my imagination to make up games. Of course, there was always lots of time for drawing.

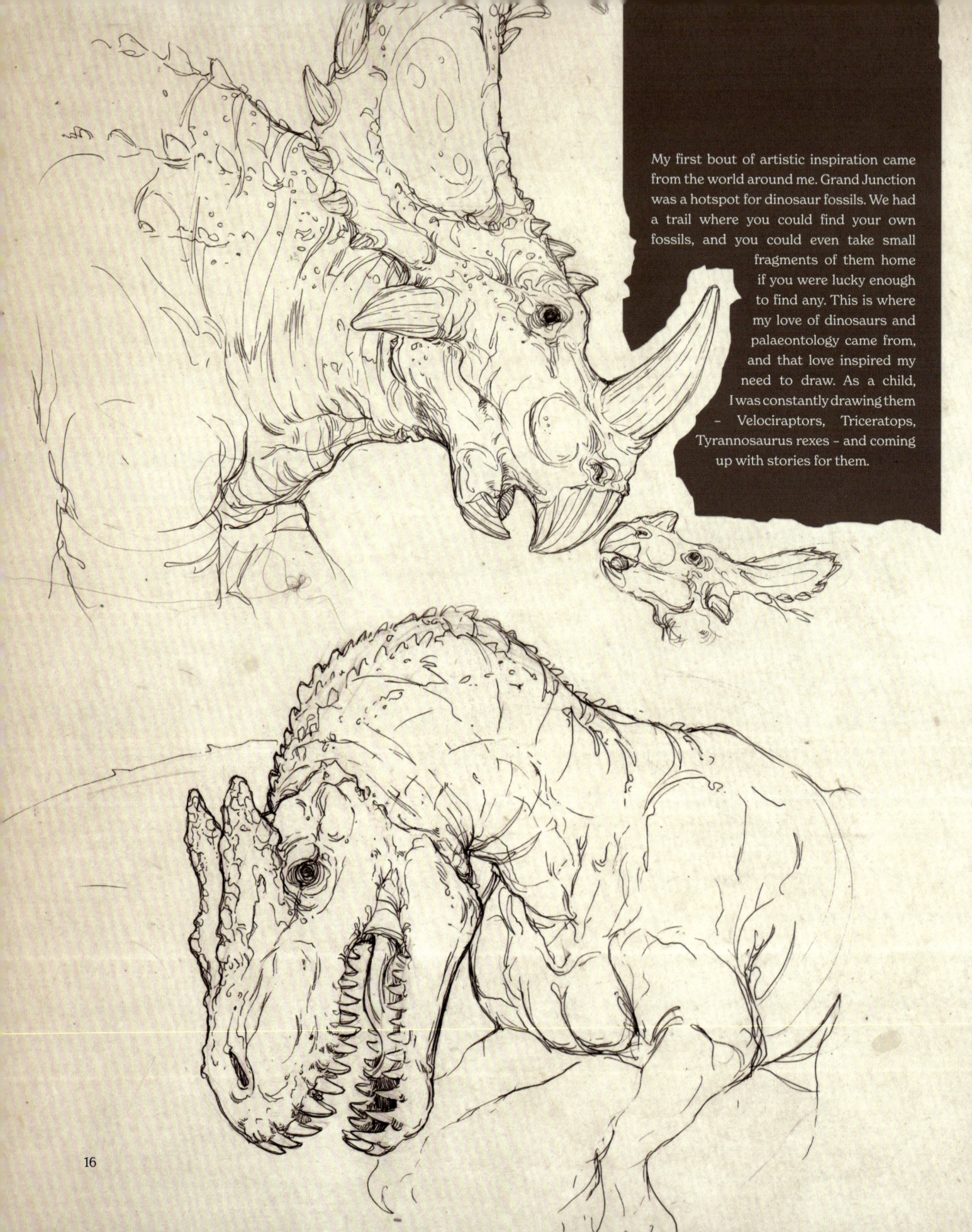

My first bout of artistic inspiration came from the world around me. Grand Junction was a hotspot for dinosaur fossils. We had a trail where you could find your own fossils, and you could even take small fragments of them home if you were lucky enough to find any. This is where my love of dinosaurs and palaeontology came from, and that love inspired my need to draw. As a child, I was constantly drawing them – Velociraptors, Triceratops, Tyrannosaurus rexes – and coming up with stories for them.

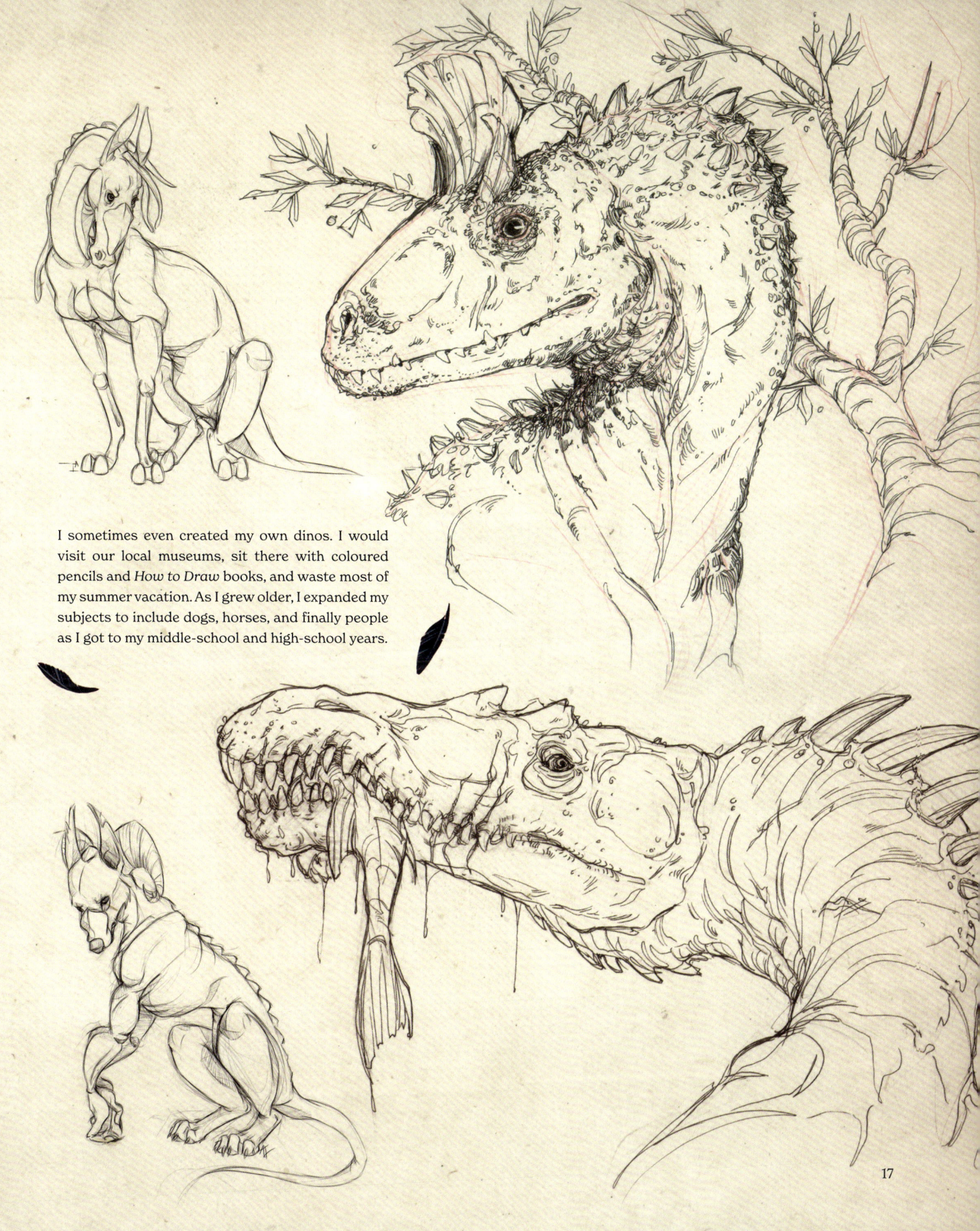

I sometimes even created my own dinos. I would visit our local museums, sit there with coloured pencils and *How to Draw* books, and waste most of my summer vacation. As I grew older, I expanded my subjects to include dogs, horses, and finally people as I got to my middle-school and high-school years.

17

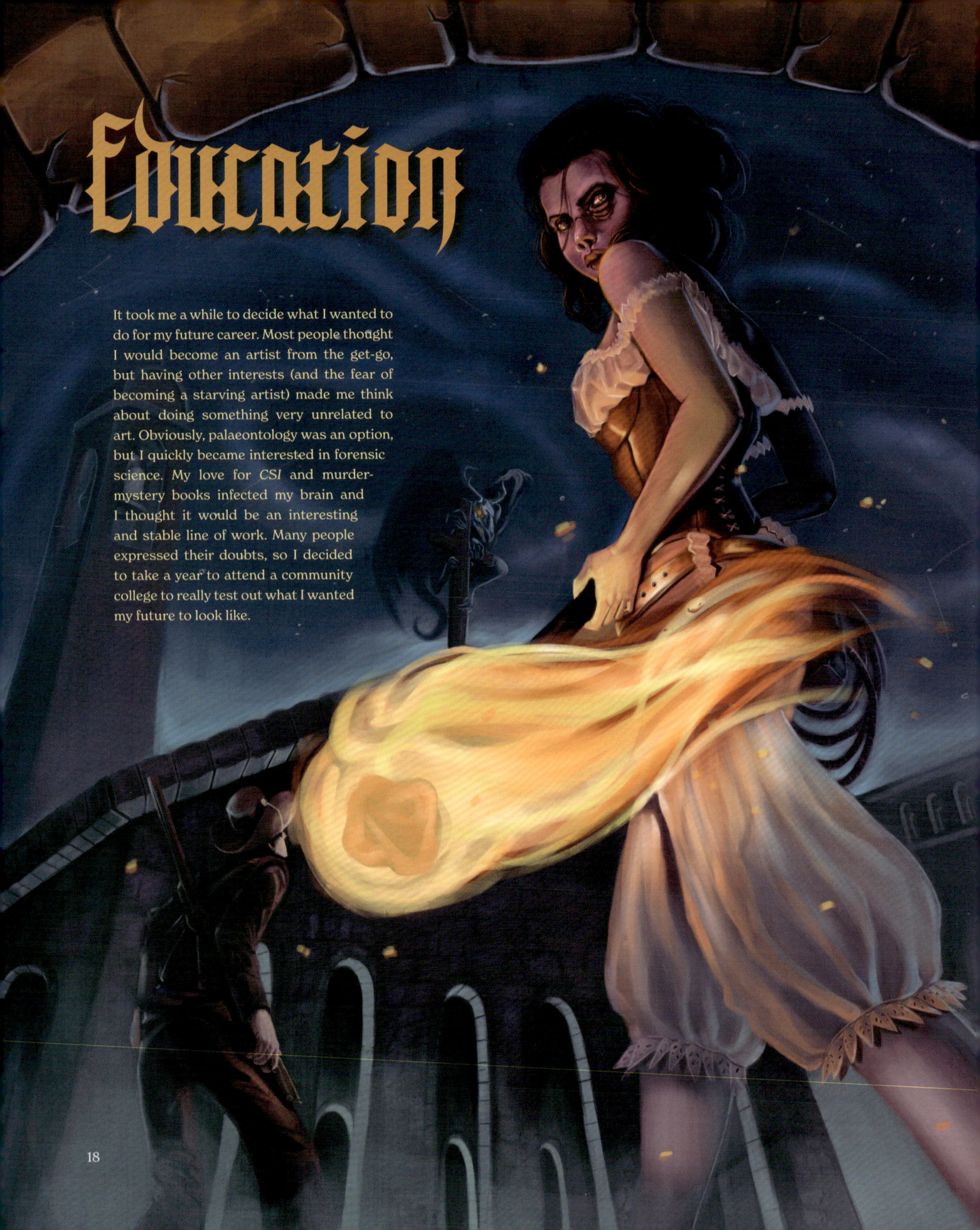

Education

It took me a while to decide what I wanted to do for my future career. Most people thought I would become an artist from the get-go, but having other interests (and the fear of becoming a starving artist) made me think about doing something very unrelated to art. Obviously, palaeontology was an option, but I quickly became interested in forensic science. My love for *CSI* and murder-mystery books infected my brain and I thought it would be an interesting and stable line of work. Many people expressed their doubts, so I decided to take a year to attend a community college to really test out what I wanted my future to look like.

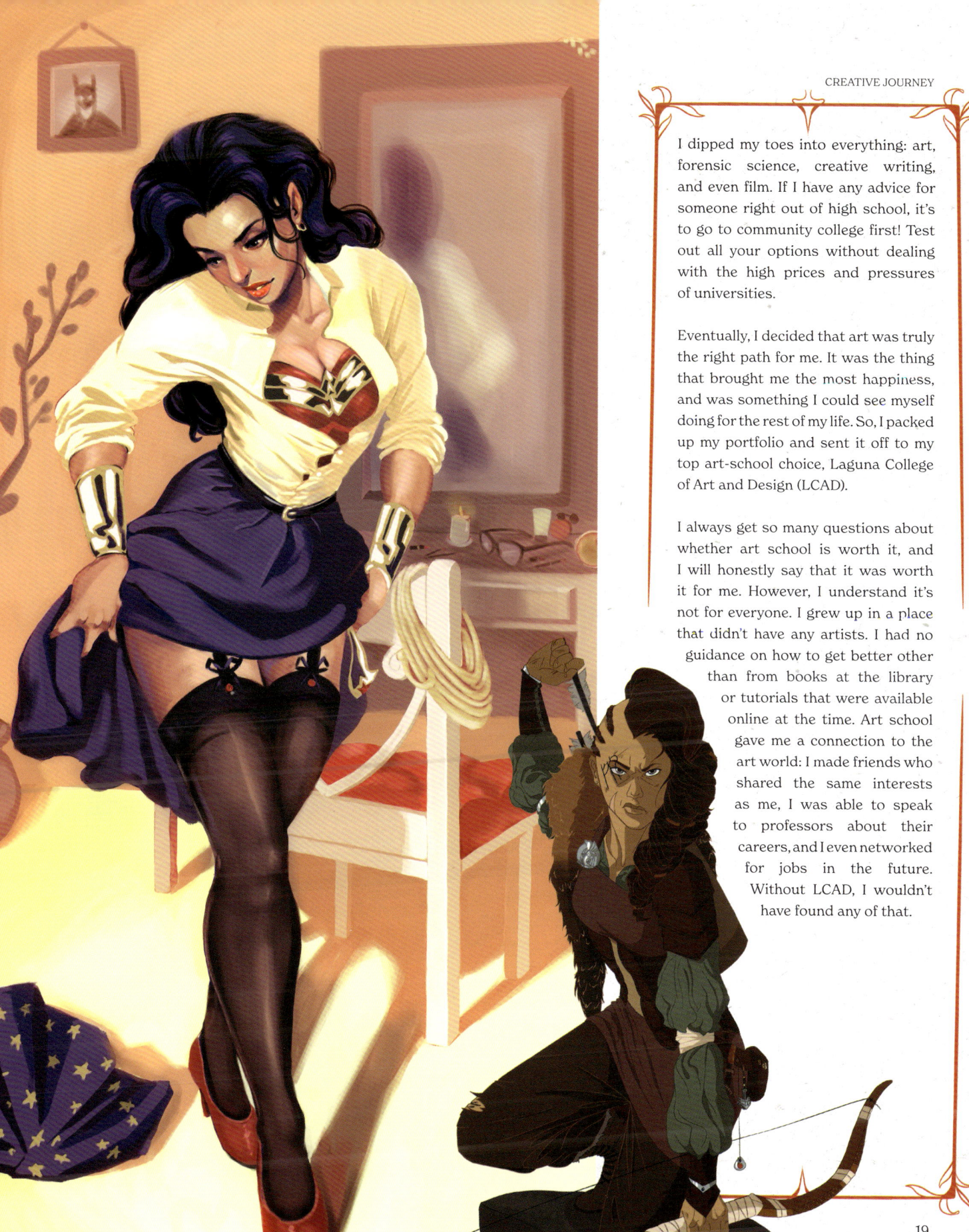

I dipped my toes into everything: art, forensic science, creative writing, and even film. If I have any advice for someone right out of high school, it's to go to community college first! Test out all your options without dealing with the high prices and pressures of universities.

Eventually, I decided that art was truly the right path for me. It was the thing that brought me the most happiness, and was something I could see myself doing for the rest of my life. So, I packed up my portfolio and sent it off to my top art-school choice, Laguna College of Art and Design (LCAD).

I always get so many questions about whether art school is worth it, and I will honestly say that it was worth it for me. However, I understand it's not for everyone. I grew up in a place that didn't have any artists. I had no guidance on how to get better other than from books at the library or tutorials that were available online at the time. Art school gave me a connection to the art world: I made friends who shared the same interests as me, I was able to speak to professors about their careers, and I even networked for jobs in the future. Without LCAD, I wouldn't have found any of that.

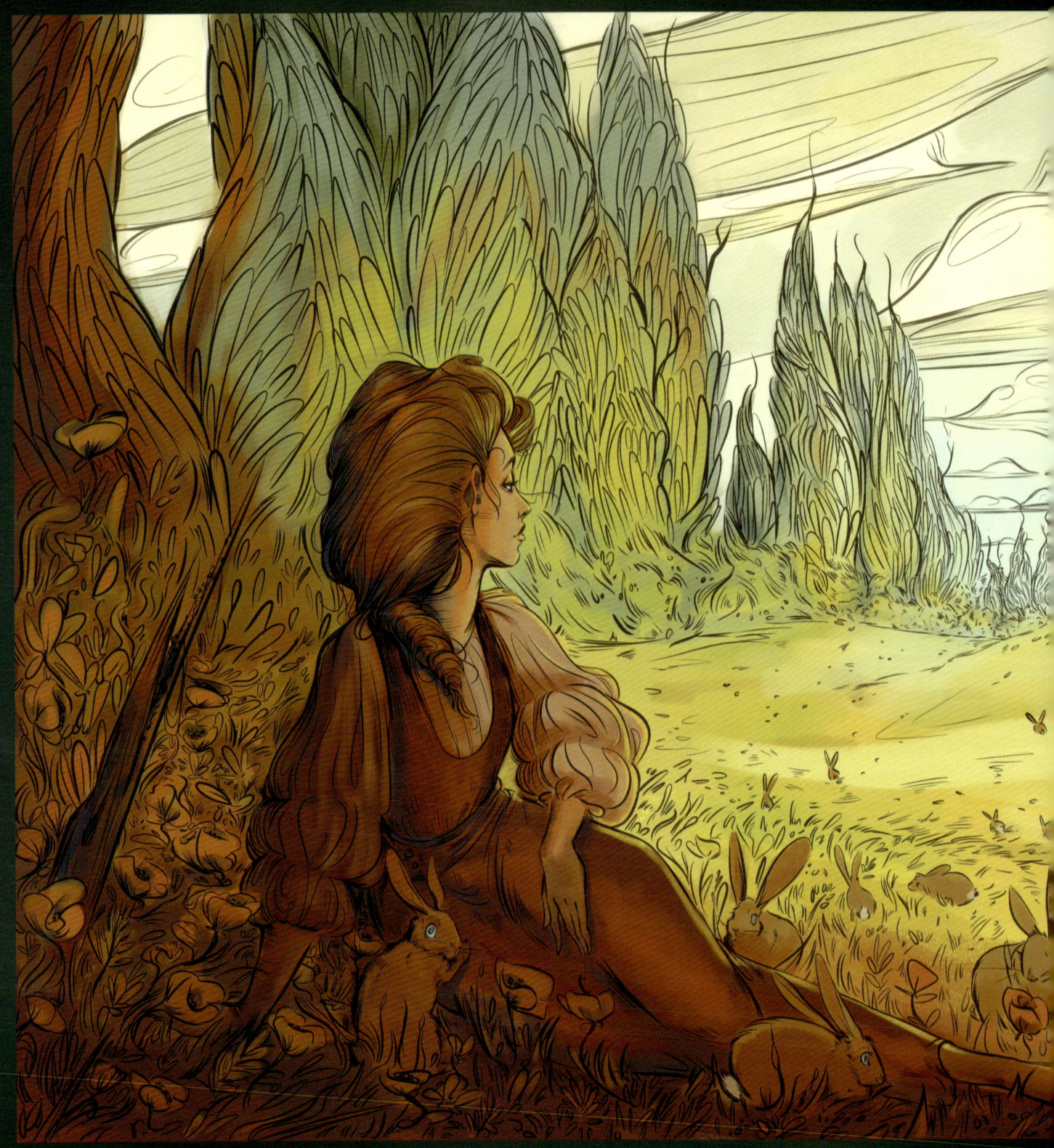

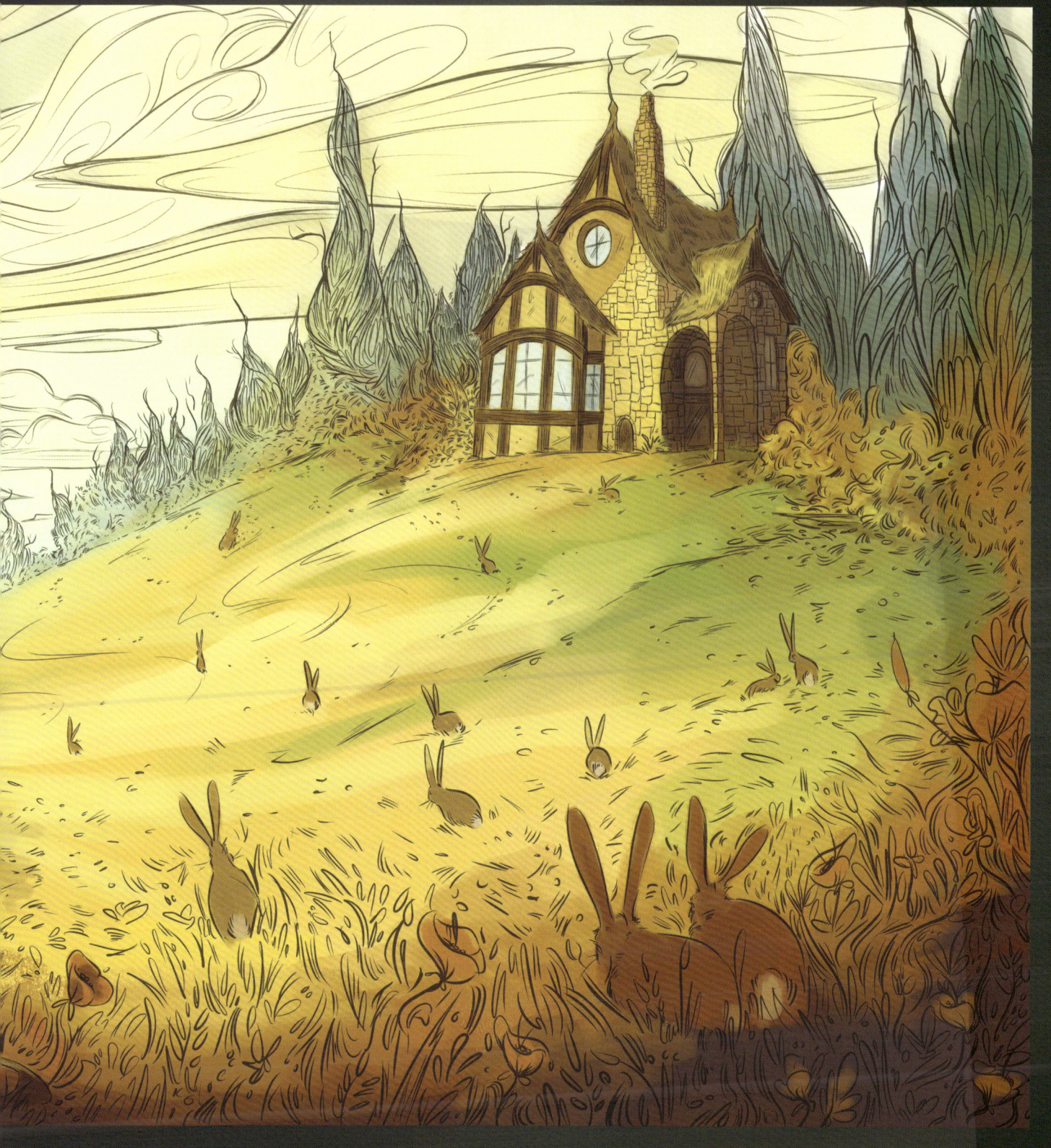

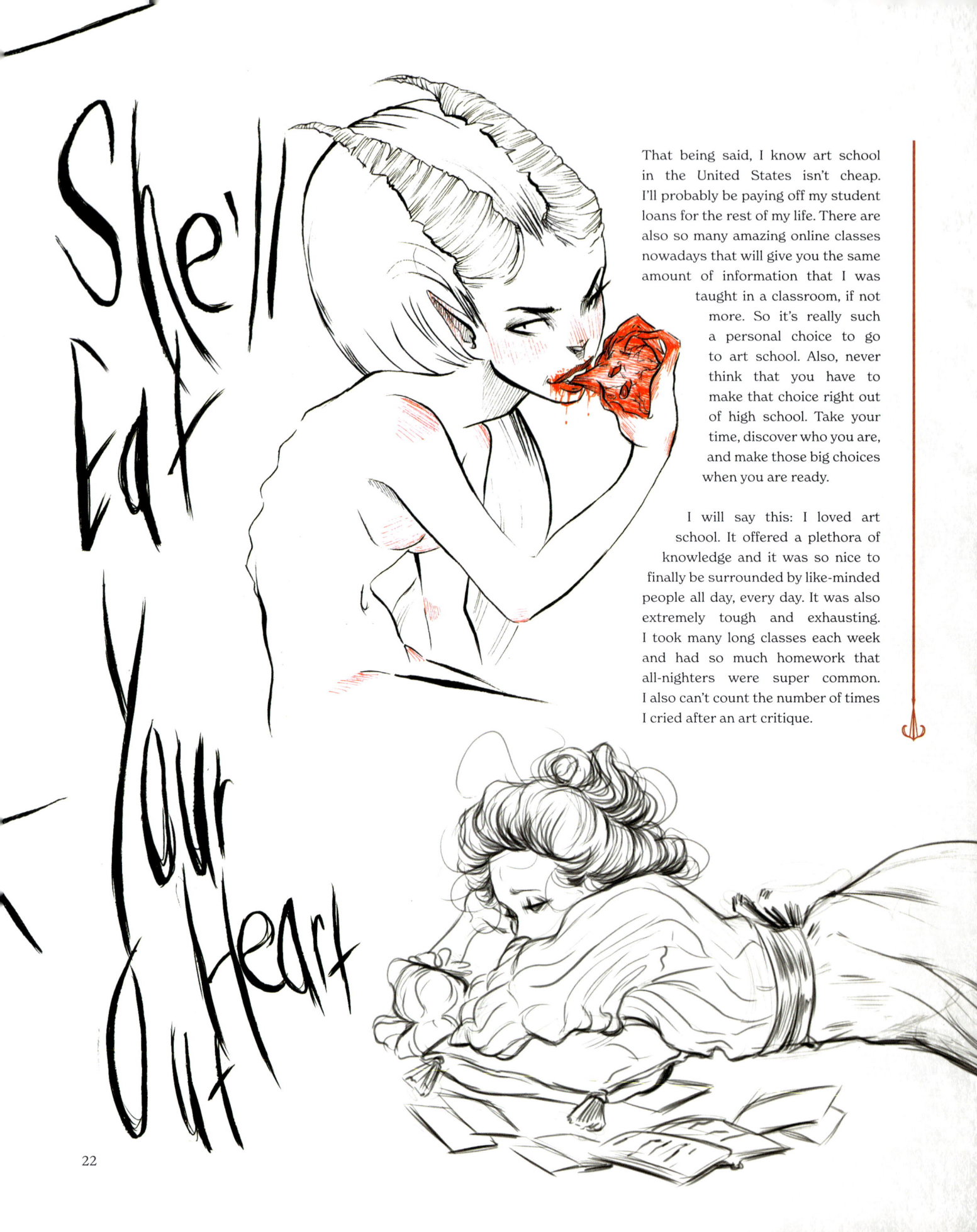

She'll Eat Your Heart Out

That being said, I know art school in the United States isn't cheap. I'll probably be paying off my student loans for the rest of my life. There are also so many amazing online classes nowadays that will give you the same amount of information that I was taught in a classroom, if not more. So it's really such a personal choice to go to art school. Also, never think that you have to make that choice right out of high school. Take your time, discover who you are, and make those big choices when you are ready.

I will say this: I loved art school. It offered a plethora of knowledge and it was so nice to finally be surrounded by like-minded people all day, every day. It was also extremely tough and exhausting. I took many long classes each week and had so much homework that all-nighters were super common. I also can't count the number of times I cried after an art critique.

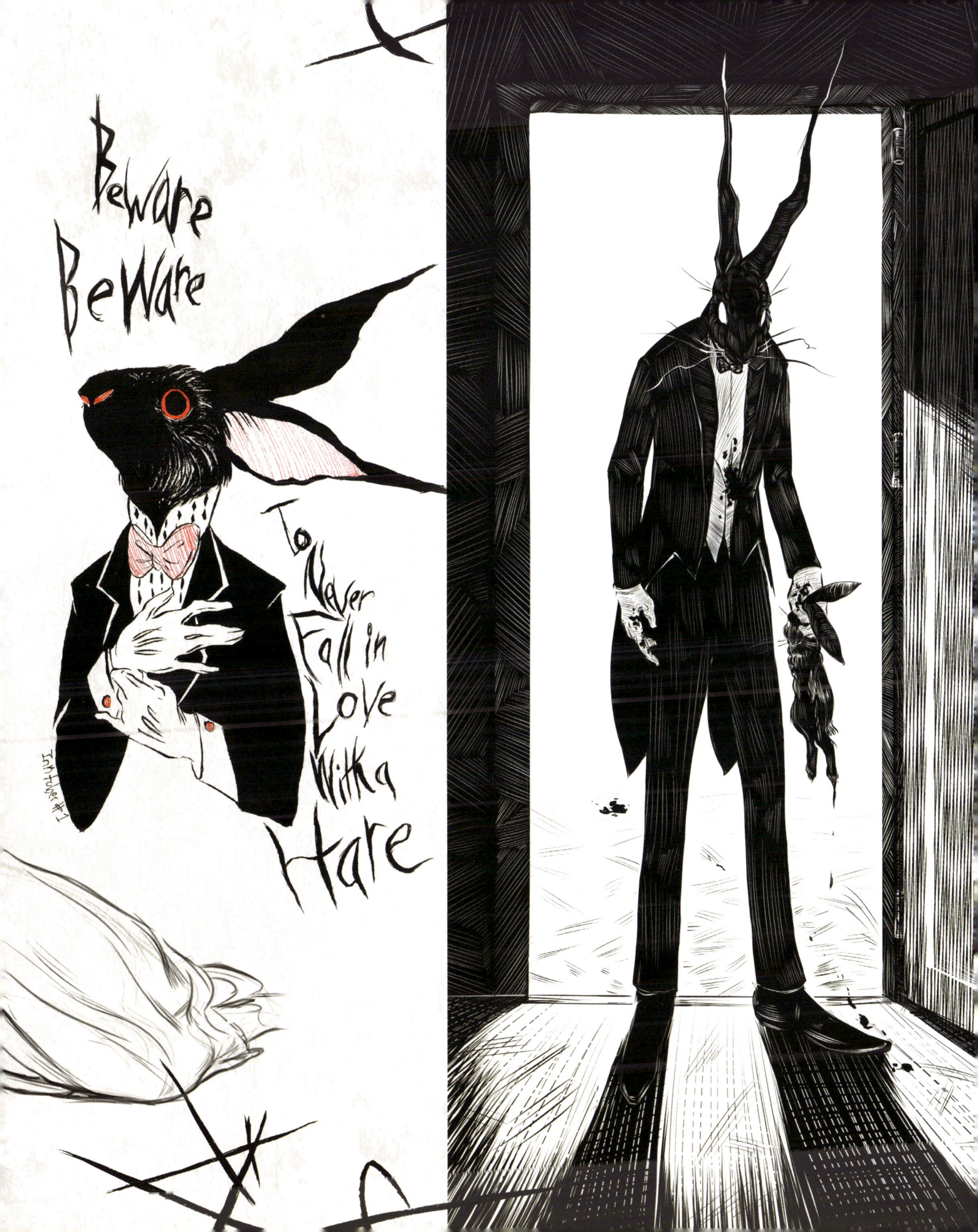

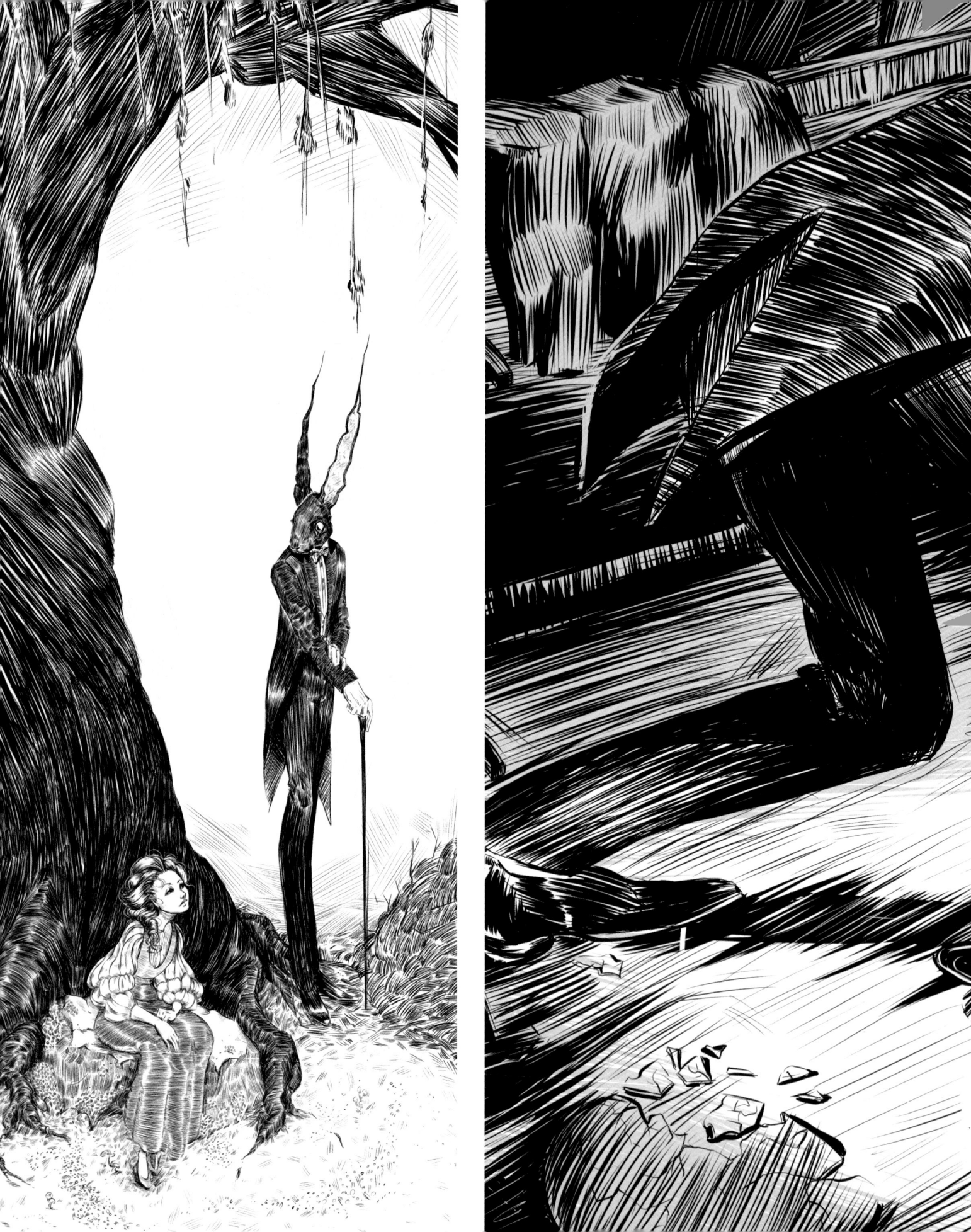

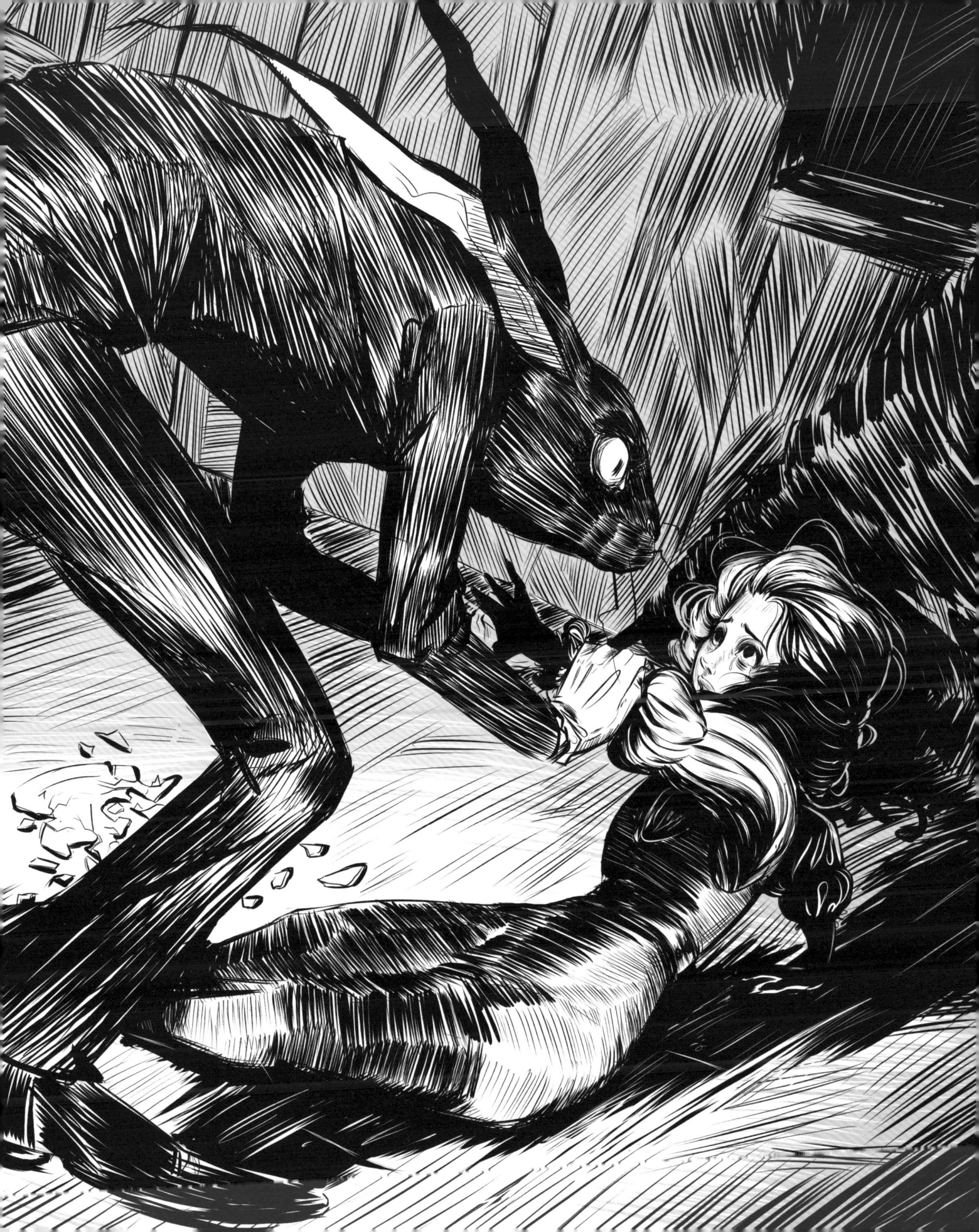

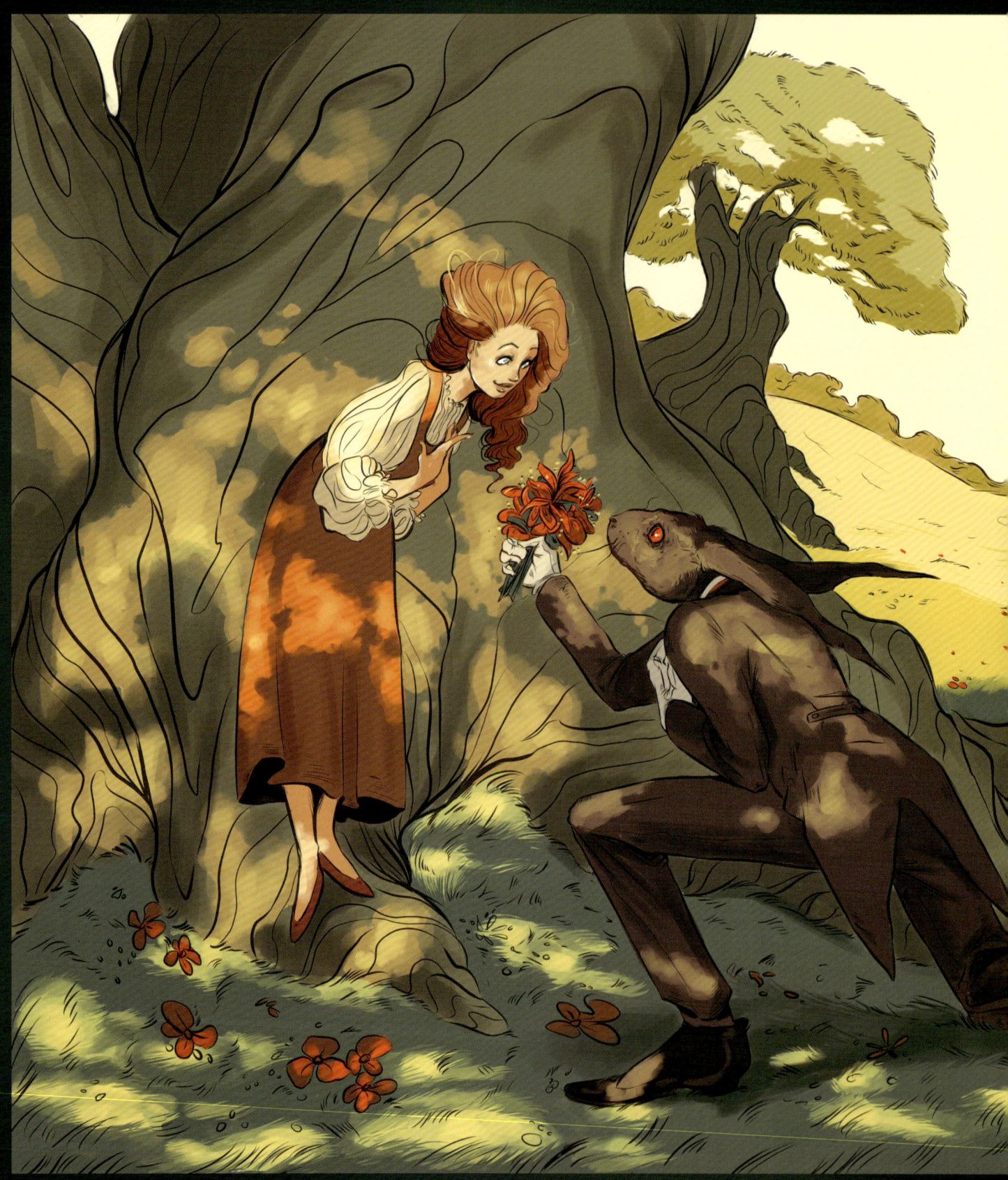

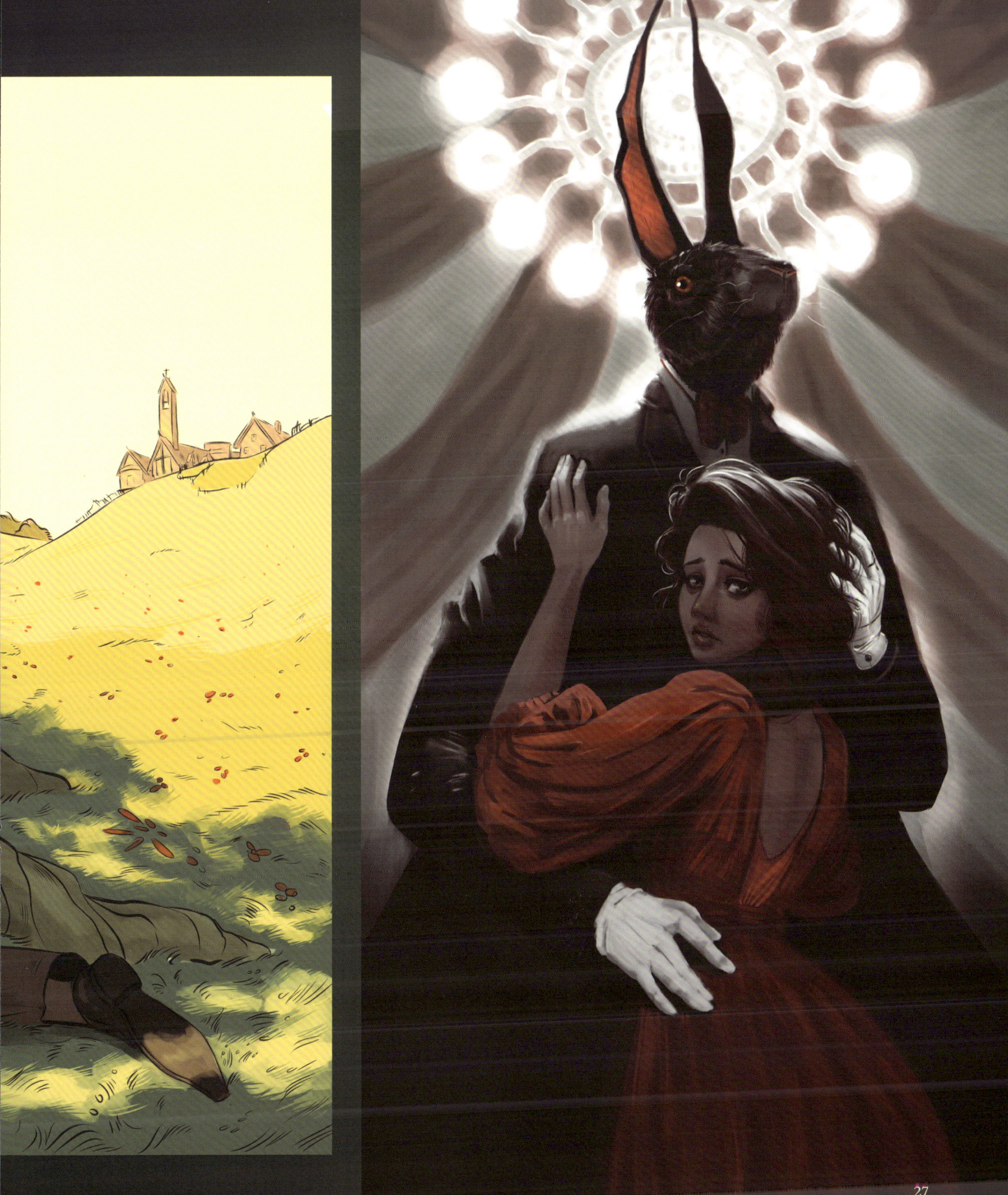

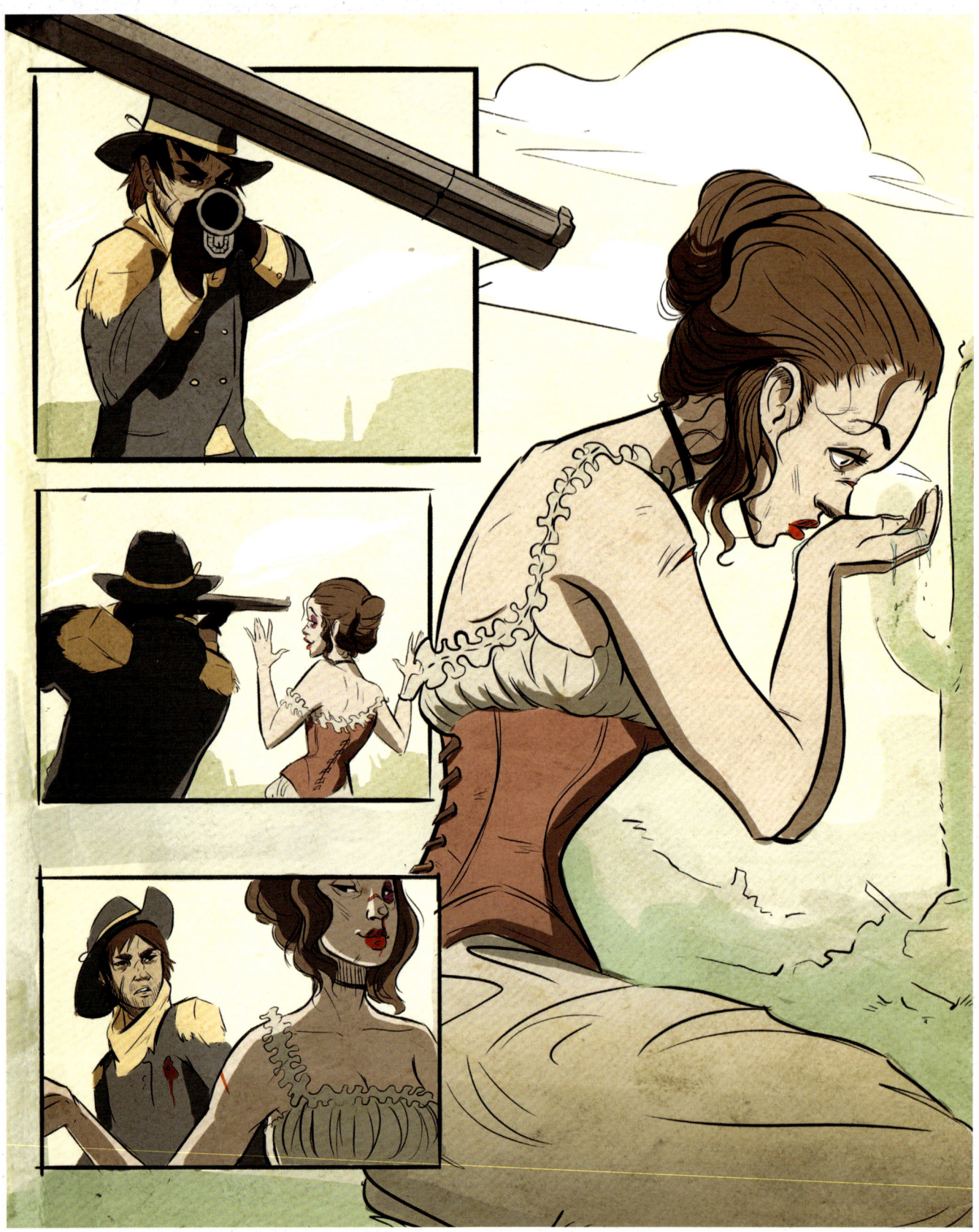

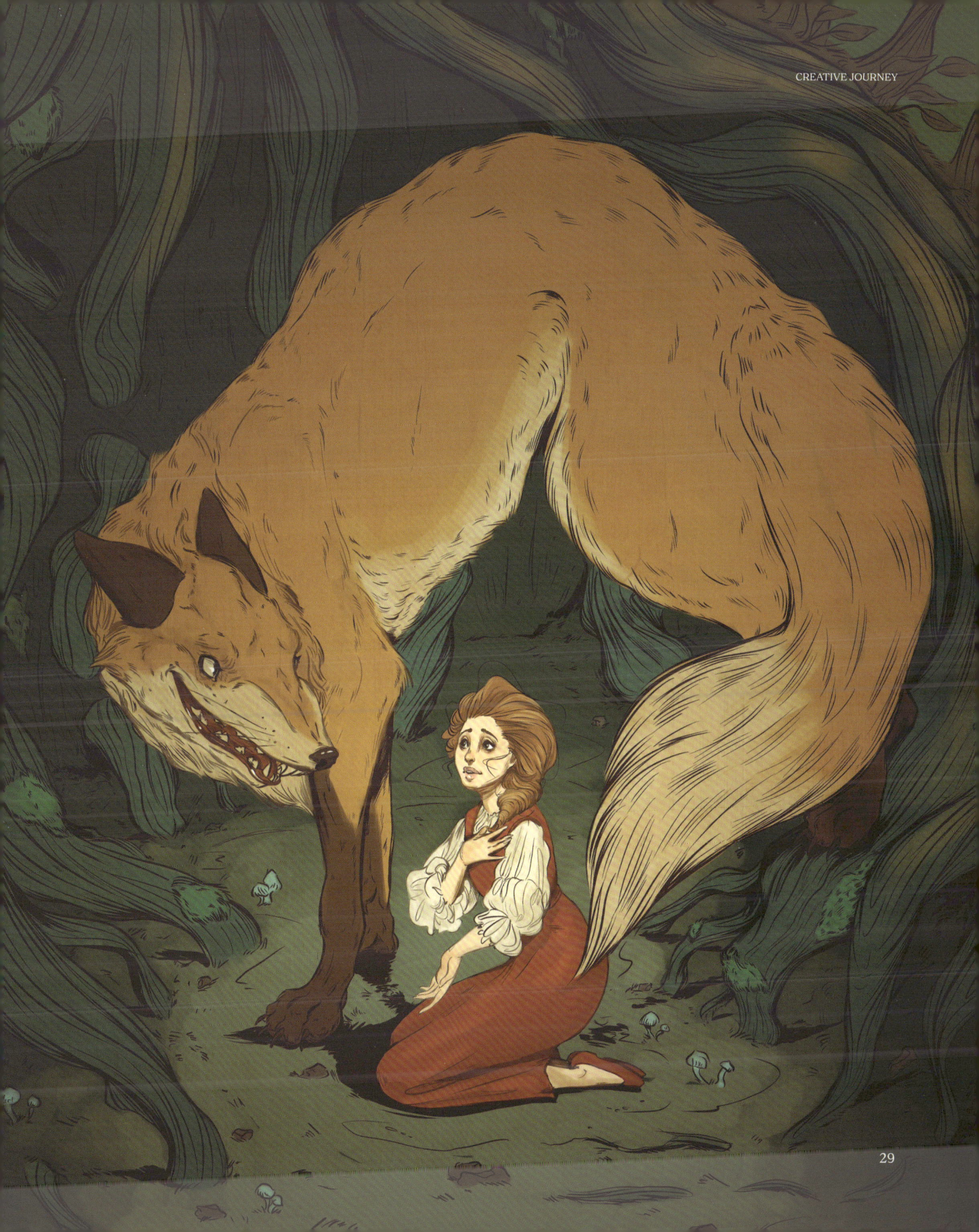

Unconventional career path

When I applied for LCAD, I wanted to pursue animation. However, when the school looked over my portfolio, they told me that I would work better as an illustrator and granted me a bigger scholarship to go into that major. So, of course, I was all for it, and I eventually learned that they had been right. I didn't really want to be an animator. It's just that illustration jobs are not easy to come by, and they typically involve so many different skills and requirements.

While I was planning my portfolio to send to big companies, I began posting my art on Instagram. I mostly posted sketches, **but** I also participated in this new drawing challenge at the time called Inktober. The goal was to create ink drawings every day for thirty days. I never made it through to the end of the challenge, but boy did I draw as much as I could to keep up with it! From there, my following really took off. It was just a matter of being in the right place at the right time. Instagram was amazing back then – you could get so many views and followers from a single post.

By the time I graduated from LCAD, I had about 100,000 followers on Instagram, which was enough for me to start my own online shop. In my tiny shared apartment with three other roommates, I made stickers and small prints to sell.

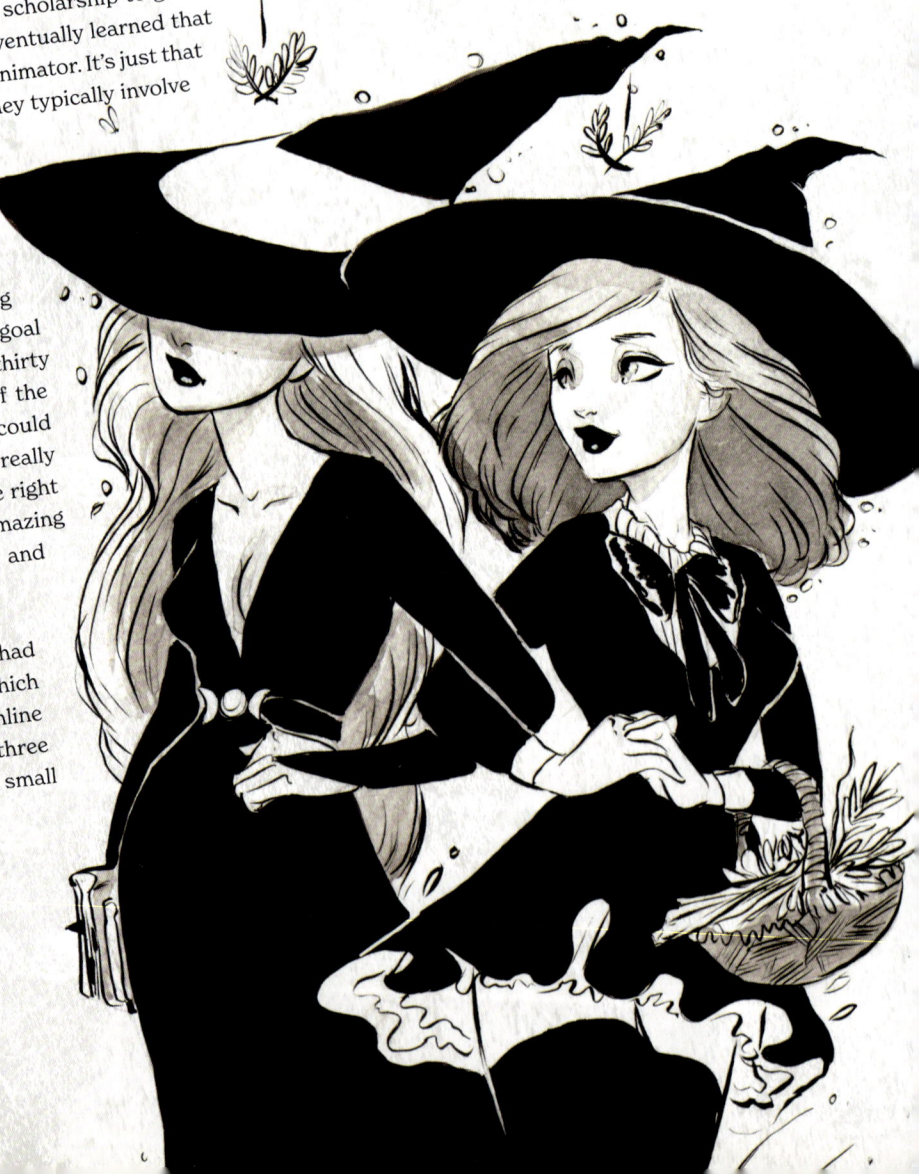

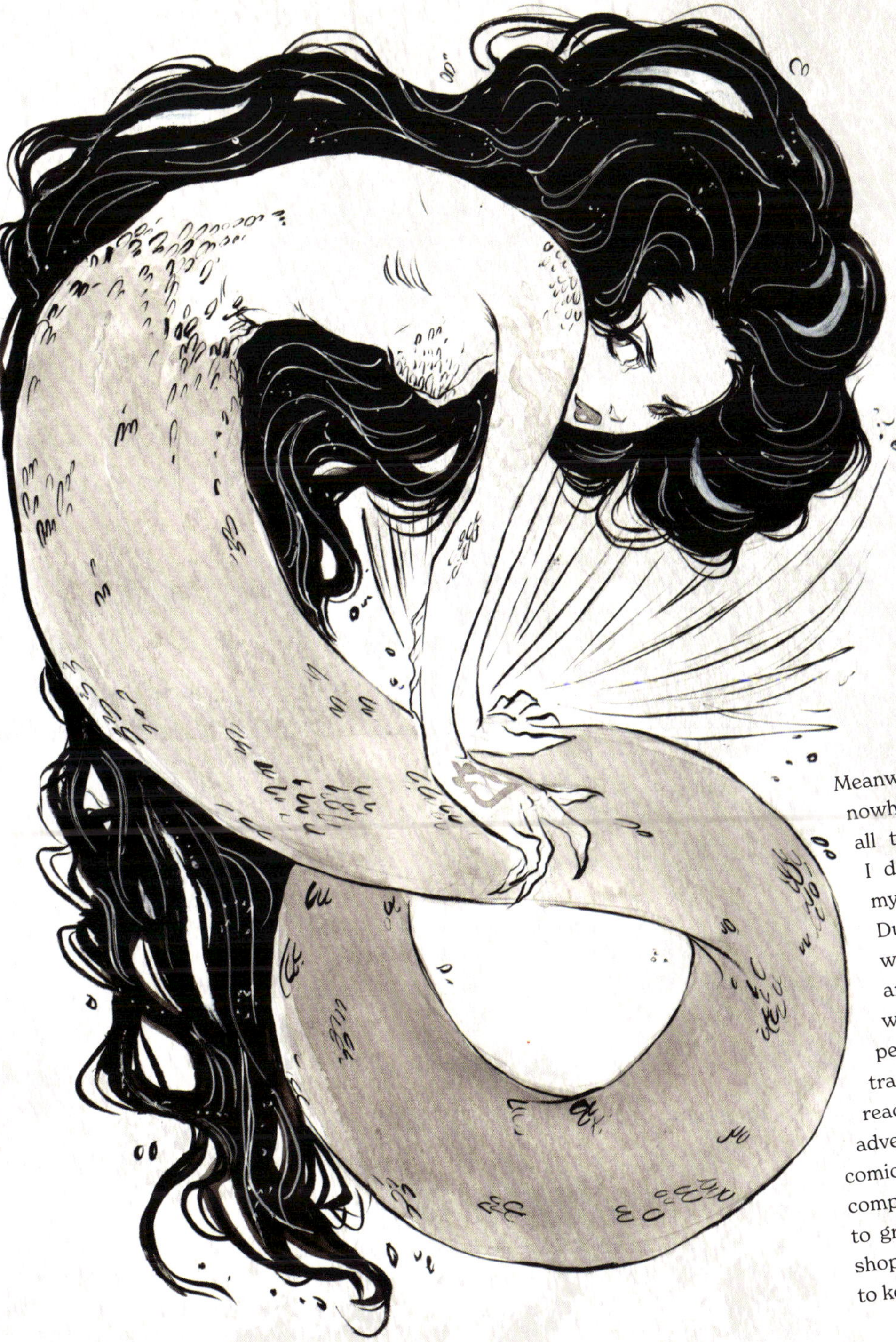

Meanwhile, the job search was leading nowhere. I kept getting rejections from all the companies I'd applied to, so I decided to move back home with my parents until I found a stable job. During that time, I still did a bunch of work on social media. I curated posts and merch, and applied for conventions where I could sell my artwork in person. My name started gaining some traction after that and people began reaching out to me for freelance jobs and advertisements. Some of these included comic-book covers and apparel for big-name companies. My online business also started to grow, and soon enough, I had to hire a shop manager because I didn't have the time to keep up with it all.

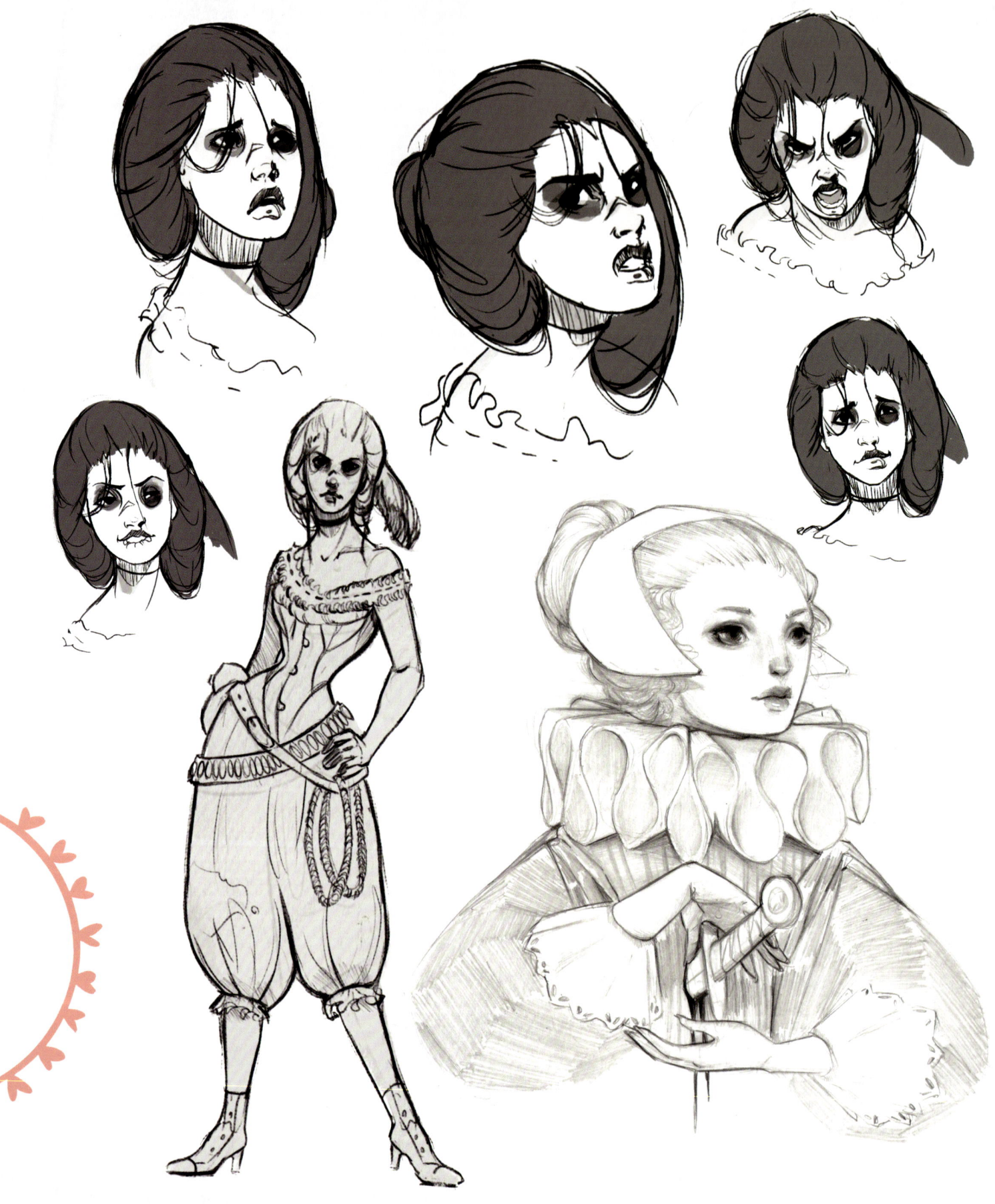

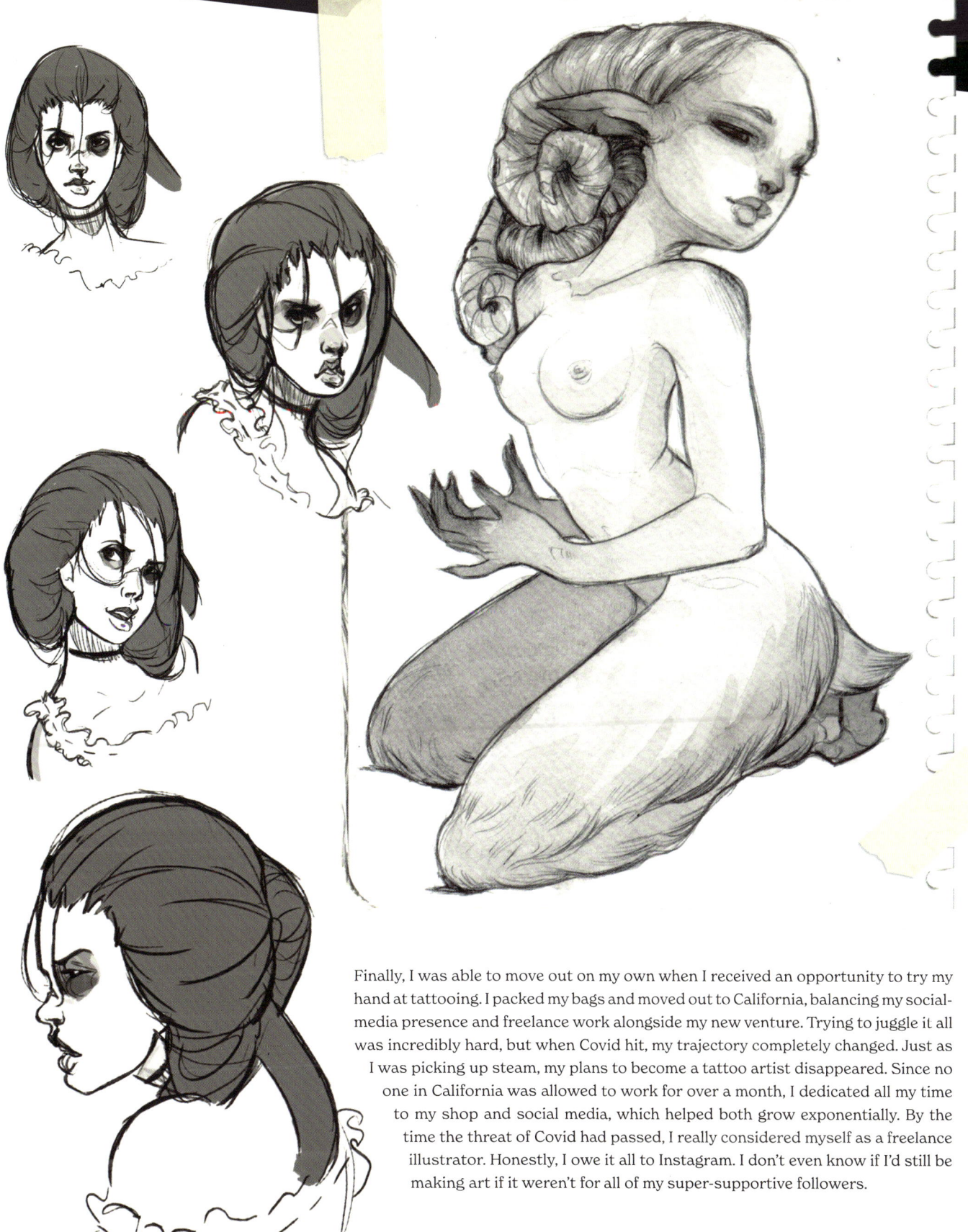

Finally, I was able to move out on my own when I received an opportunity to try my hand at tattooing. I packed my bags and moved out to California, balancing my social-media presence and freelance work alongside my new venture. Trying to juggle it all was incredibly hard, but when Covid hit, my trajectory completely changed. Just as I was picking up steam, my plans to become a tattoo artist disappeared. Since no one in California was allowed to work for over a month, I dedicated all my time to my shop and social media, which helped both grow exponentially. By the time the threat of Covid had passed, I really considered myself as a freelance illustrator. Honestly, I owe it all to Instagram. I don't even know if I'd still be making art if it weren't for all of my super-supportive followers.

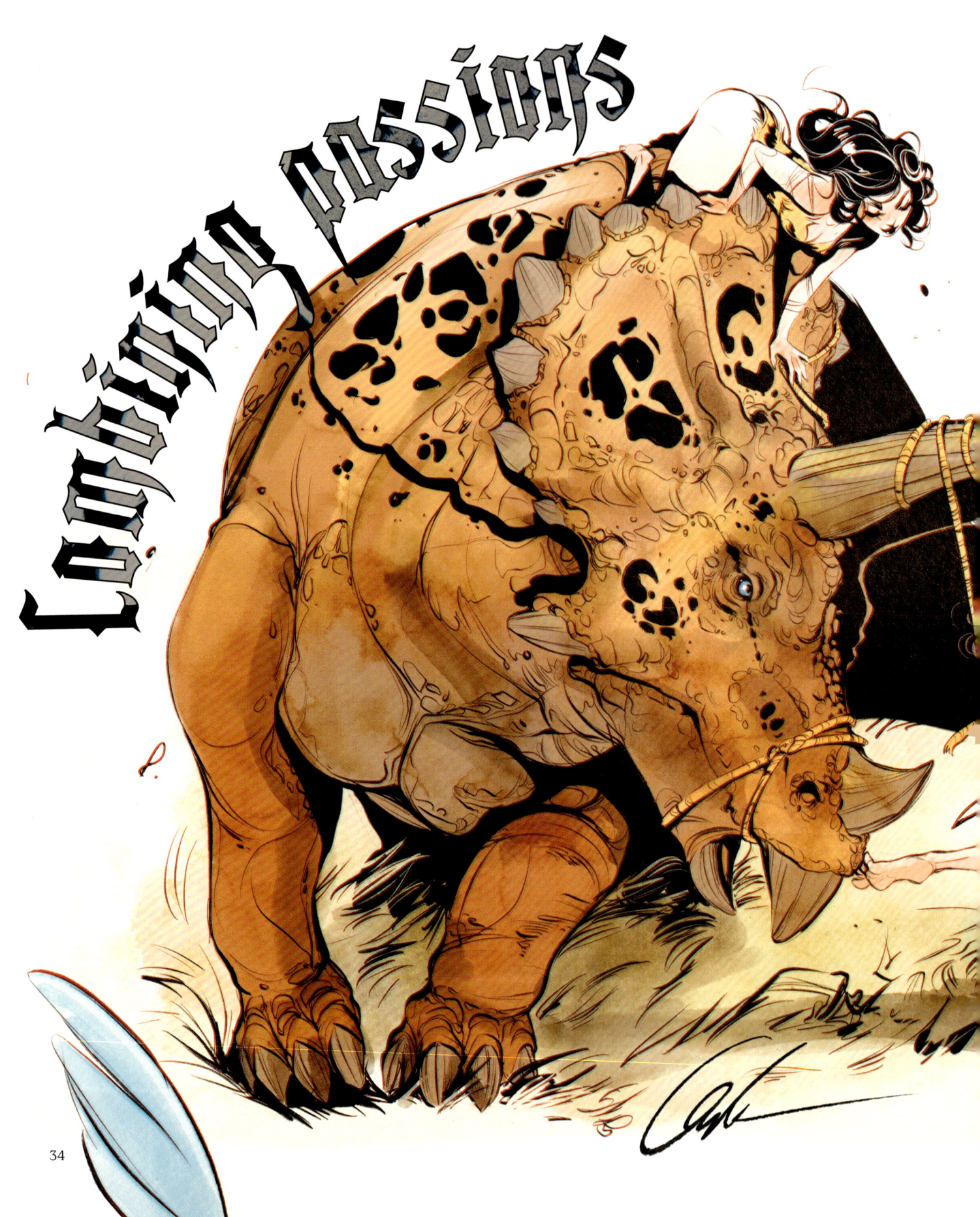

Combining passions

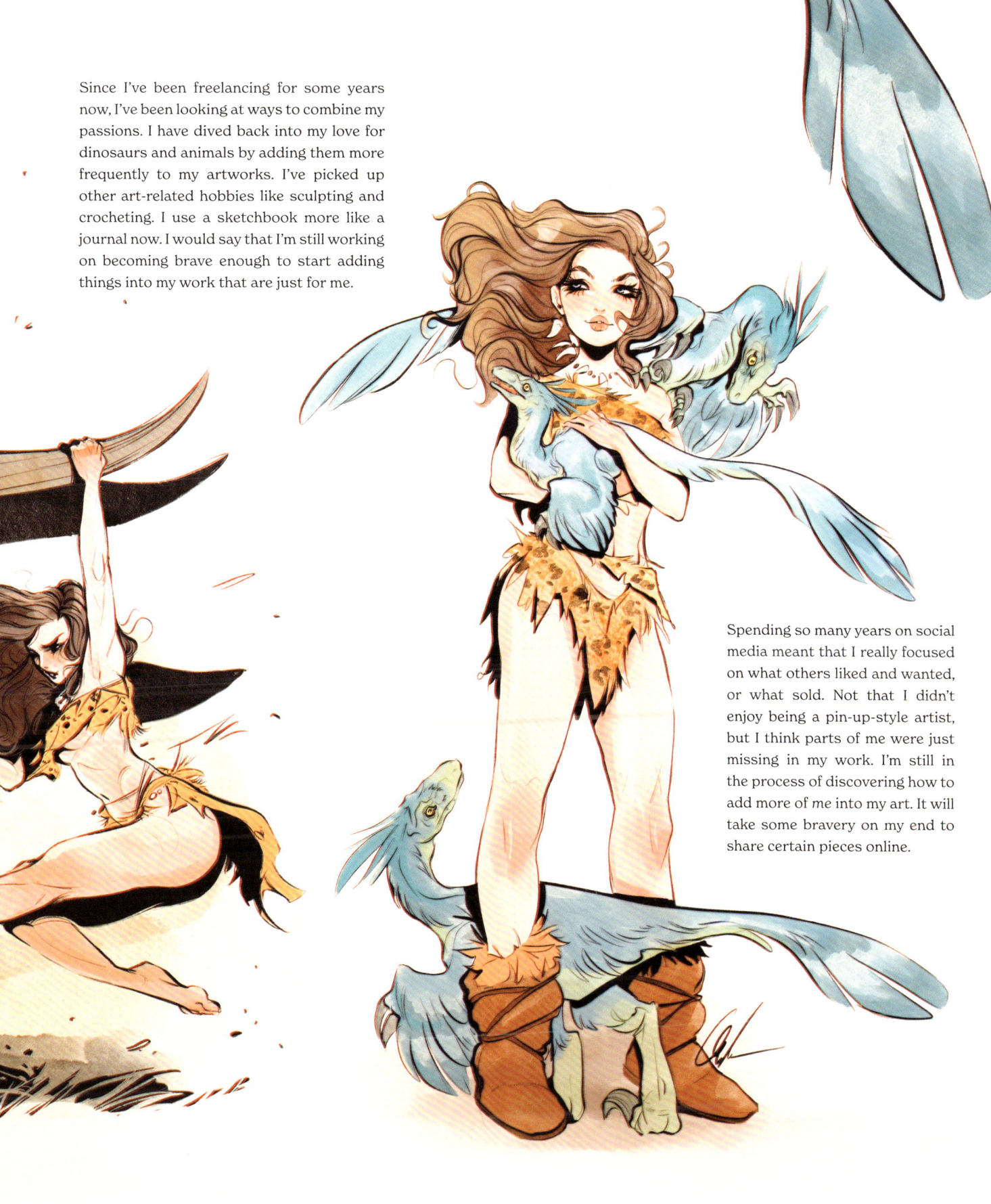

Since I've been freelancing for some years now, I've been looking at ways to combine my passions. I have dived back into my love for dinosaurs and animals by adding them more frequently to my artworks. I've picked up other art-related hobbies like sculpting and crocheting. I use a sketchbook more like a journal now. I would say that I'm still working on becoming brave enough to start adding things into my work that are just for me.

Spending so many years on social media meant that I really focused on what others liked and wanted, or what sold. Not that I didn't enjoy being a pin-up-style artist, but I think parts of me were just missing in my work. I'm still in the process of discovering how to add more of *me* into my art. It will take some bravery on my end to share certain pieces online.

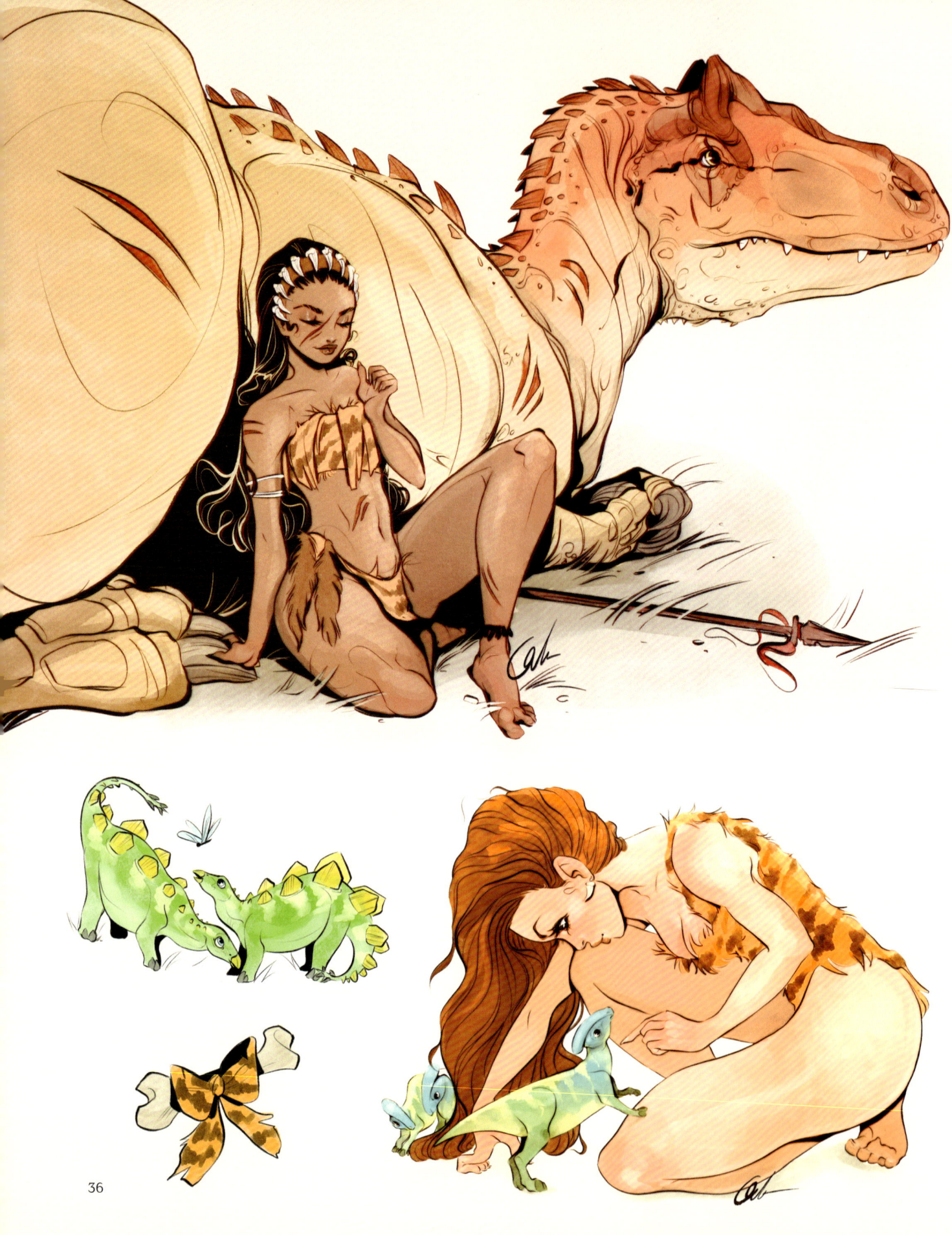

I will say that it's been quite fun to connect with people on a new level through my more personal pieces. I love it when people come up to me at conventions to point out the pieces they love the most, especially when the artwork is personal to me – something that was a little self-indulgent – and they still connect with it.

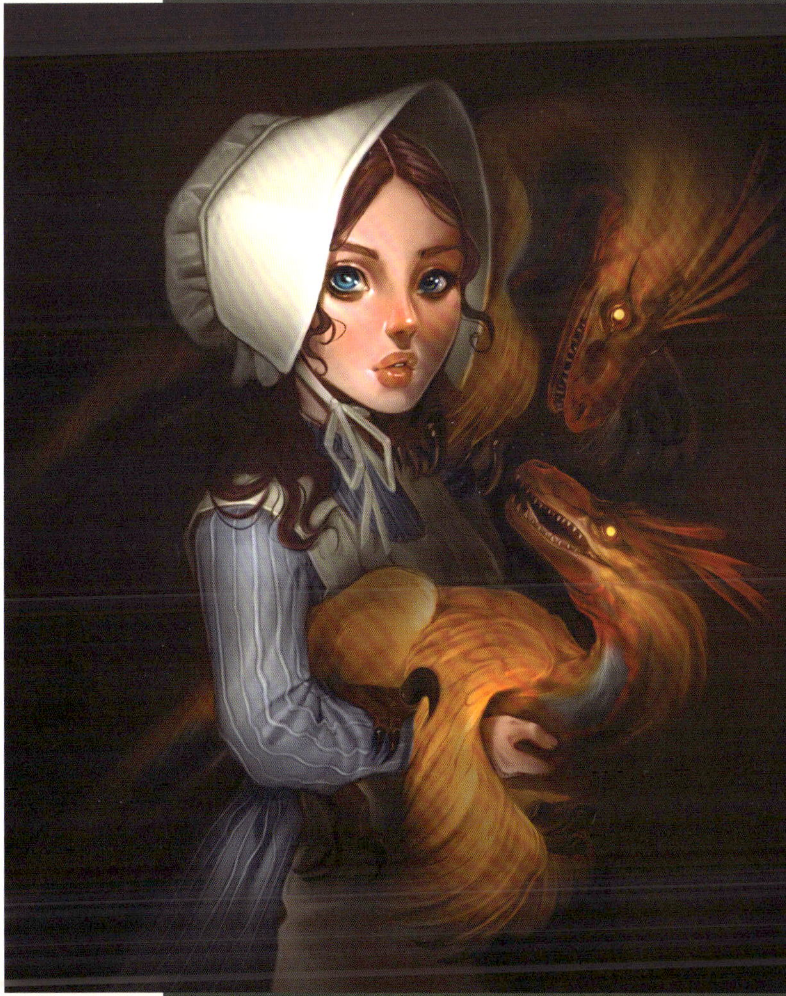

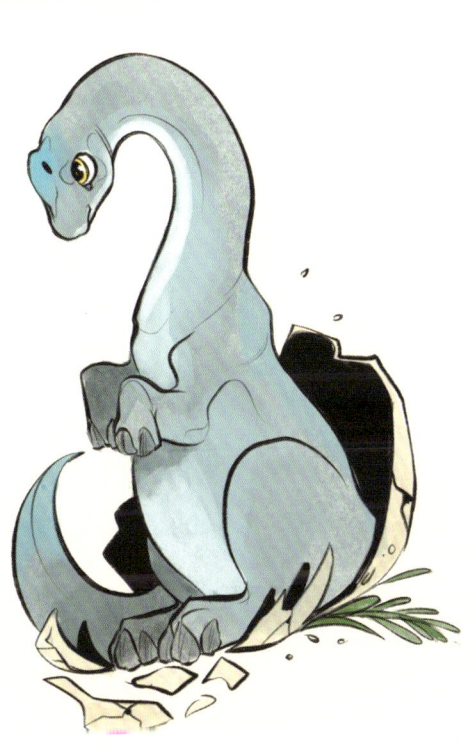

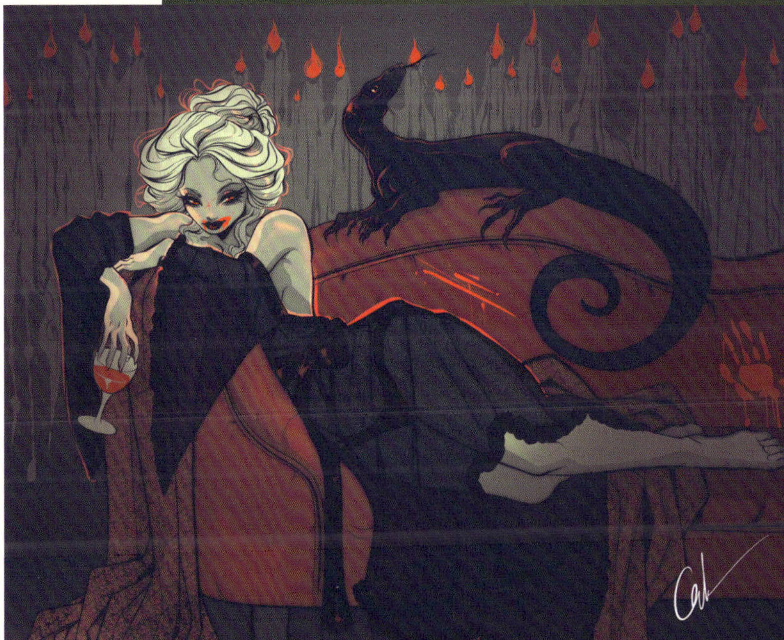

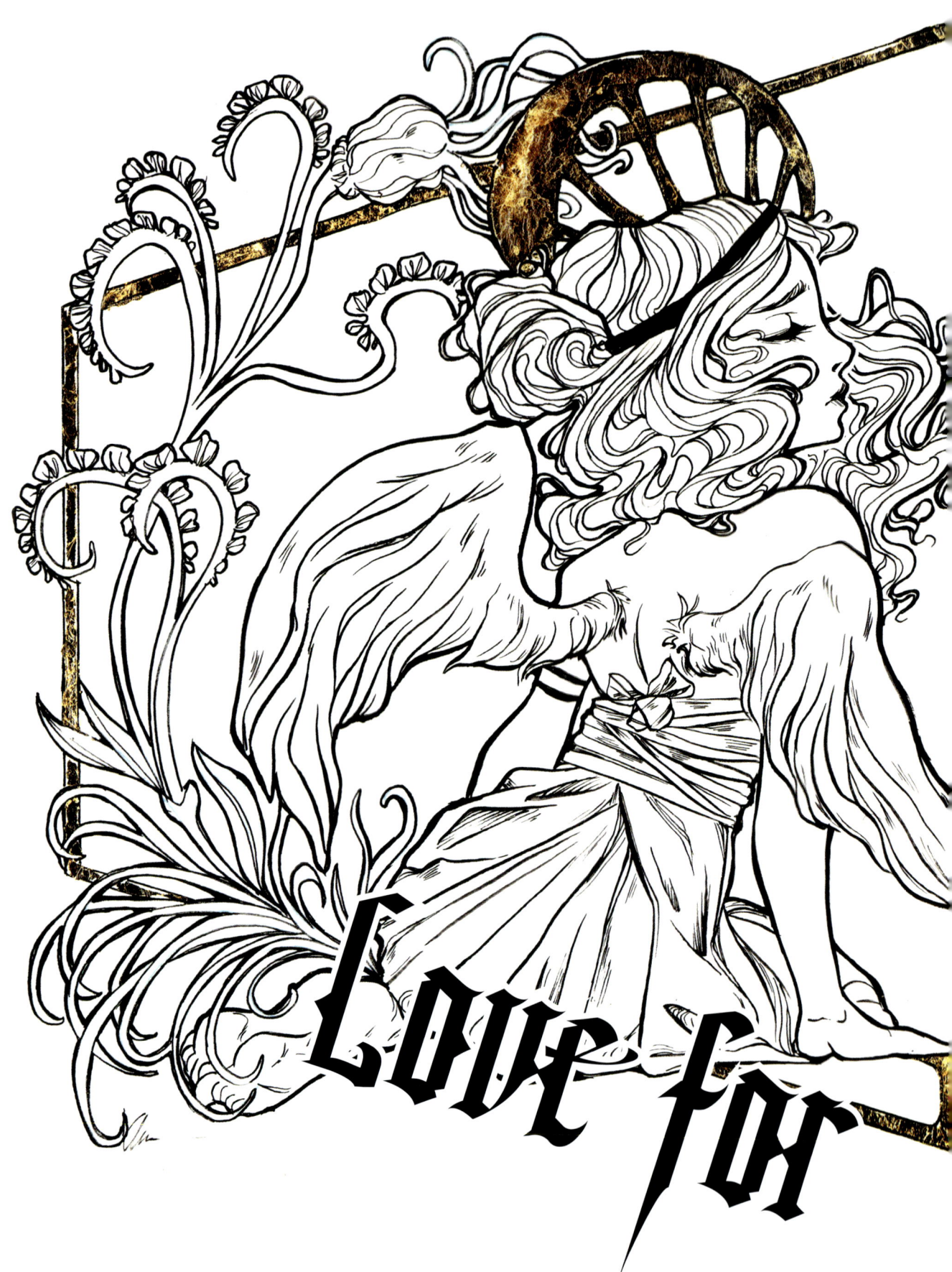

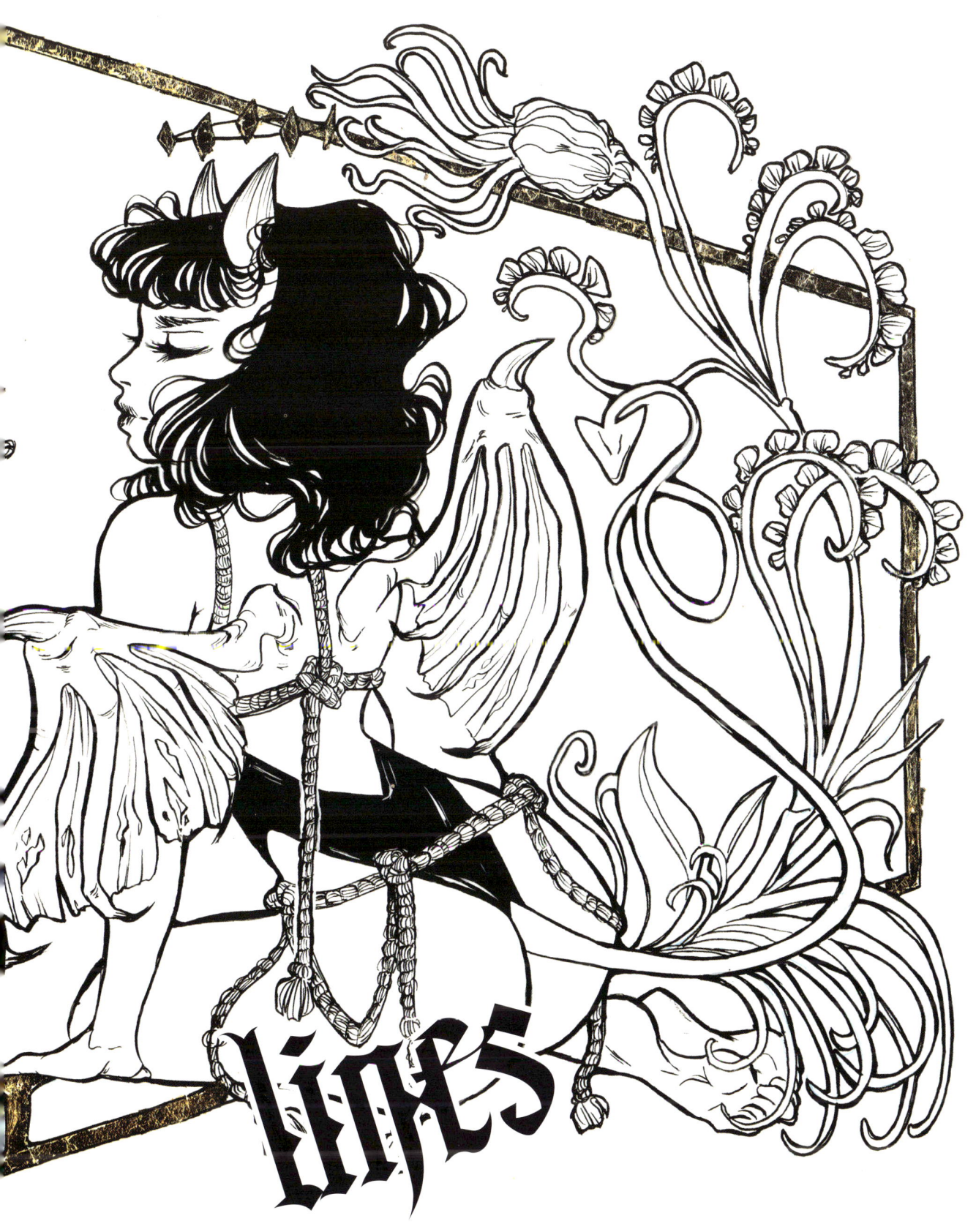

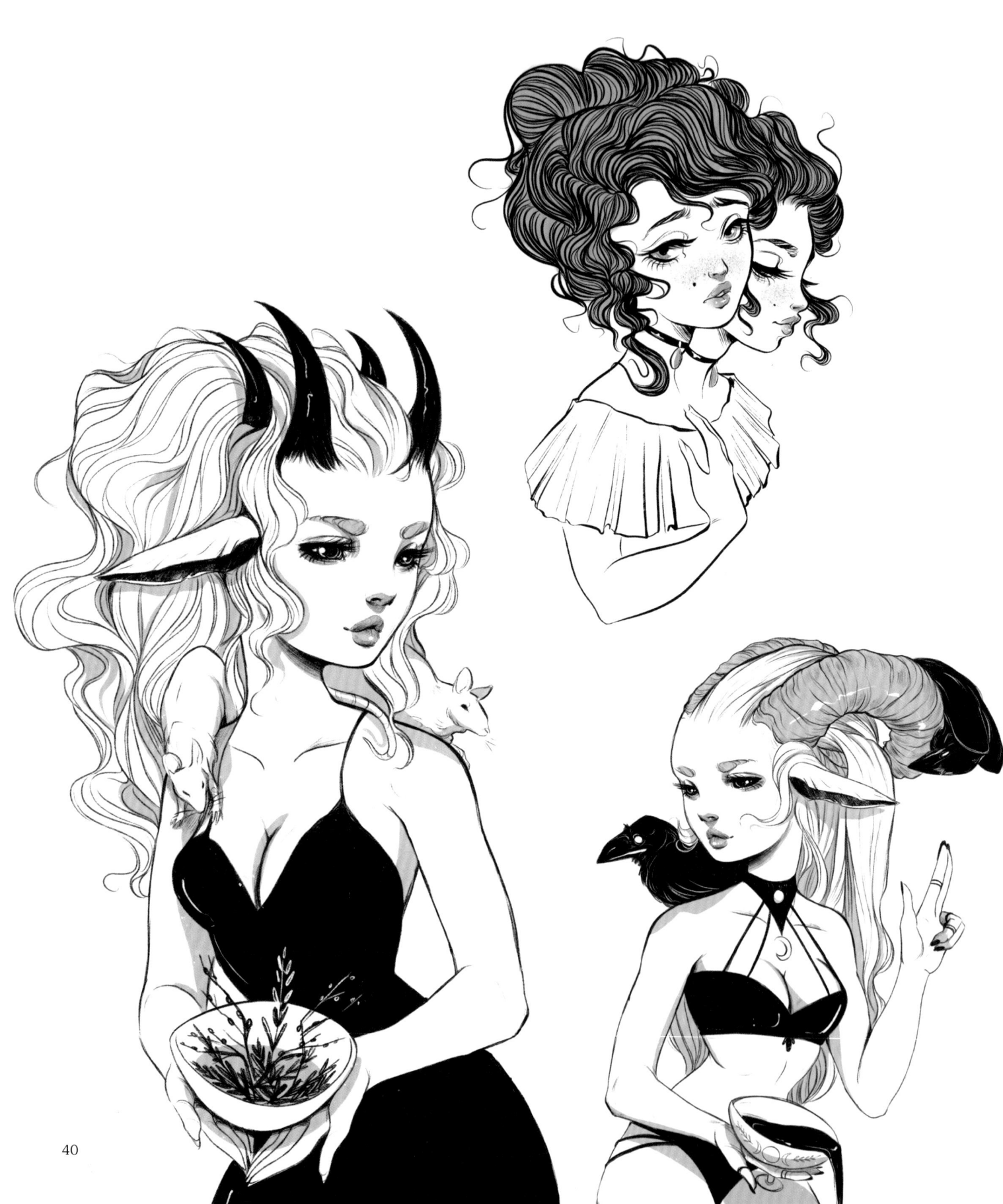

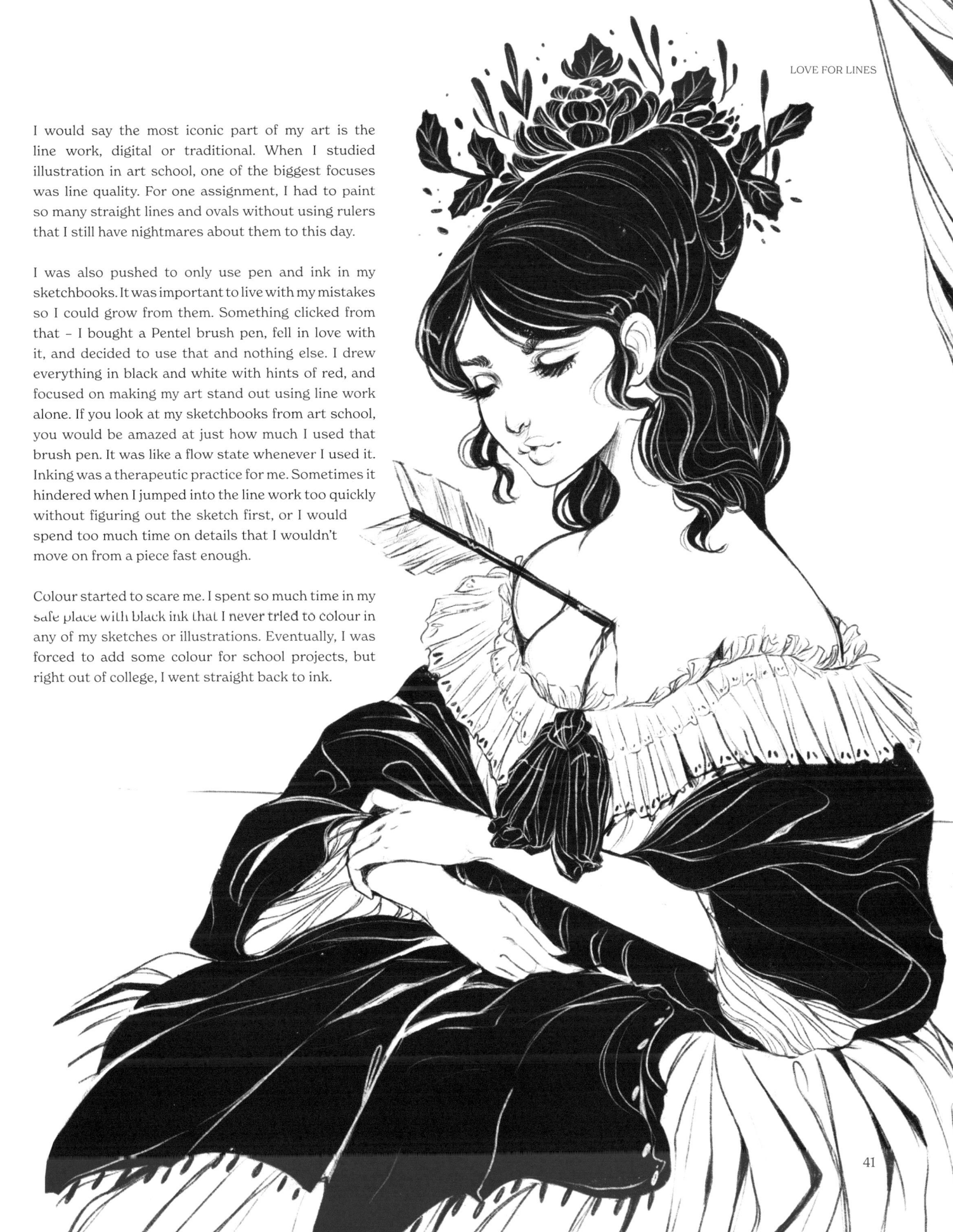

I would say the most iconic part of my art is the line work, digital or traditional. When I studied illustration in art school, one of the biggest focuses was line quality. For one assignment, I had to paint so many straight lines and ovals without using rulers that I still have nightmares about them to this day.

I was also pushed to only use pen and ink in my sketchbooks. It was important to live with my mistakes so I could grow from them. Something clicked from that – I bought a Pentel brush pen, fell in love with it, and decided to use that and nothing else. I drew everything in black and white with hints of red, and focused on making my art stand out using line work alone. If you look at my sketchbooks from art school, you would be amazed at just how much I used that brush pen. It was like a flow state whenever I used it. Inking was a therapeutic practice for me. Sometimes it hindered when I jumped into the line work too quickly without figuring out the sketch first, or I would spend too much time on details that I wouldn't move on from a piece fast enough.

Colour started to scare me. I spent so much time in my safe place with black ink that I never tried to colour in any of my sketches or illustrations. Eventually, I was forced to add some colour for school projects, but right out of college, I went straight back to ink.

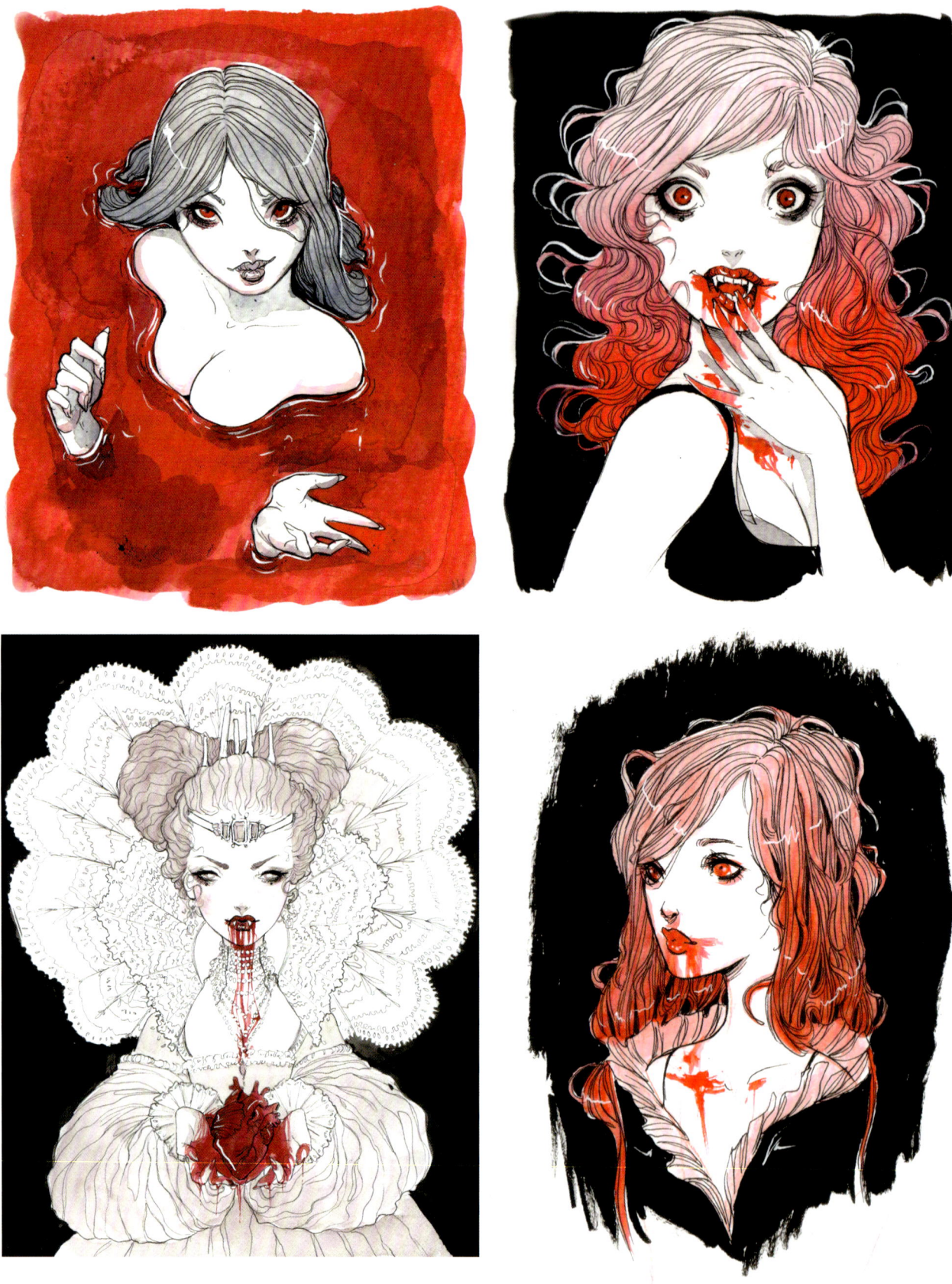

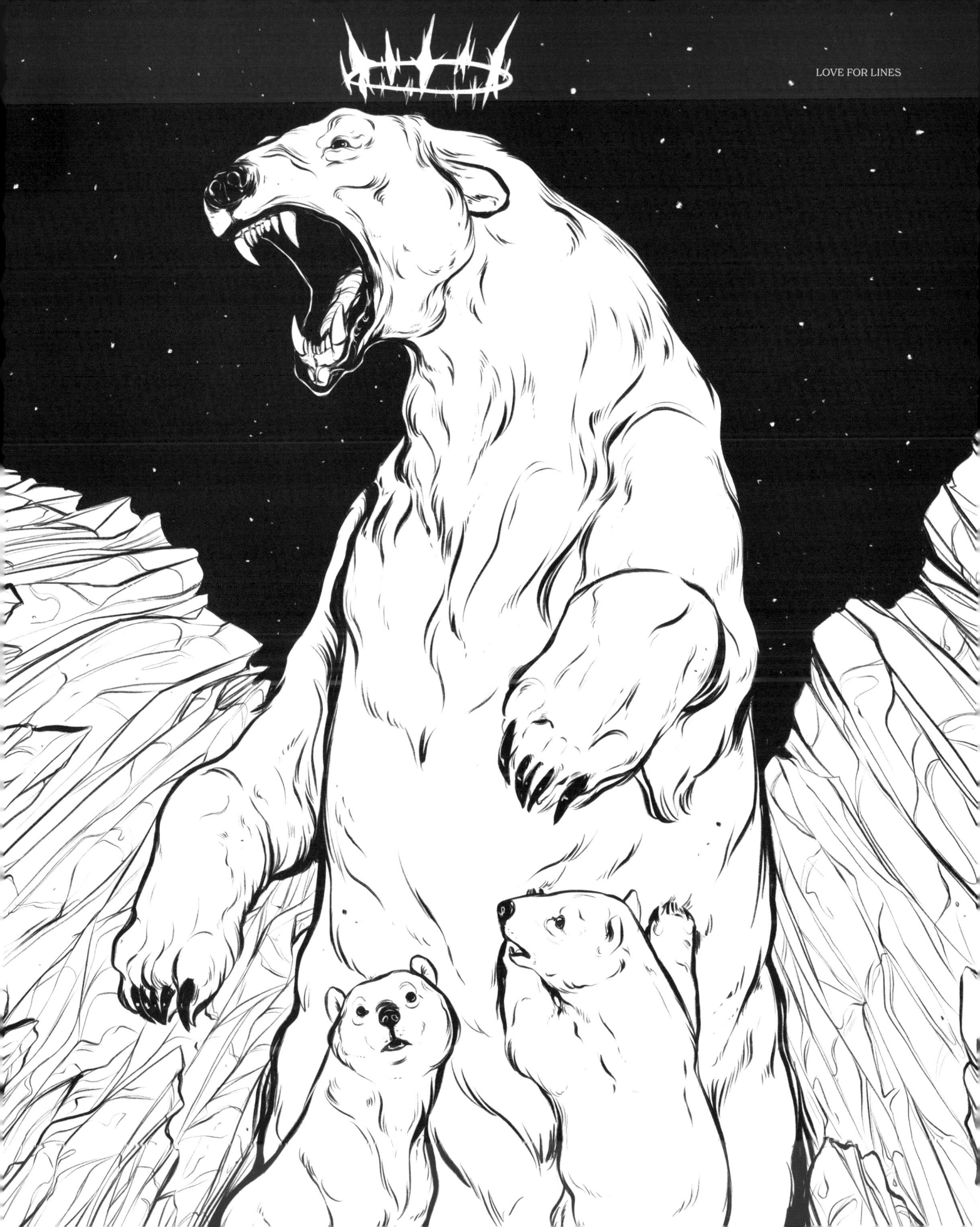

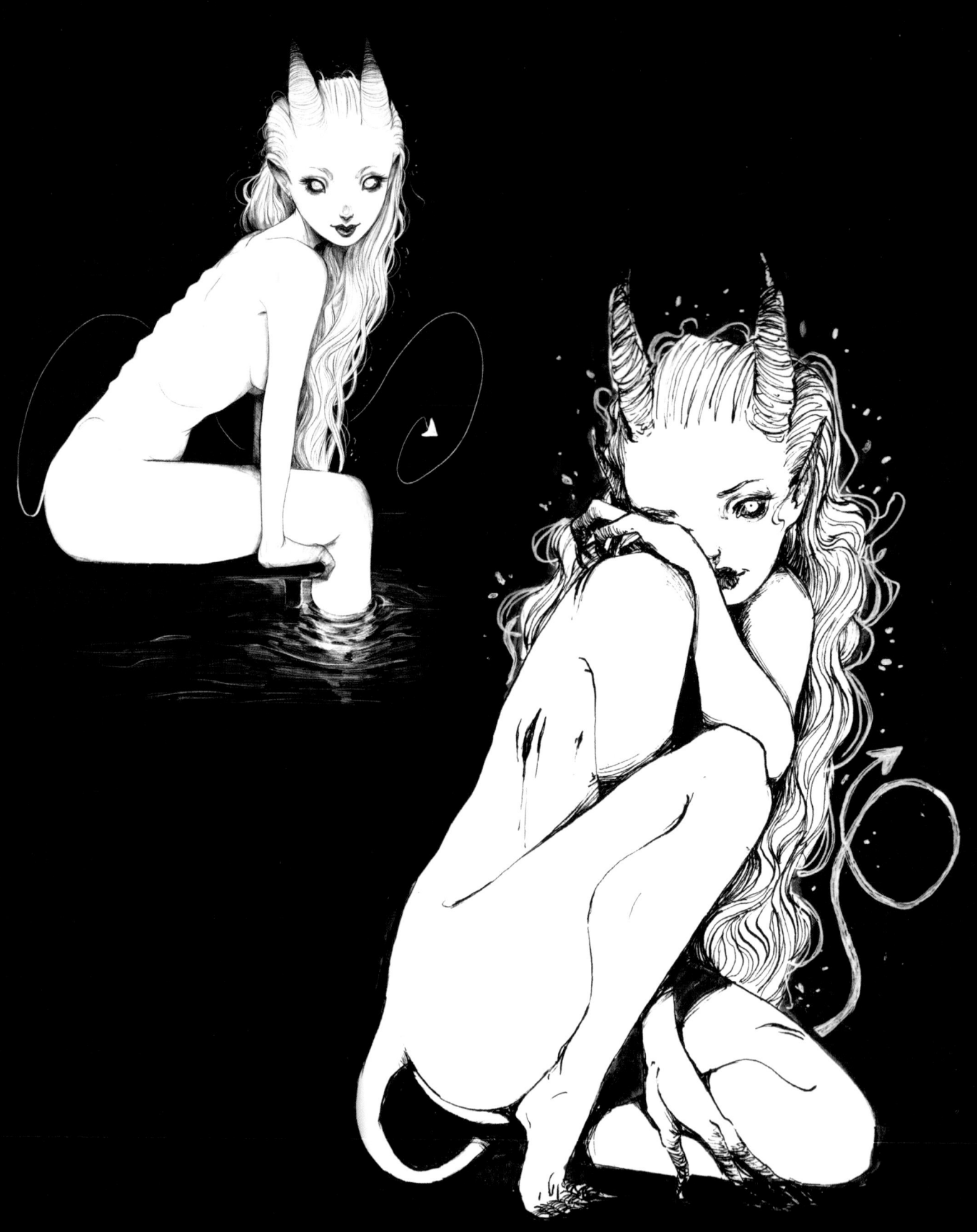

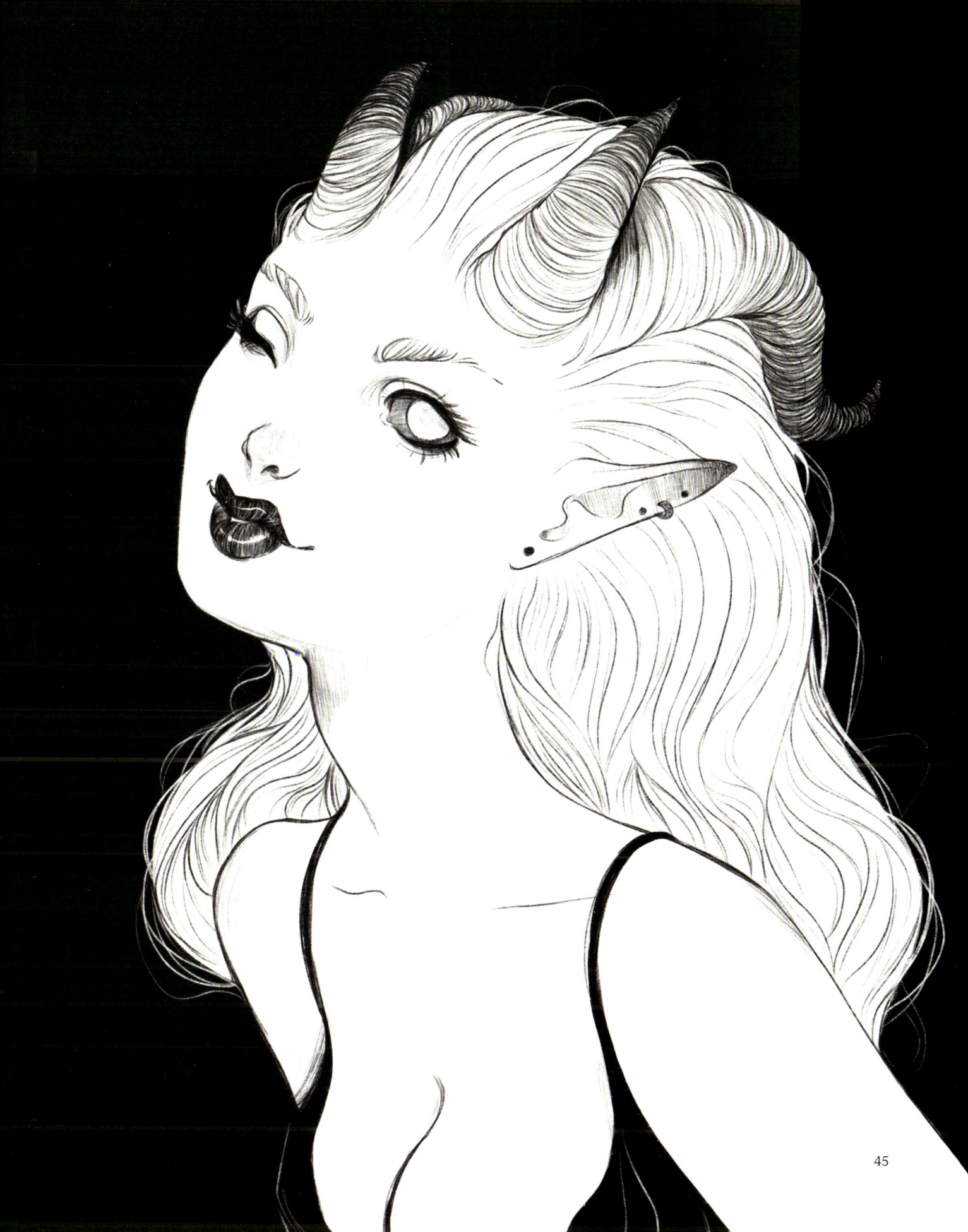

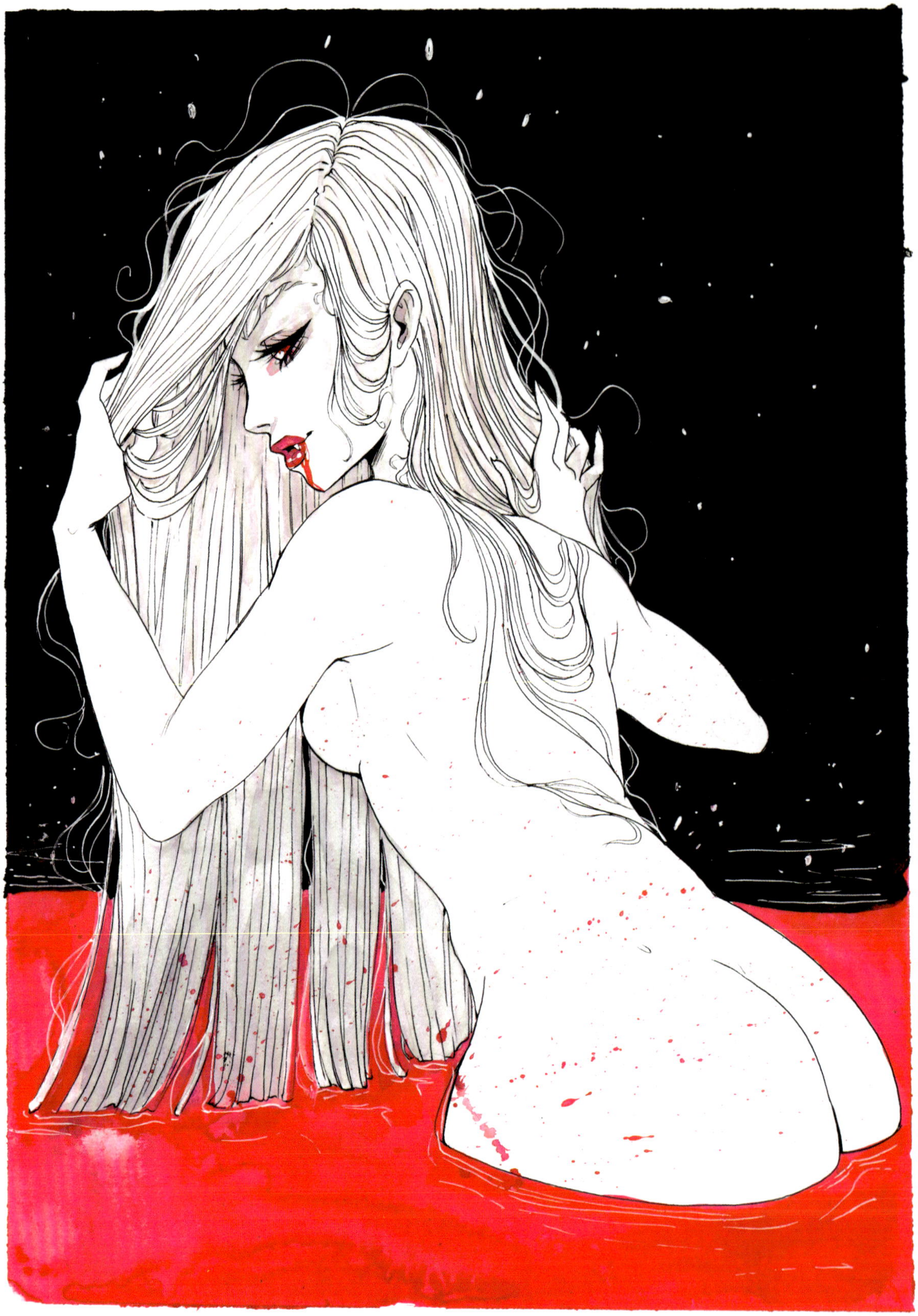

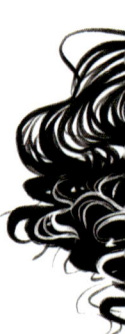

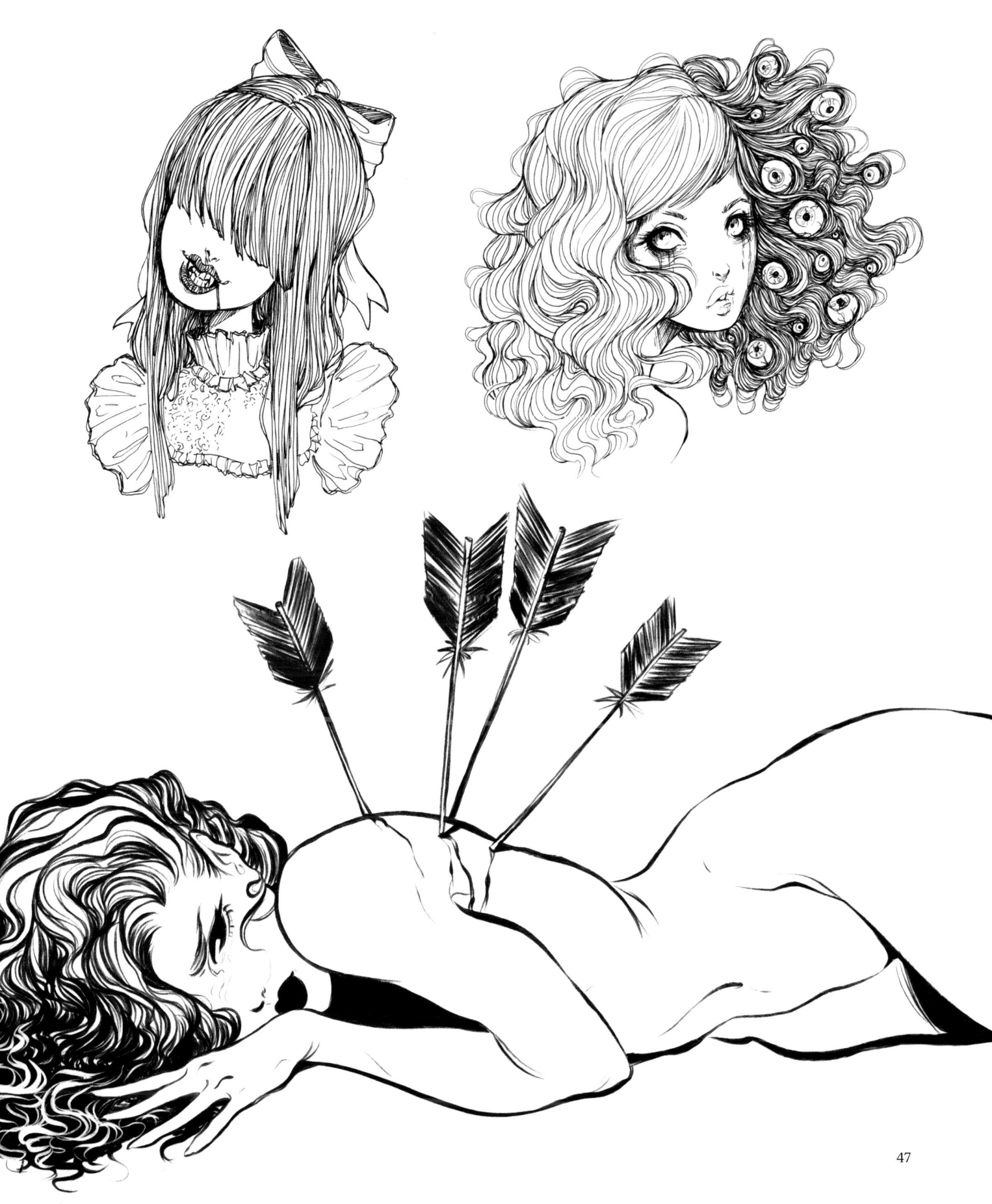

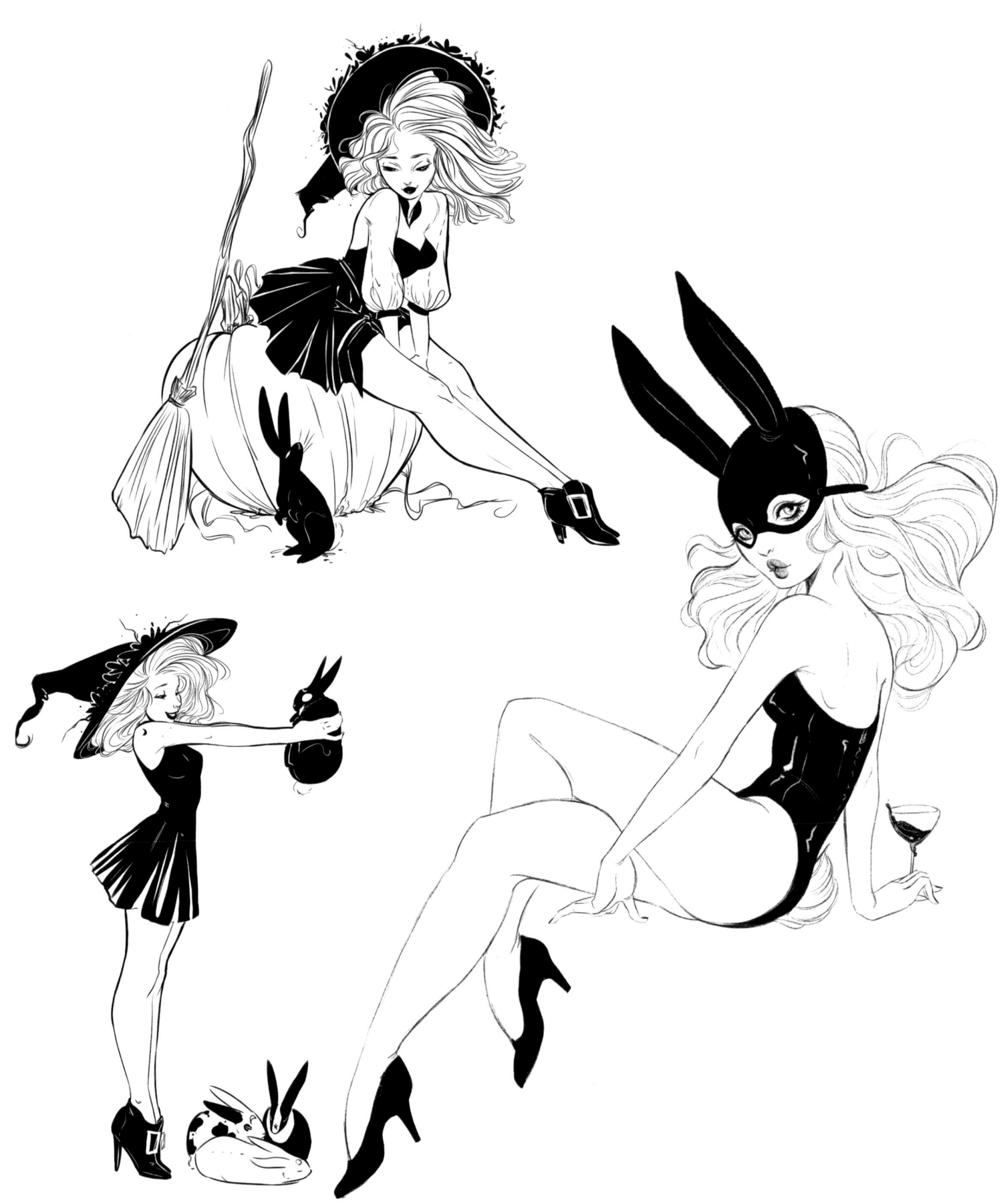

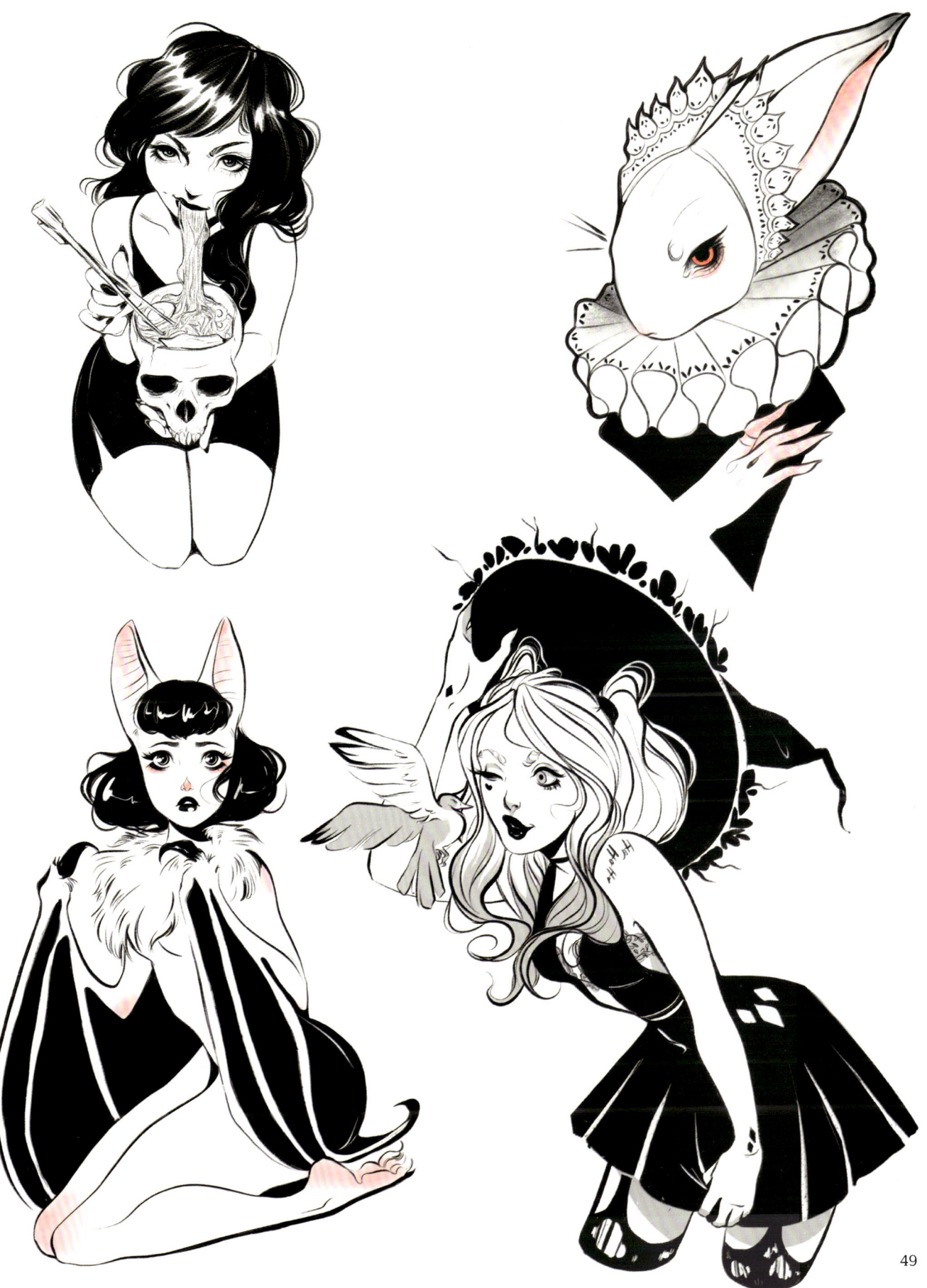

49

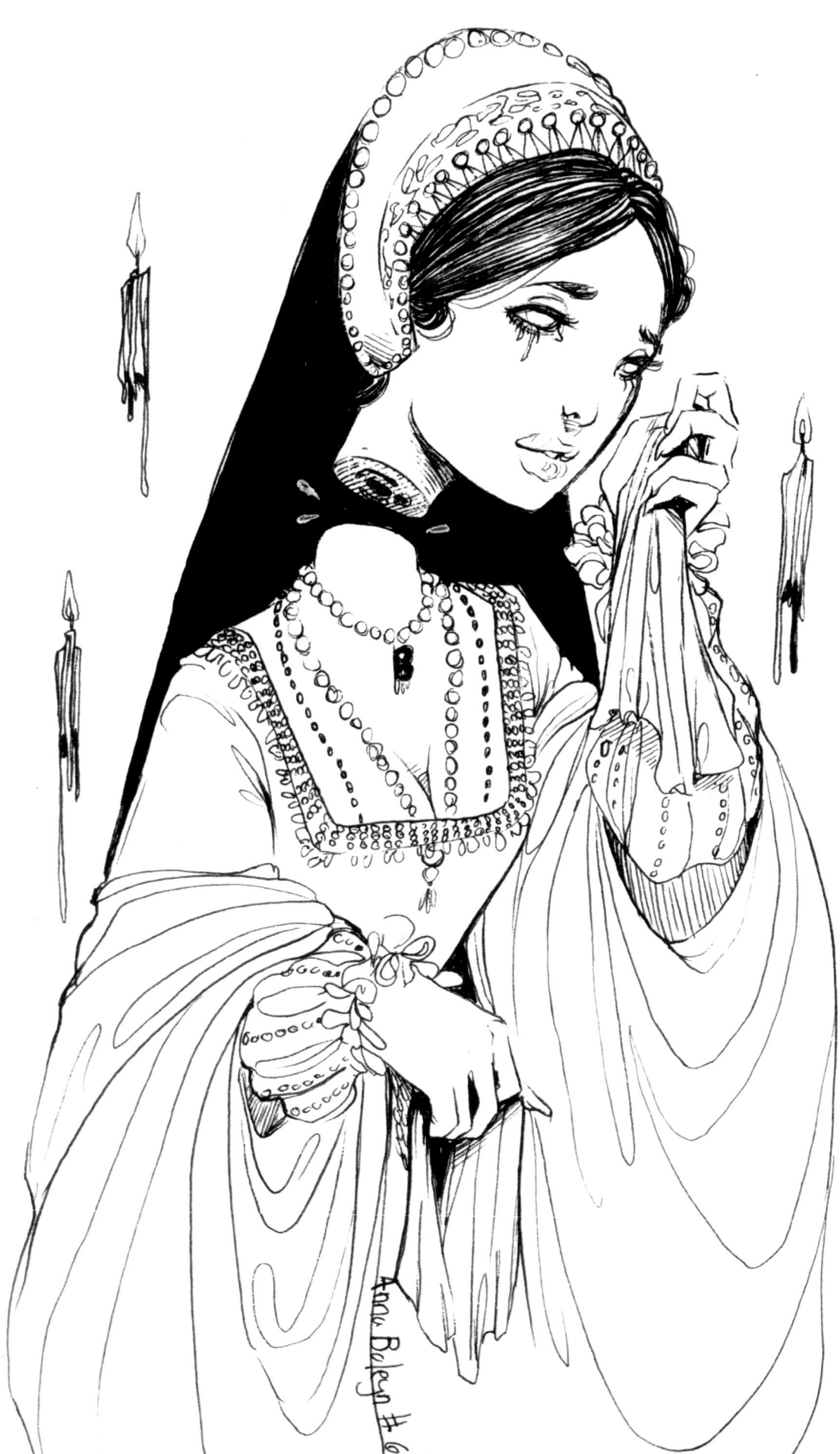

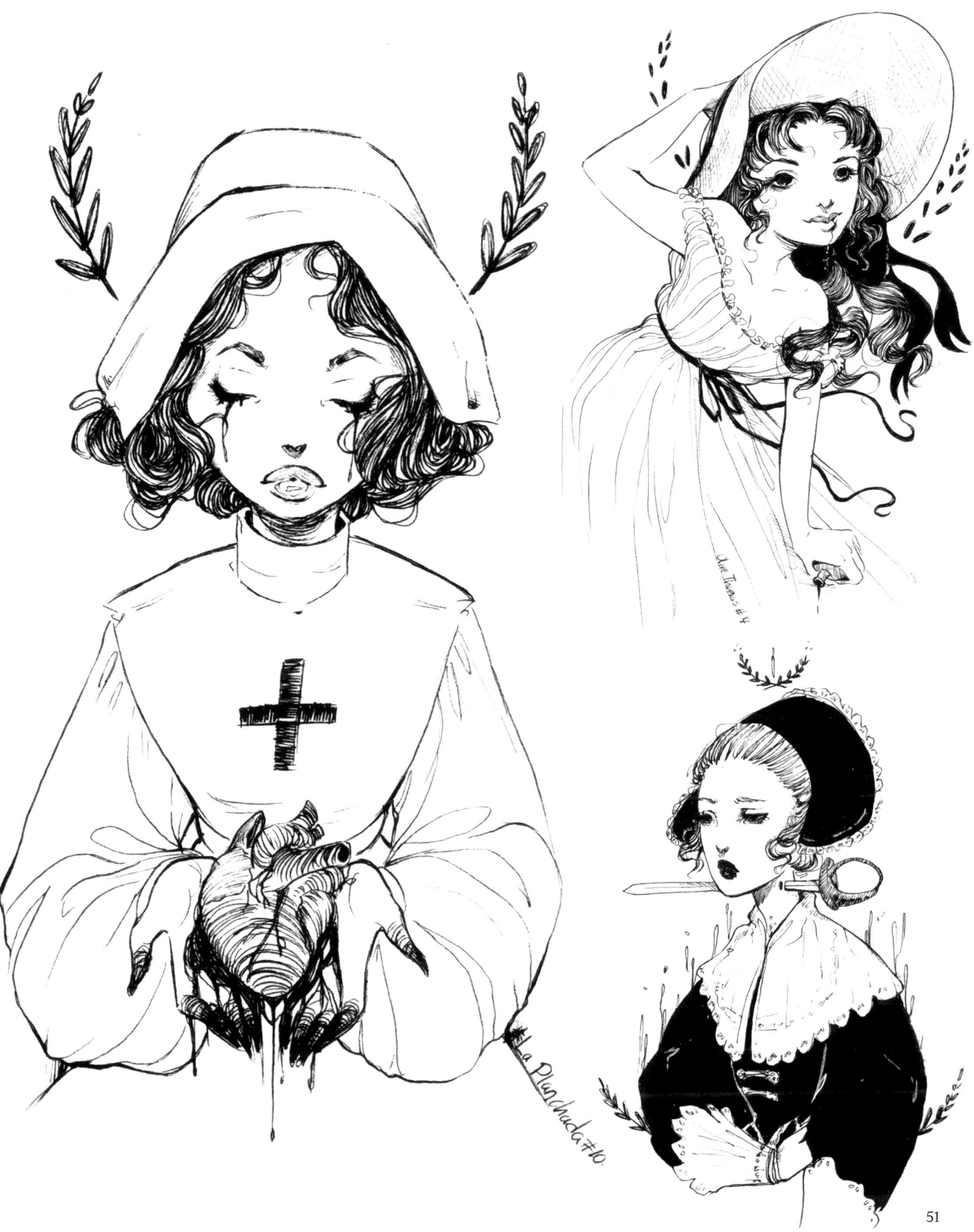

51

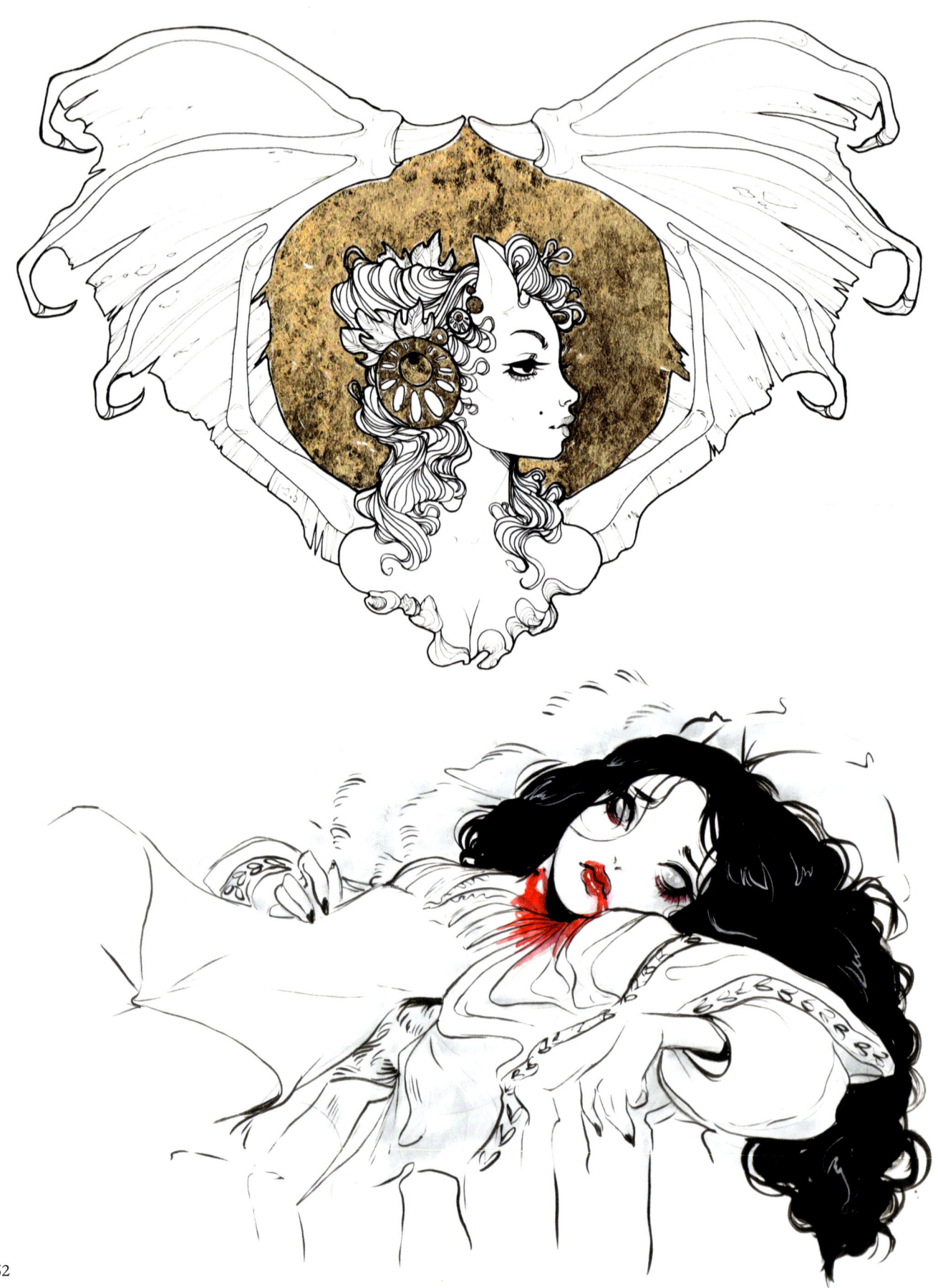

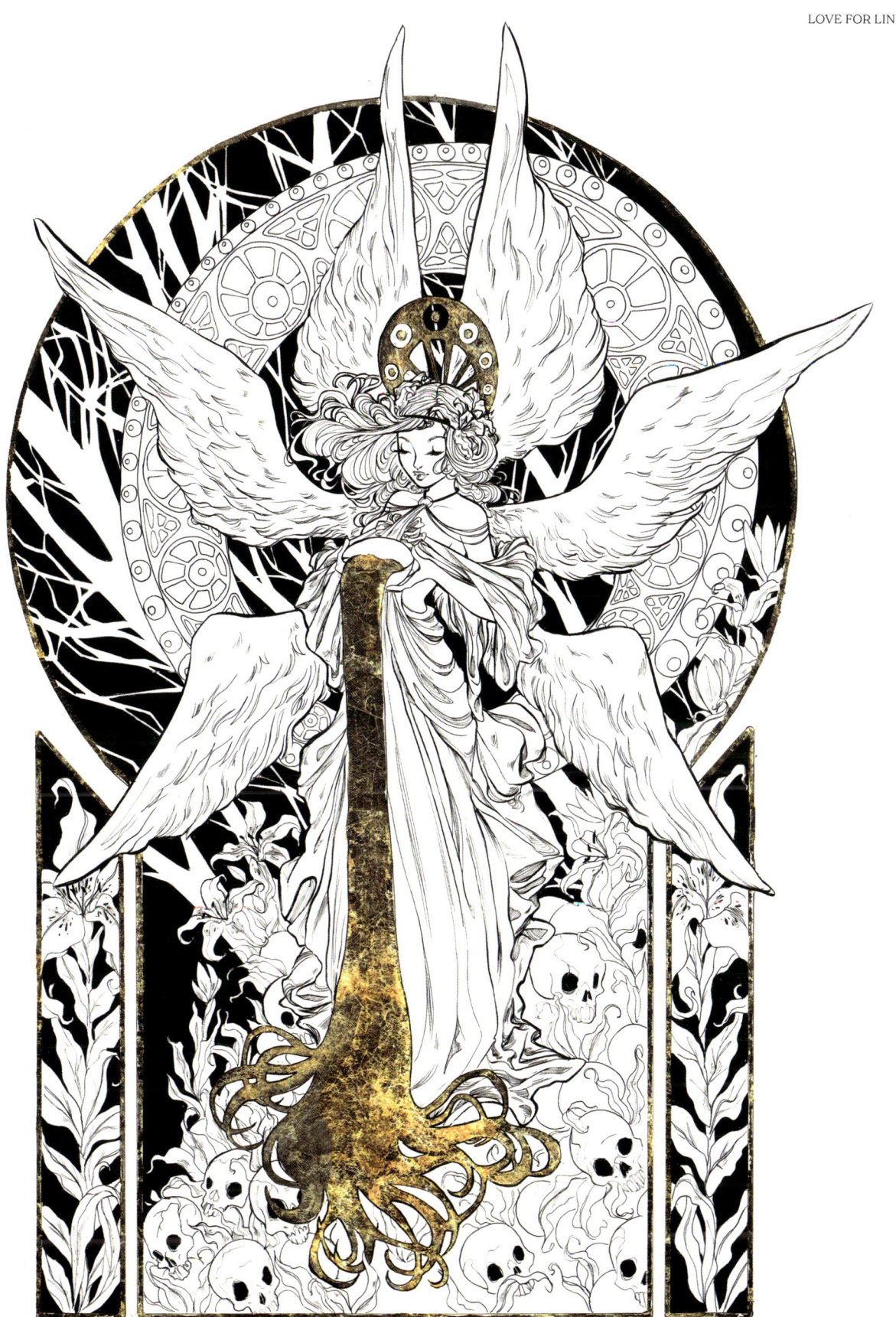

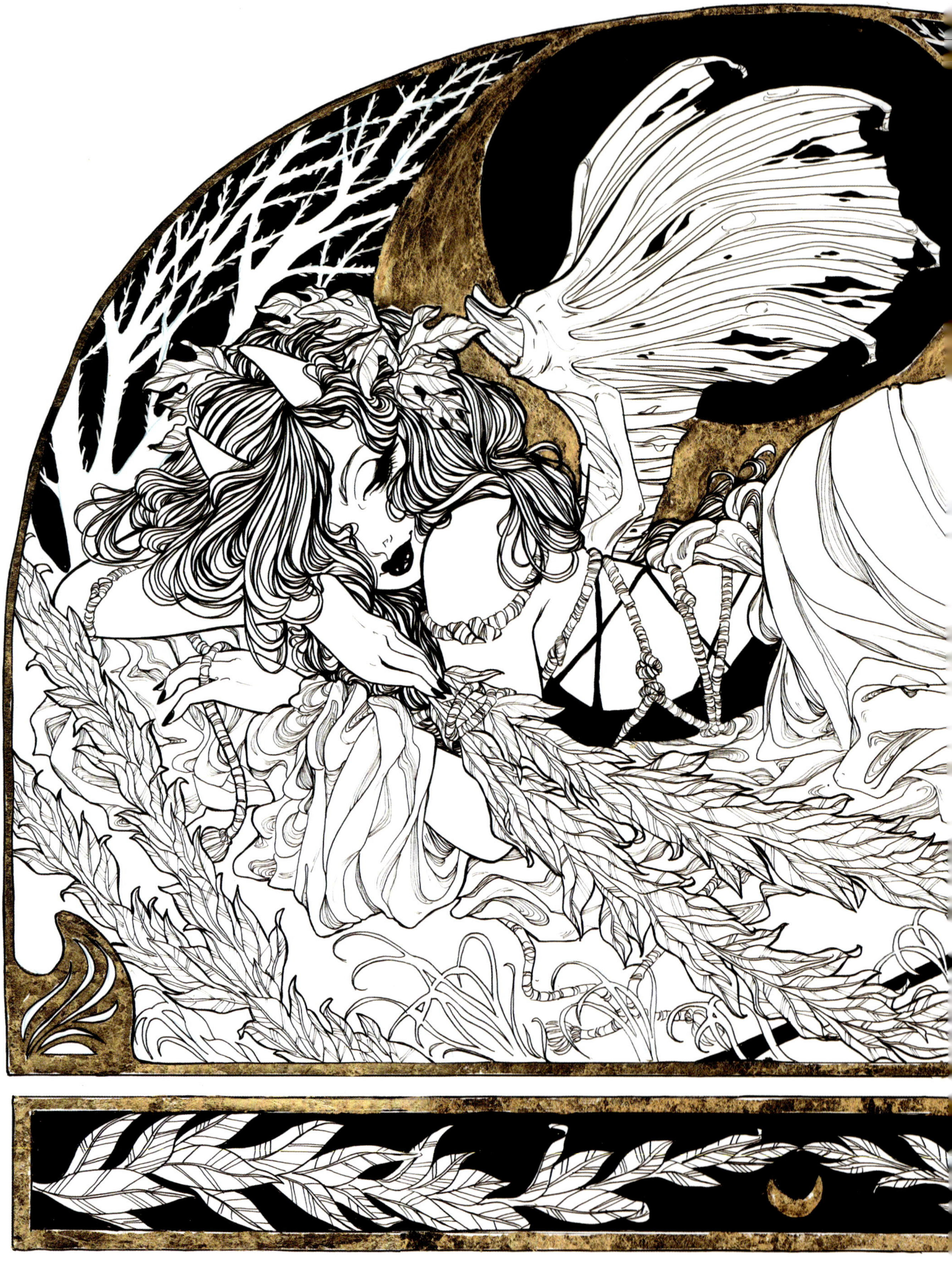

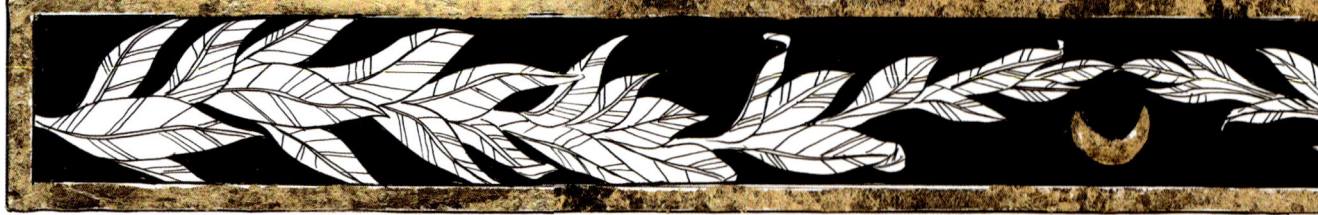

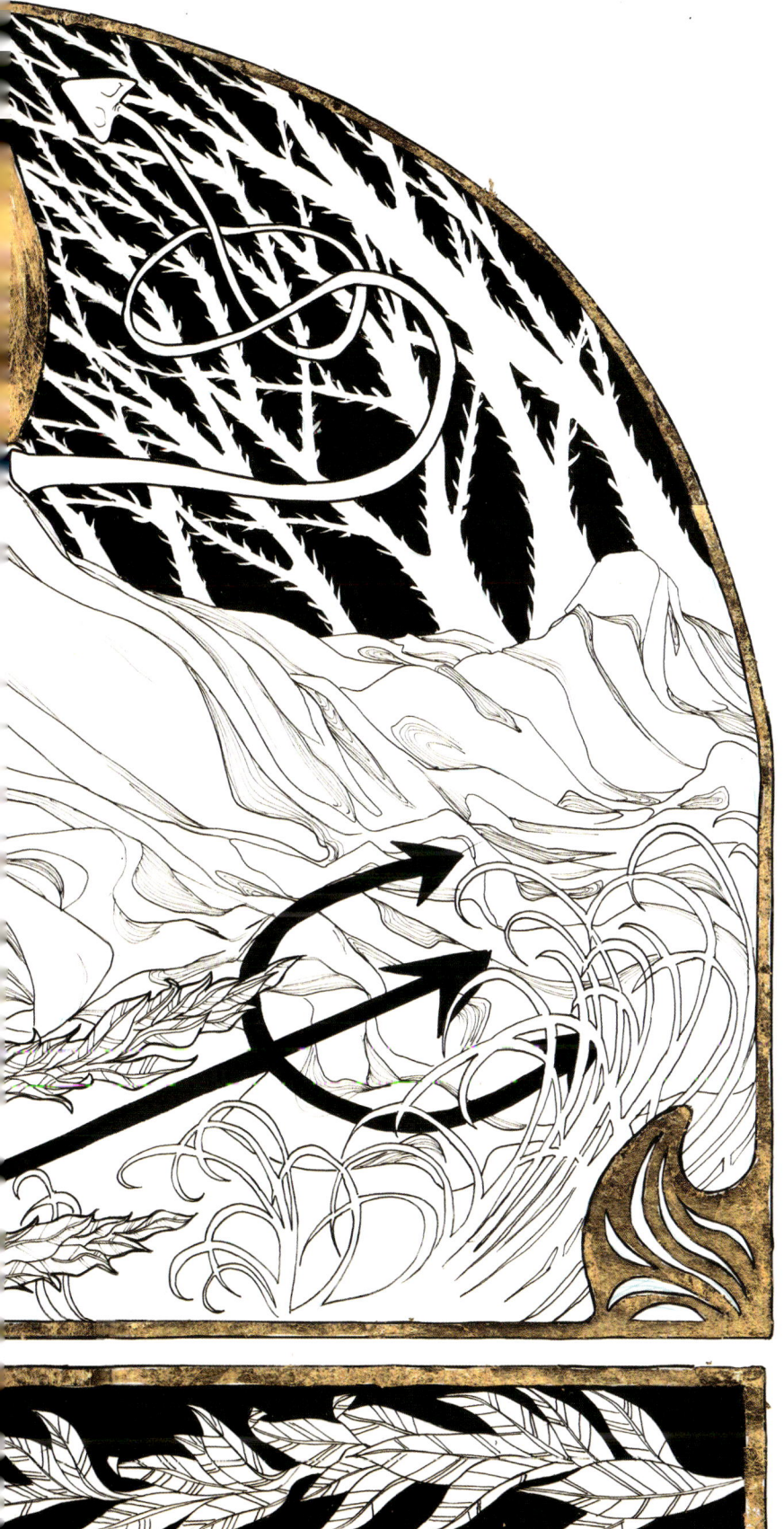

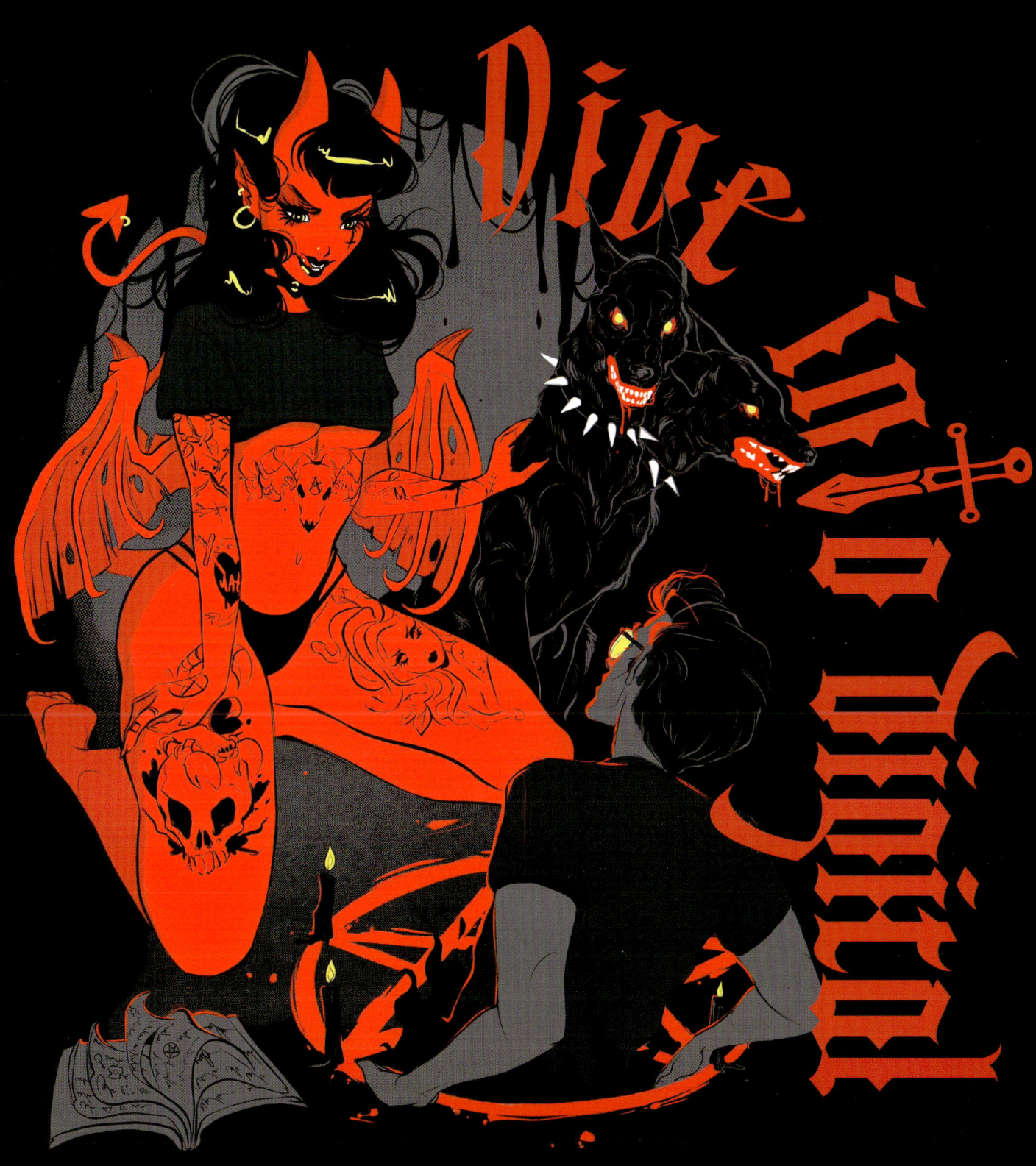

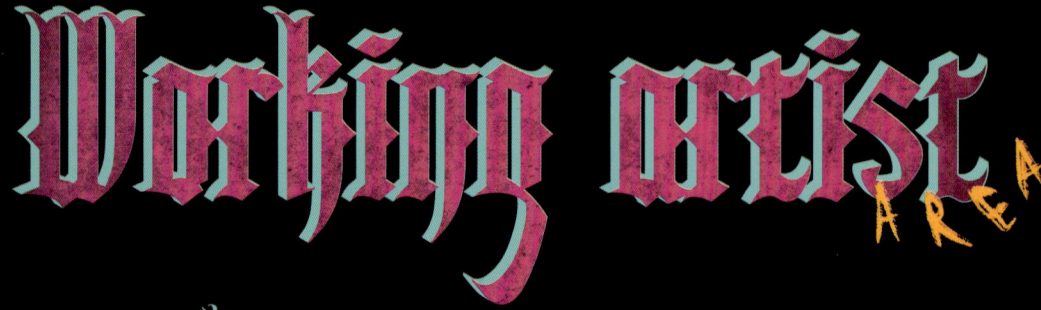

Working artist AREA

Choosing a career in art is risky. You have to take many chances and grab opportunities whenever you stumble upon them to build up your career. I've worked on character design, apparel concepts, and comic-book covers, and even dabbled in tattooing. Whenever I saw the chance to better myself as an artist, especially if it involved paid work, I took it. Not all jobs were fun and not all jobs really went anywhere. For example, one of my favourite jobs from years ago just died suddenly, and now those works will never see the light of day.

I've also designed plenty of things that will never have a name attached to them. They are now just out there in the universe as their own thing. I think that's the craziest thing about freelancing: watching your art take on a life of its own, or seeing it die without anyone ever knowing it existed.

Freelancing is so unsteady, too. You can get months that come with huge workloads and months that don't have any. You really have to be prepared for that uncertainty. However, the biggest positive is working on so many fun and varied projects. I've learned and grown so much from each job, and without them, I wouldn't be the artist I am today.

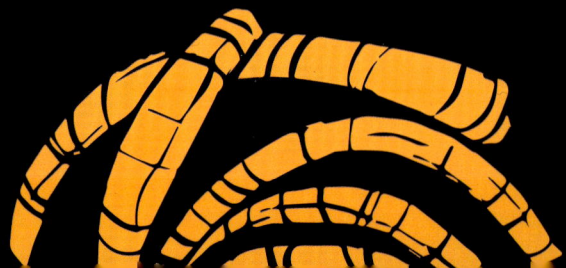

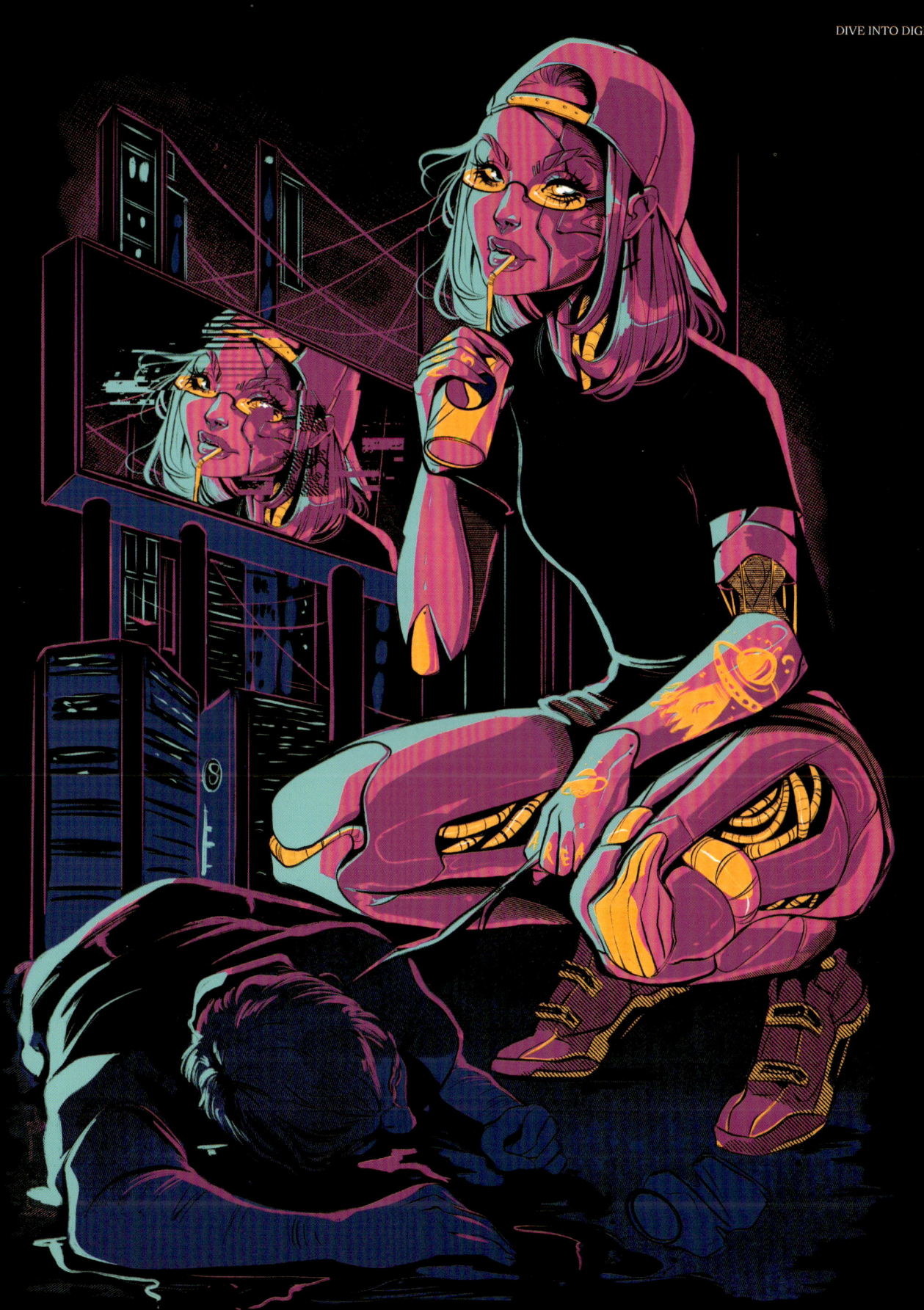

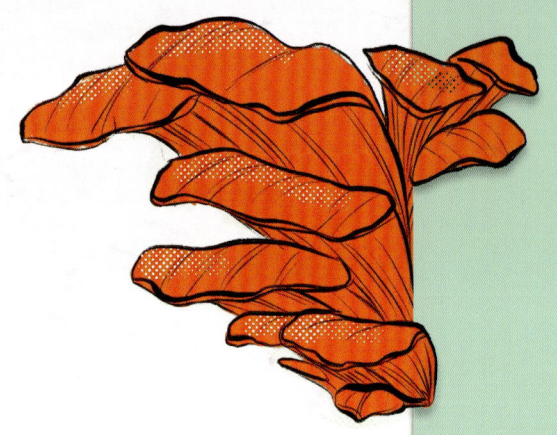

Connecting with an audience

I think one of the most important things for artists to do is connect with an audience. Your audience is going to be the biggest key to your success. I learned this very early on and, once I started my Patreon, that really validated it for me. Most of my income comes from my patrons. Even the smallest contributions from supporters who give what they can makes all the difference.

Patreon is also a place for me to form better connections with my followers. I learn what they want to see from me and get to bounce ideas off them. Each month I let my patrons pick a theme for me to work on, giving them a chance to tell me what they want to see me draw, and in return, I get to send them some exclusive goodies like prints, stickers, and a whole lot more. It also gives me the chance to share videos and do livestreams with a smaller number of people. Even if you don't have a Patreon, it's a good idea to connect with supporters in this way. Ask them questions, find out what it is that made them fall in love with your work. In today's society, people want that connection, so fostering that will really make you stand out and keep your audience around for a lot longer.

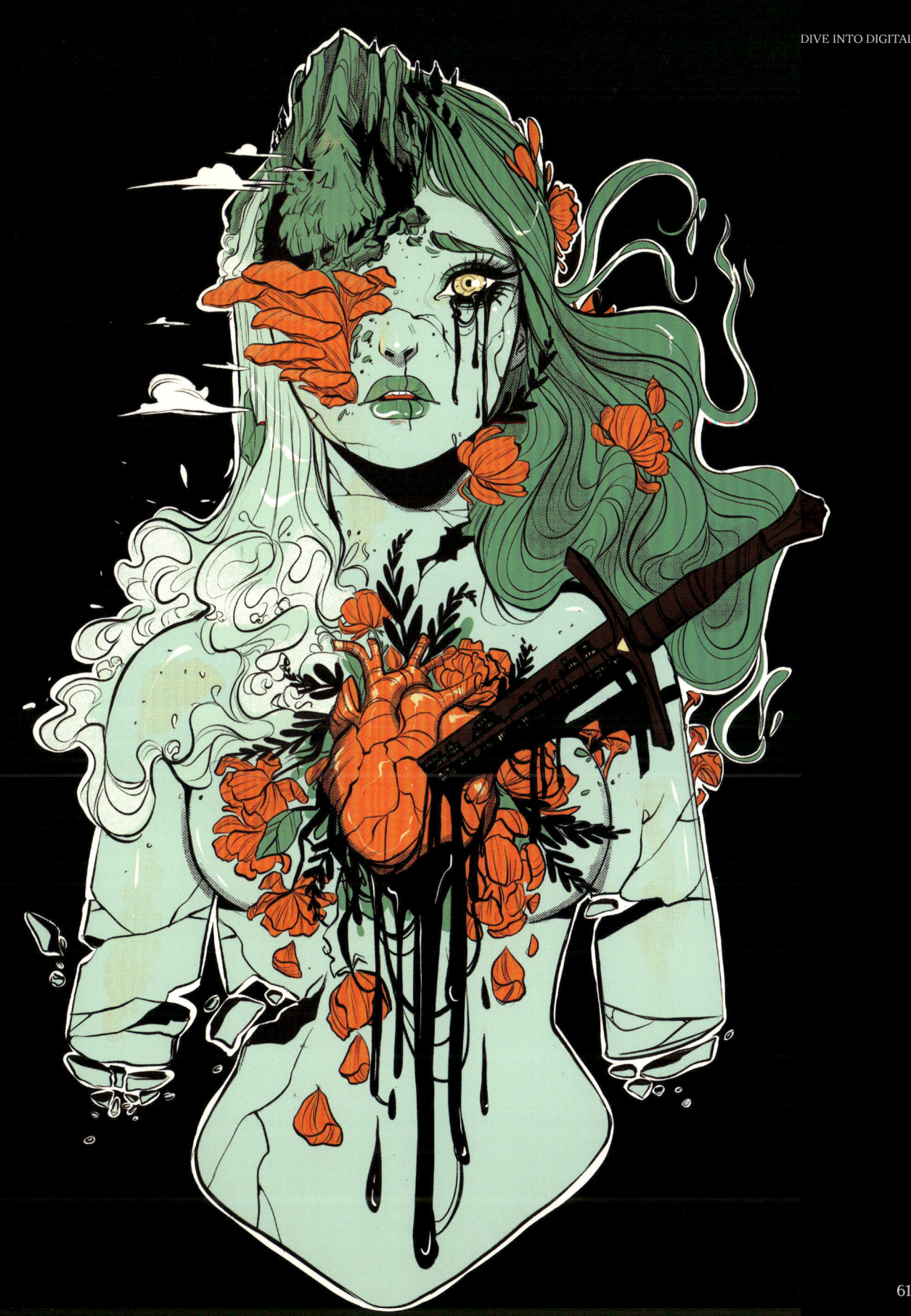

Connecting with other artists

One of the best things I've done this year is collaborate with other artists. When you're a freelance artist who works from home, it can get super lonely. I hardly see anyone all day, let alone other artists. When I go to conventions, I come away feeling so inspired and rejuvenated by being around other like-minded people. So that got me thinking: why don't I just make other fun things with my artist friends? I started reaching out to people I was close with to see if they wanted to make some sort of illustration together.

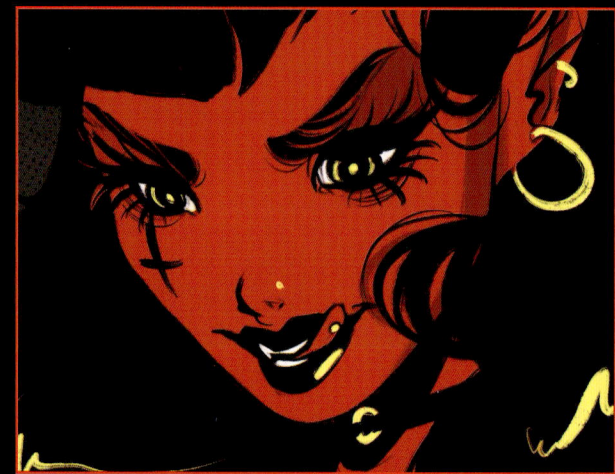

Some of my favourite projects ended up being collabs, especially the ones I had with Jijidraws. We used to live in Las Vegas together, and we would always set up our booths next to each other at conventions, so we decided to start doing fun collabs for all future conventions. We got such a great response from both of our respective audiences that we kept it up, and even did some online-shop drops, too. I think doing this and having a back-and-forth with another artist is so inspiring and helpful for improving your skills. Other artists can see what you can't in your own work, and can give you helpful feedback. You can bounce ideas off them to see what works, and you can even let them help you with parts of your piece that aren't your strong suit. Also, it's just nice to work with a friend sometimes! The artist's path can be so lonely, but it doesn't have to be like that all the time. I think it's important to reach out and talk to other creators. Fill your world with art in every way possible!

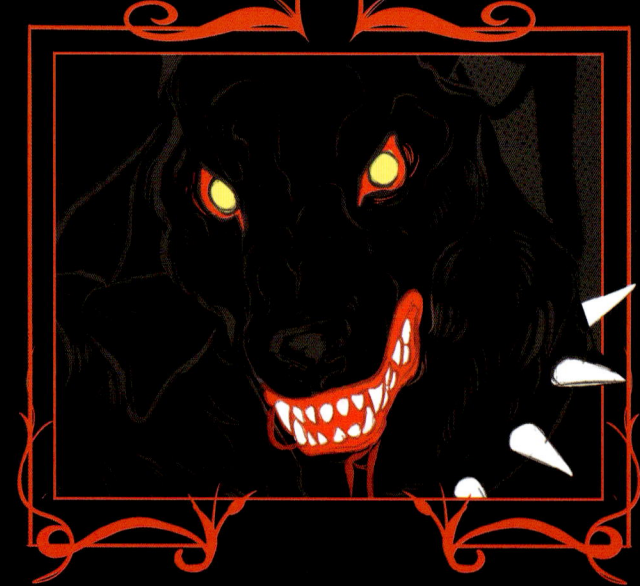

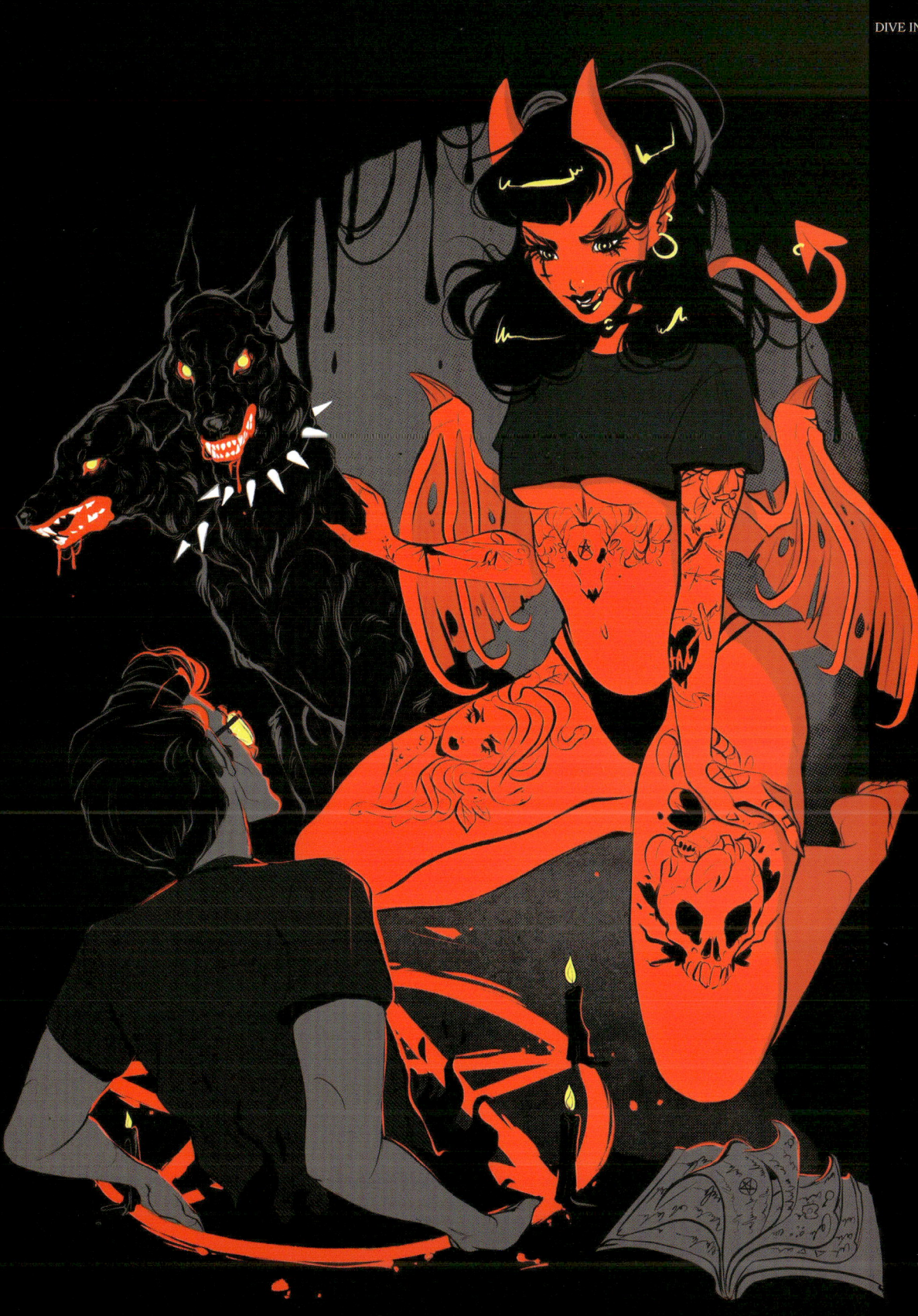

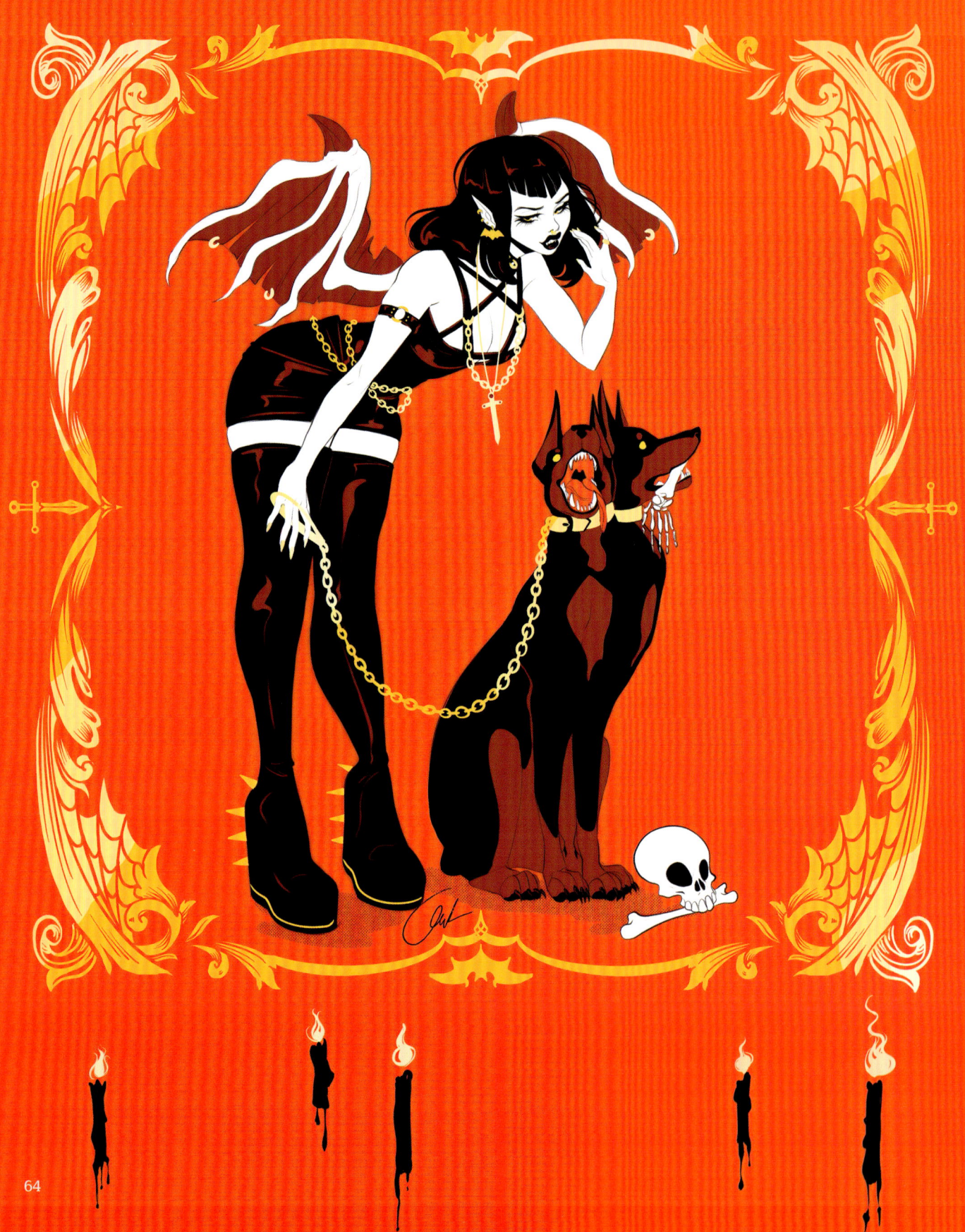

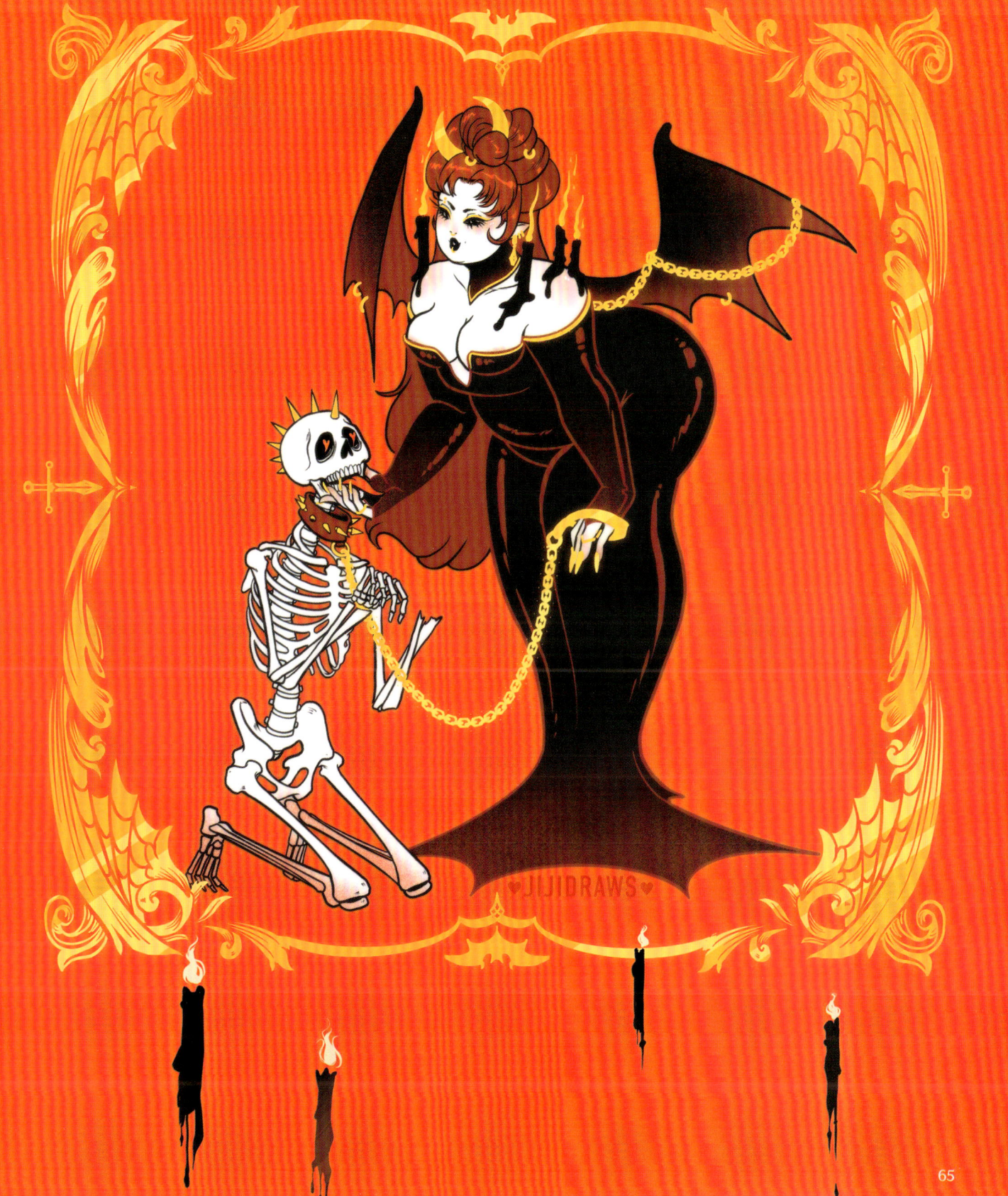

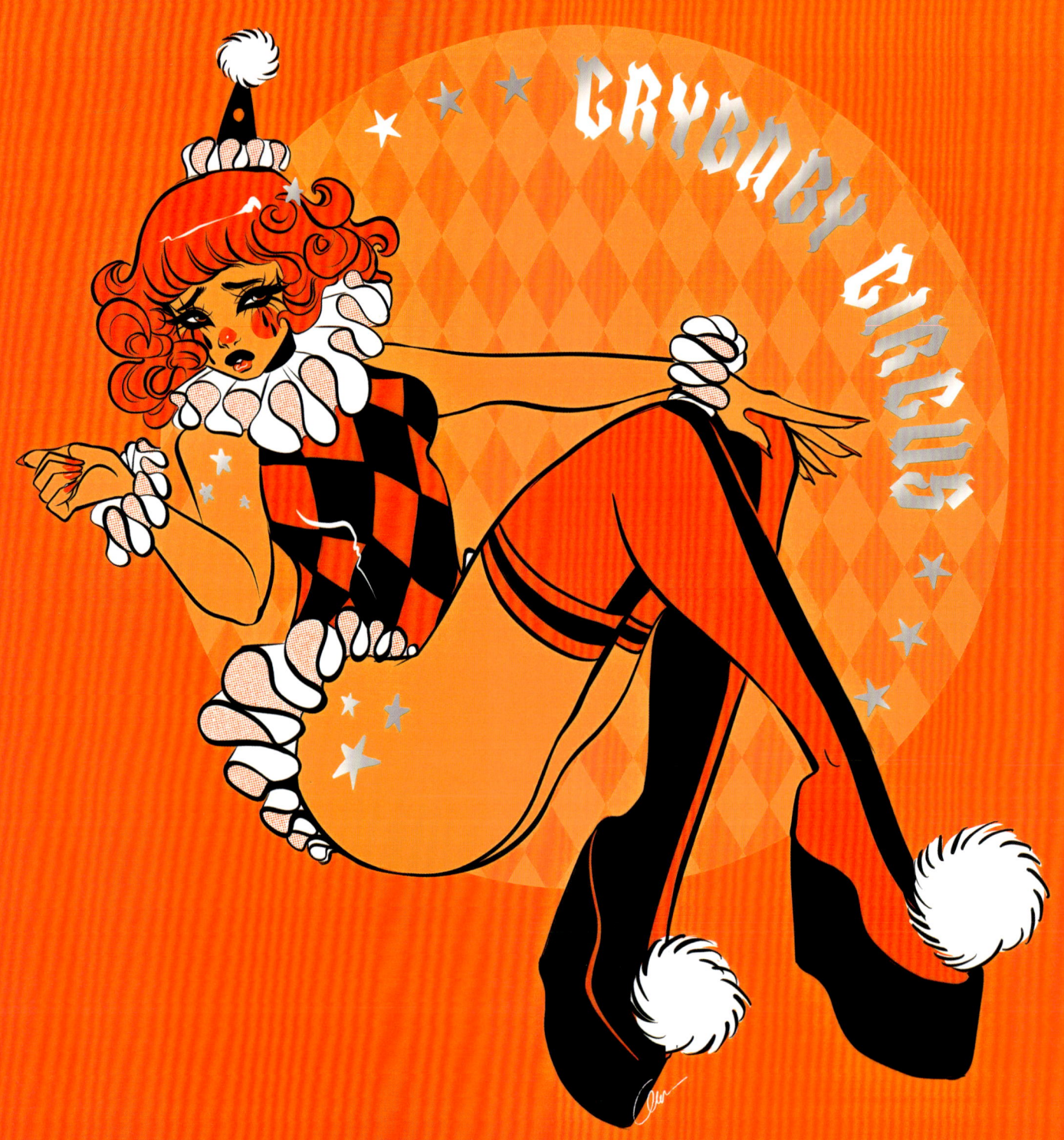

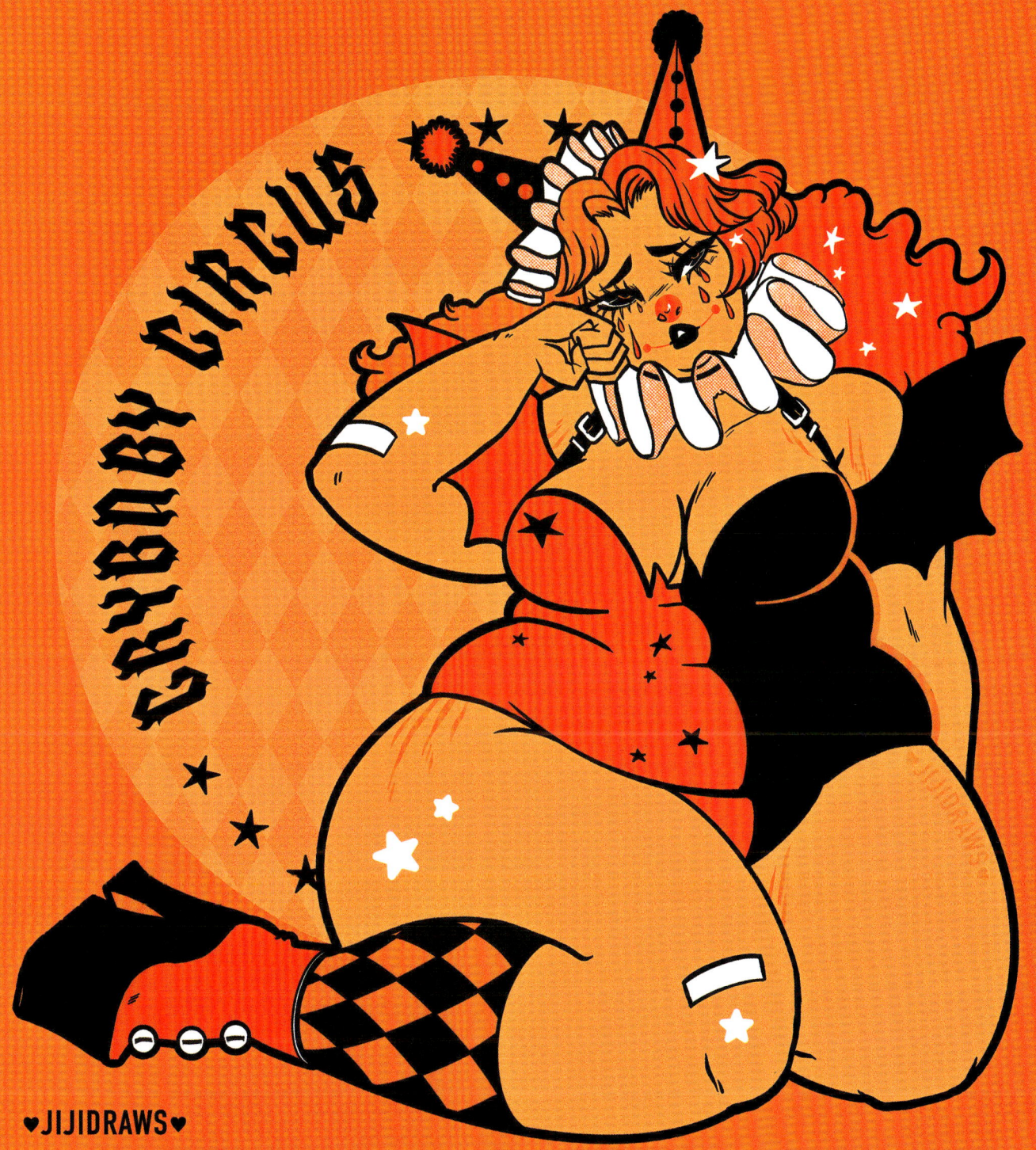

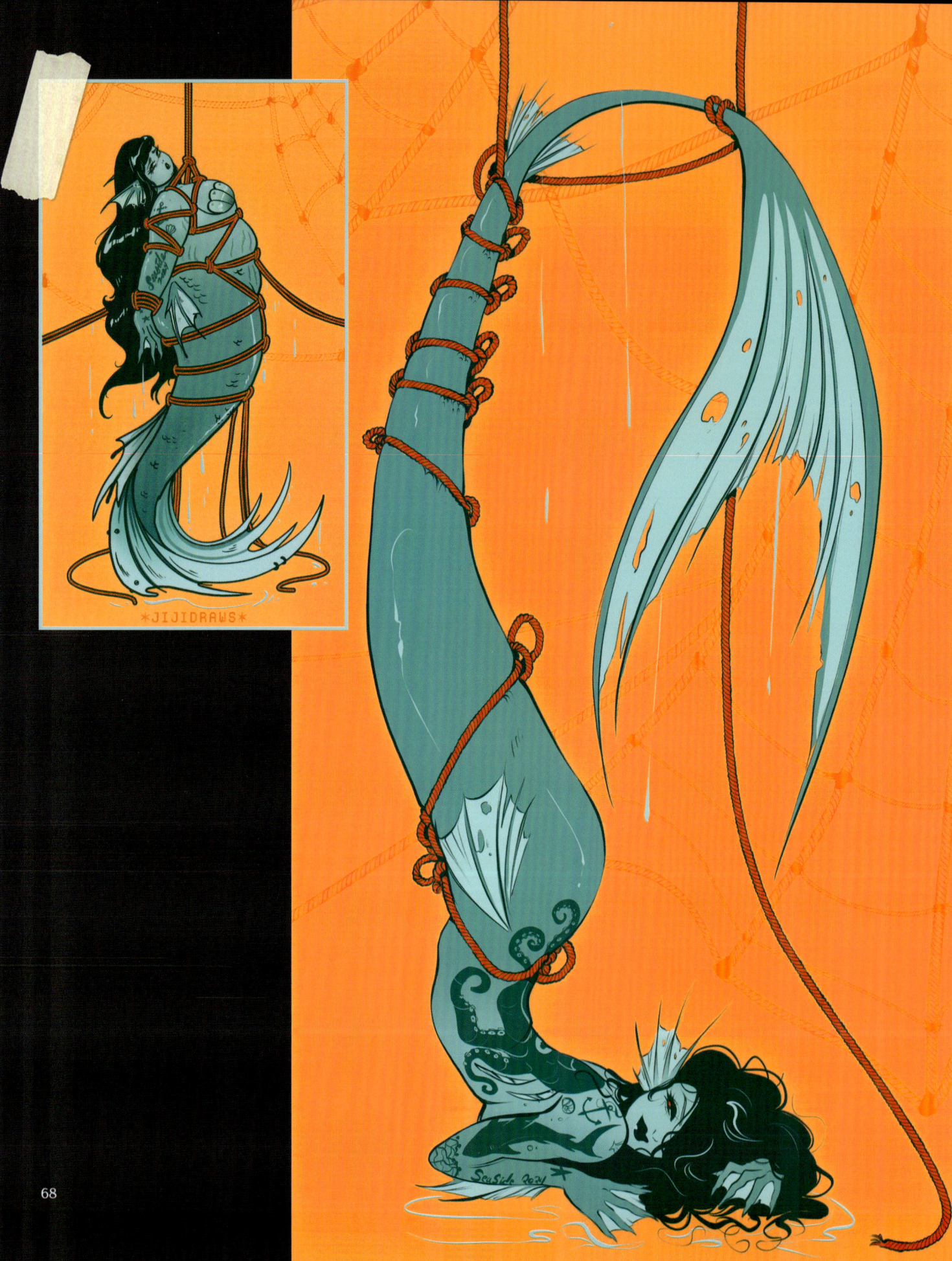

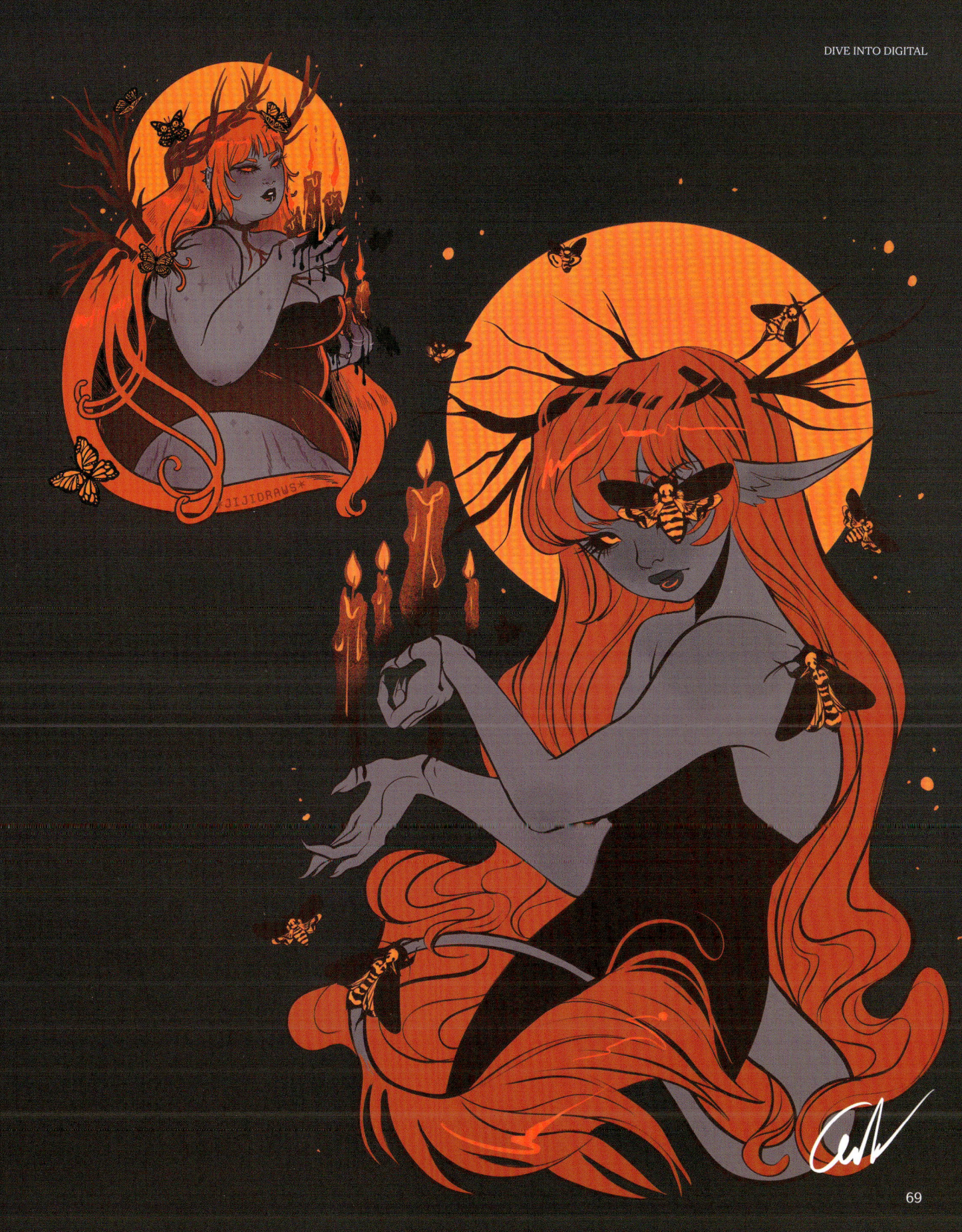

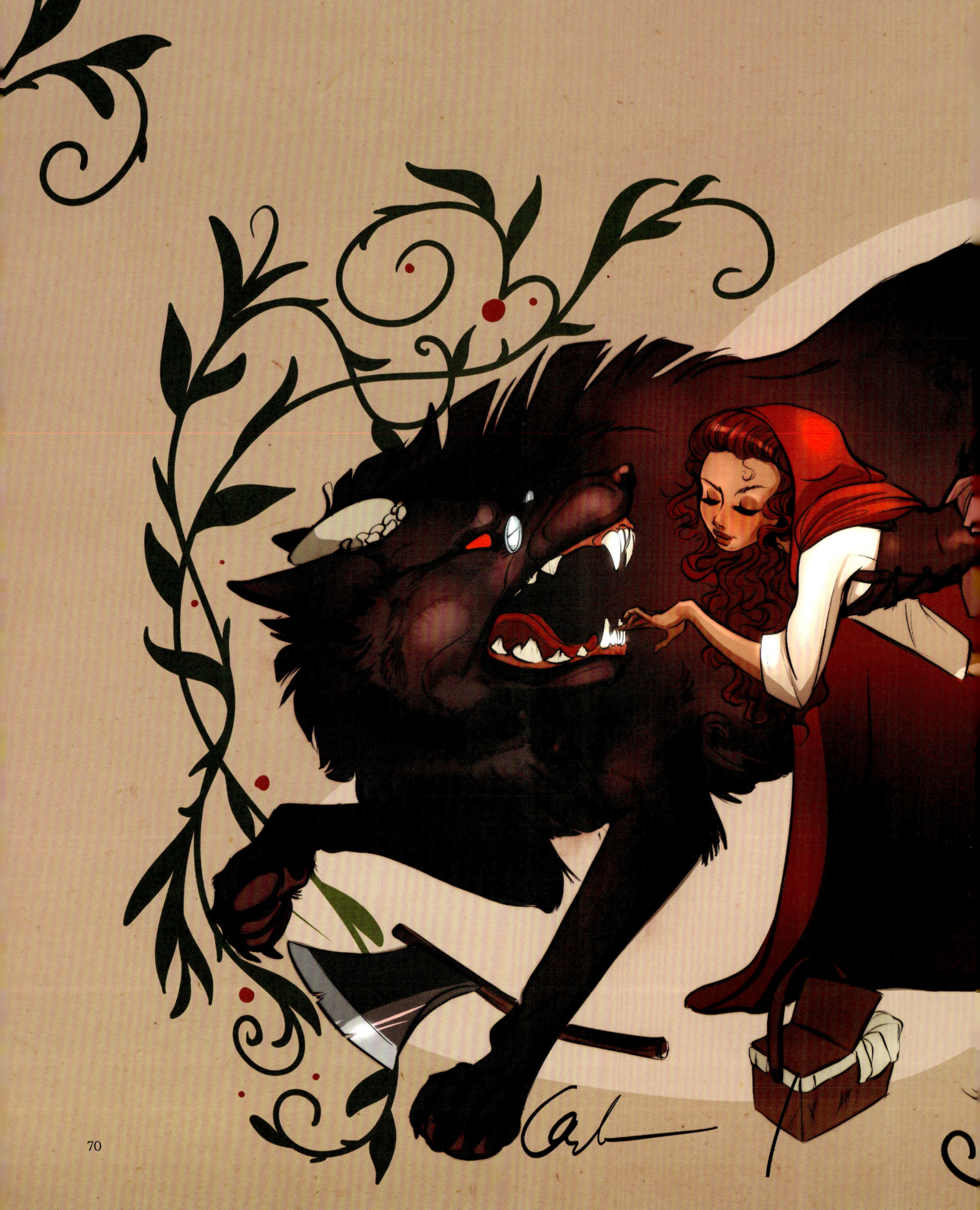

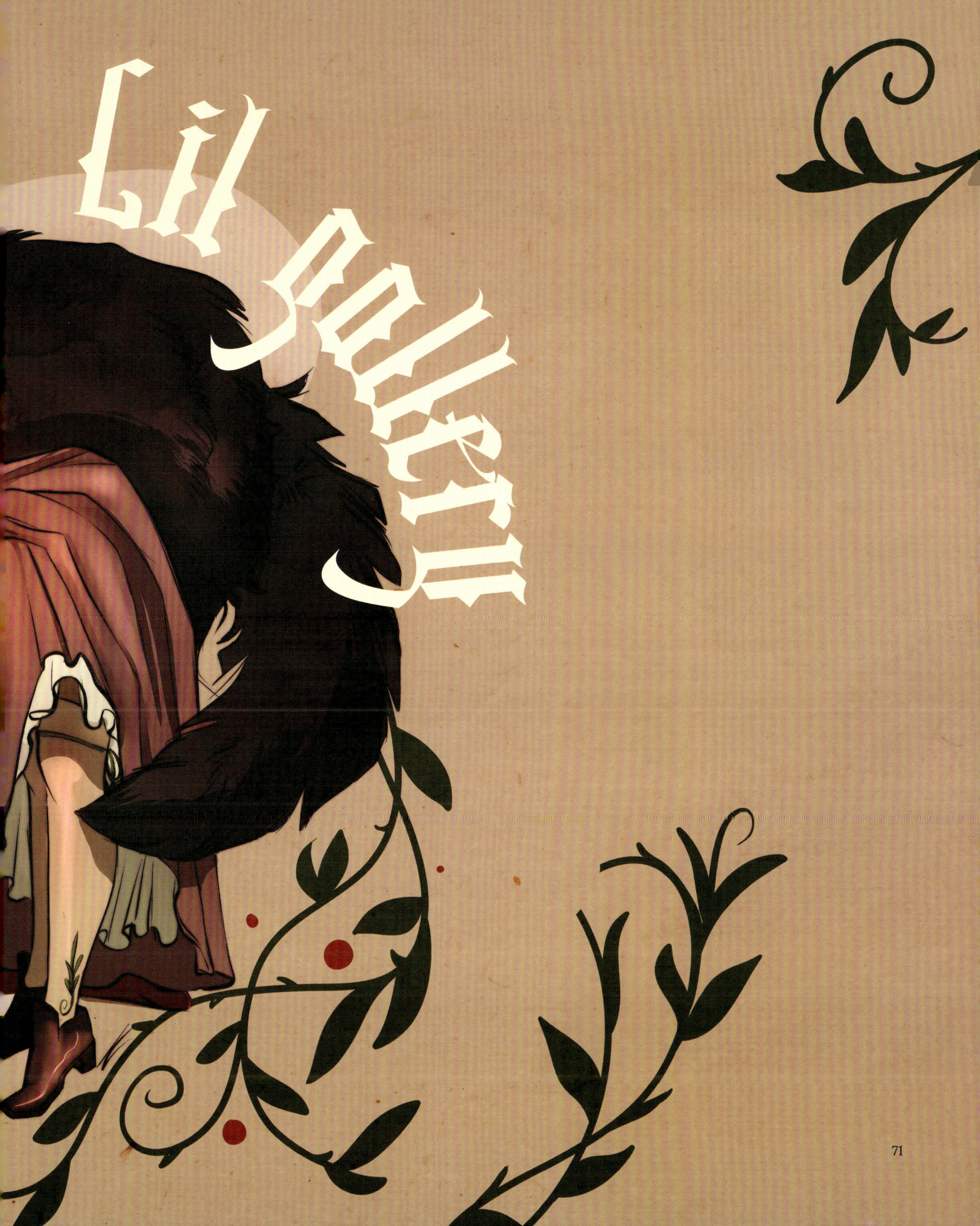

Lil gallery

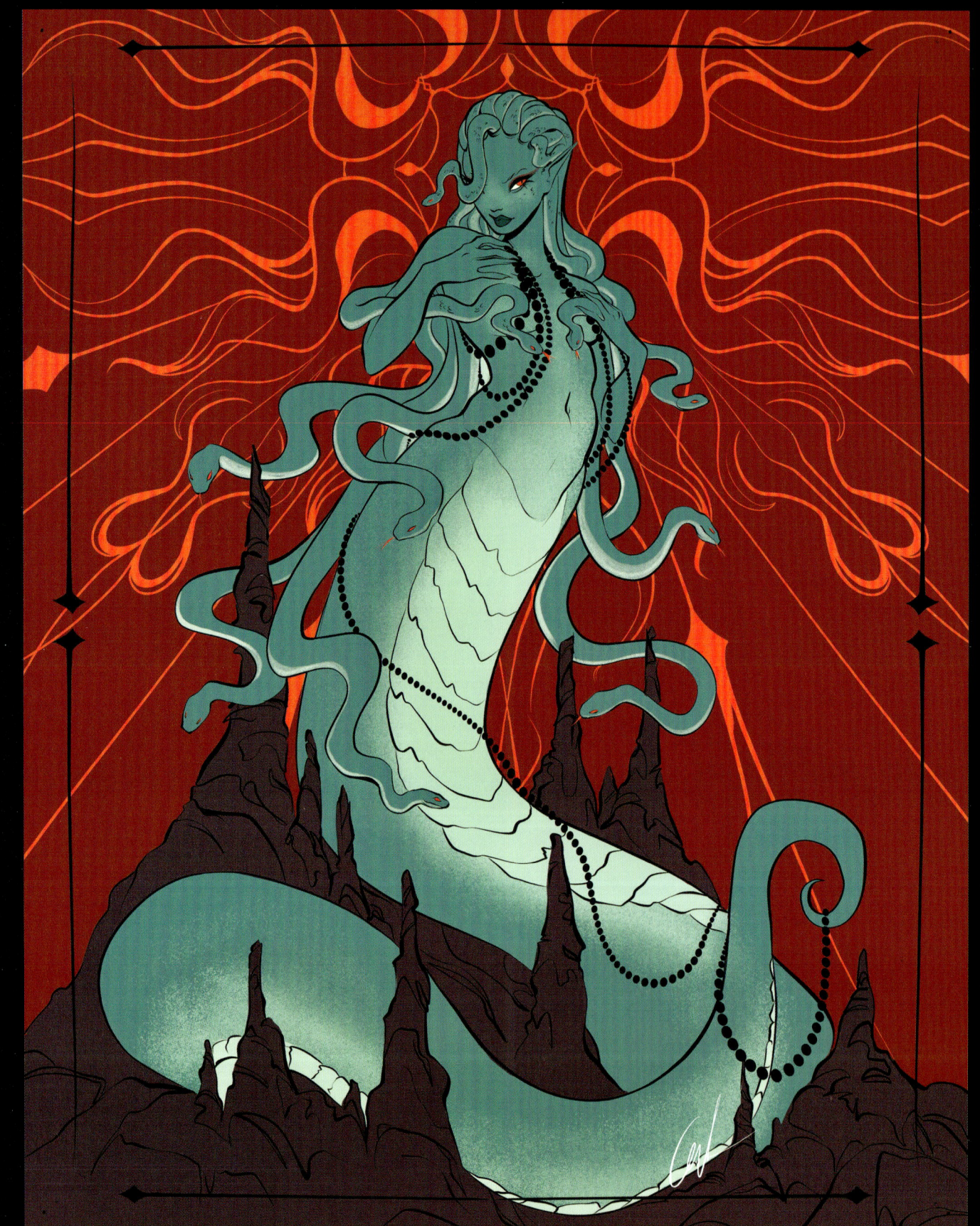

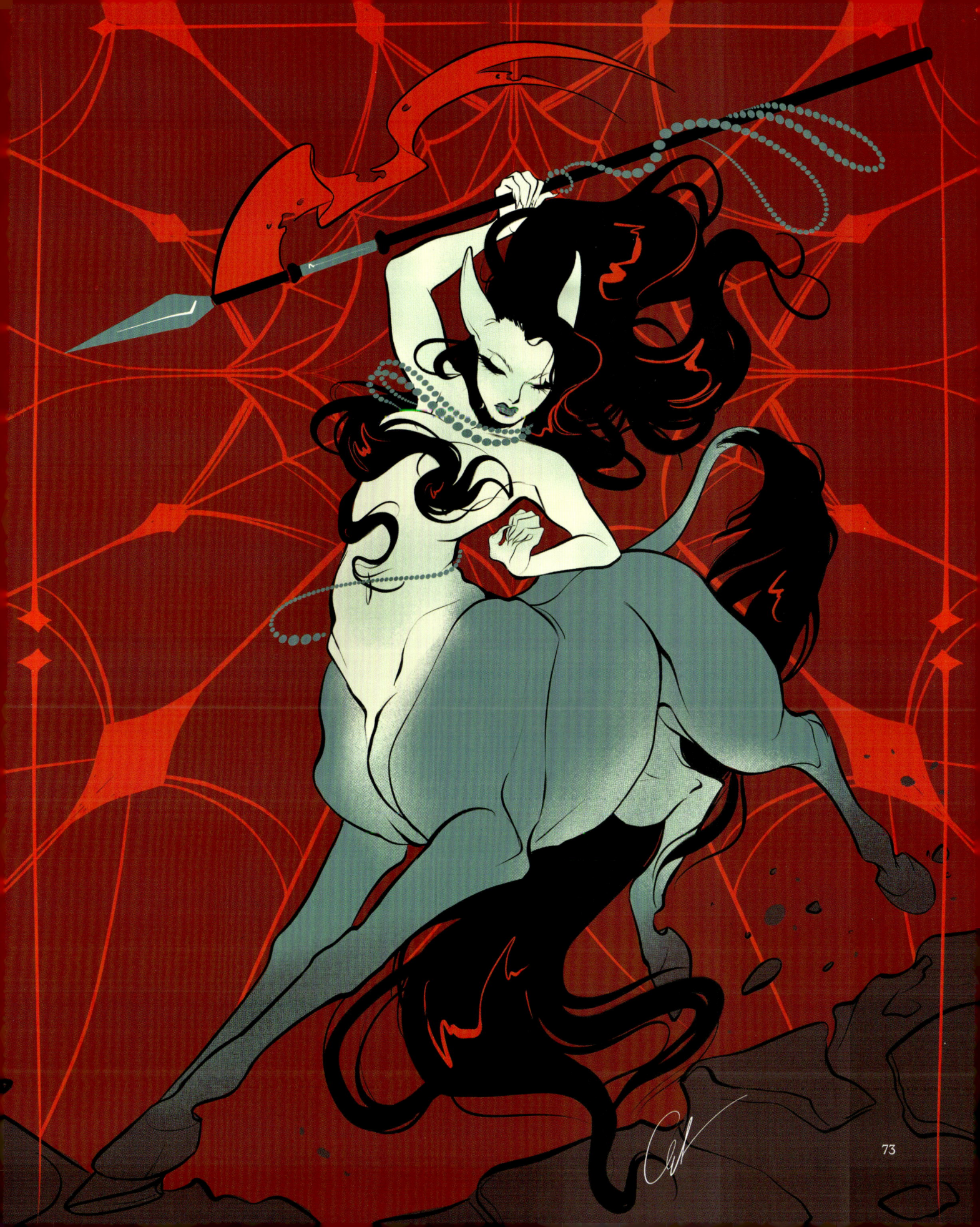

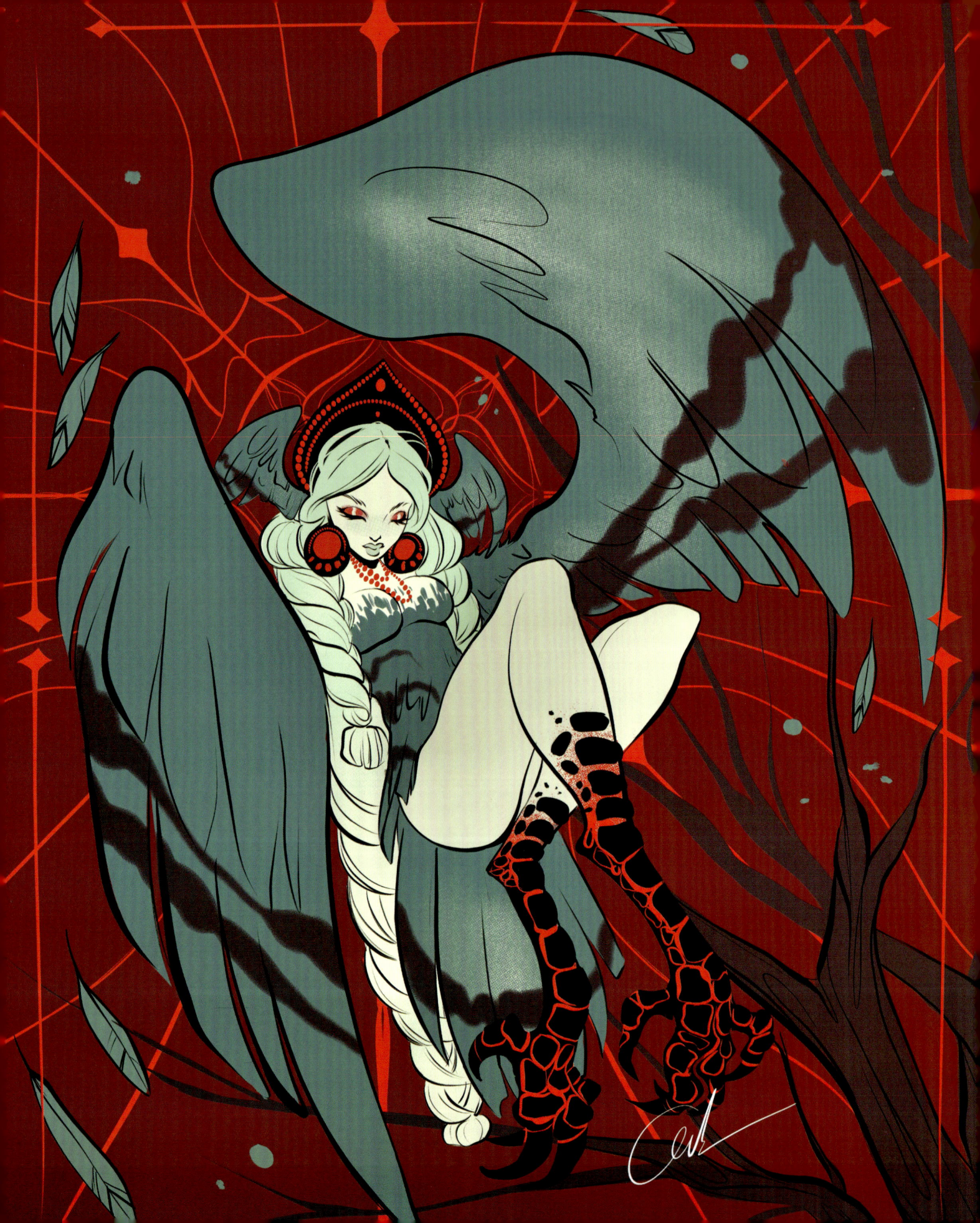

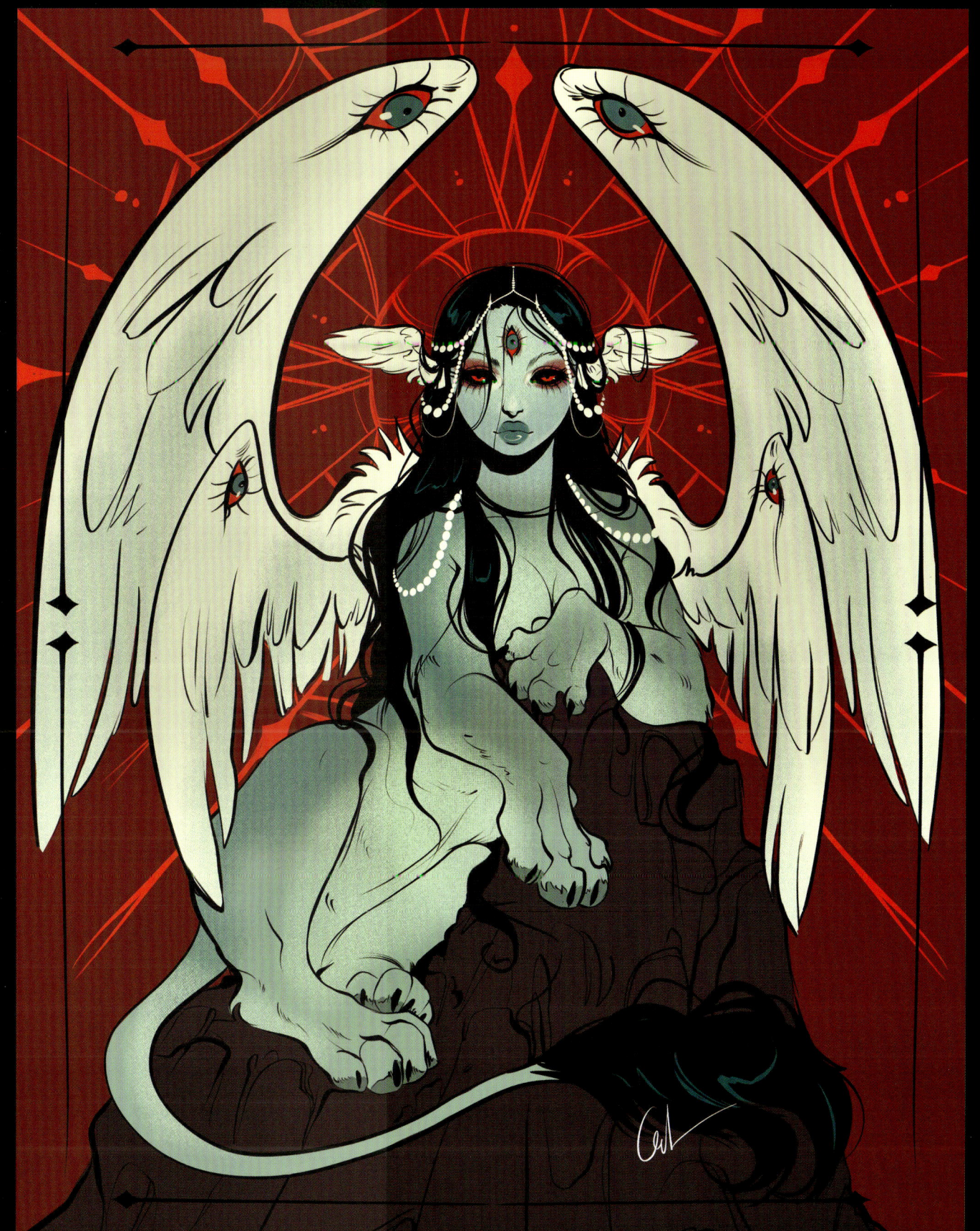

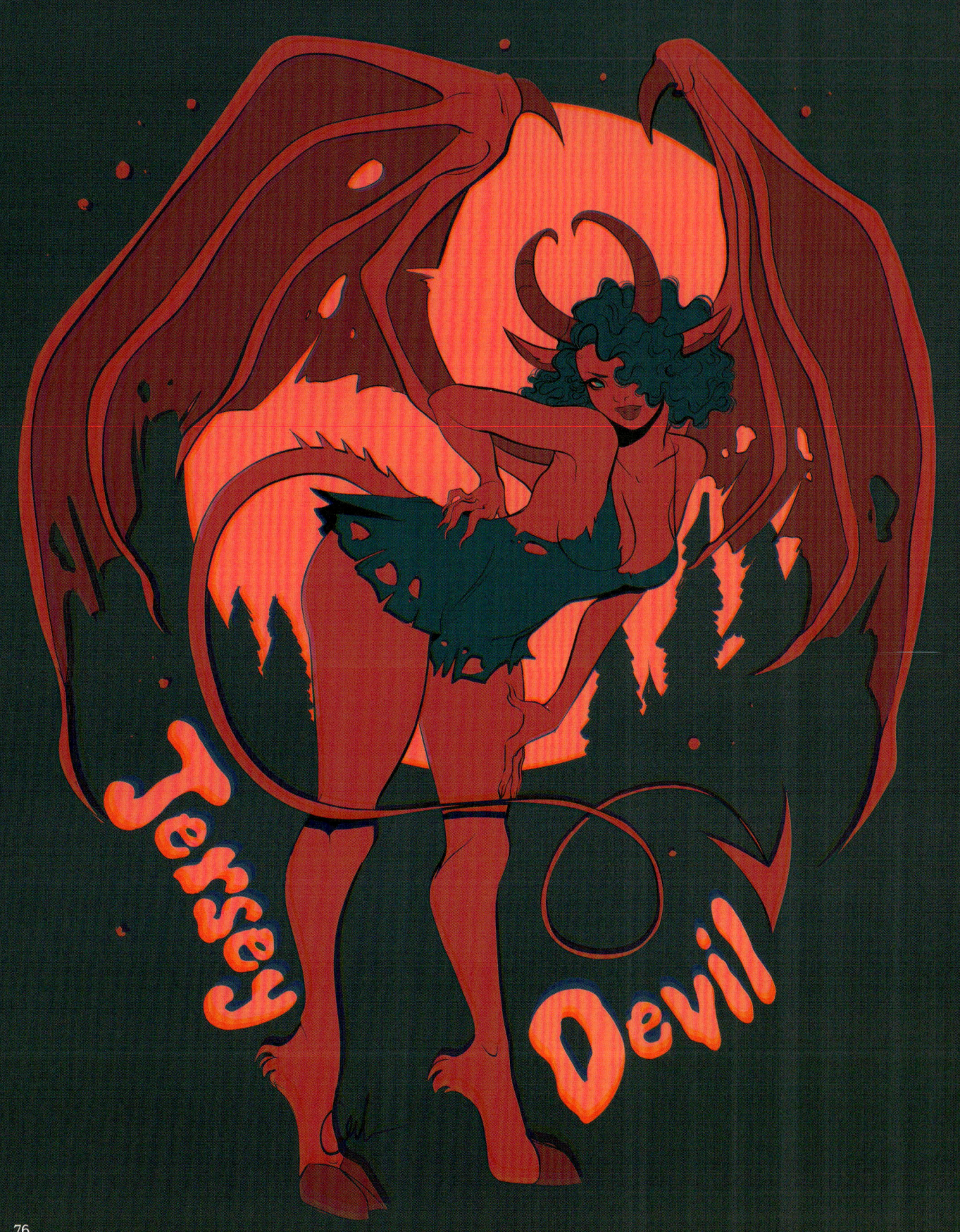

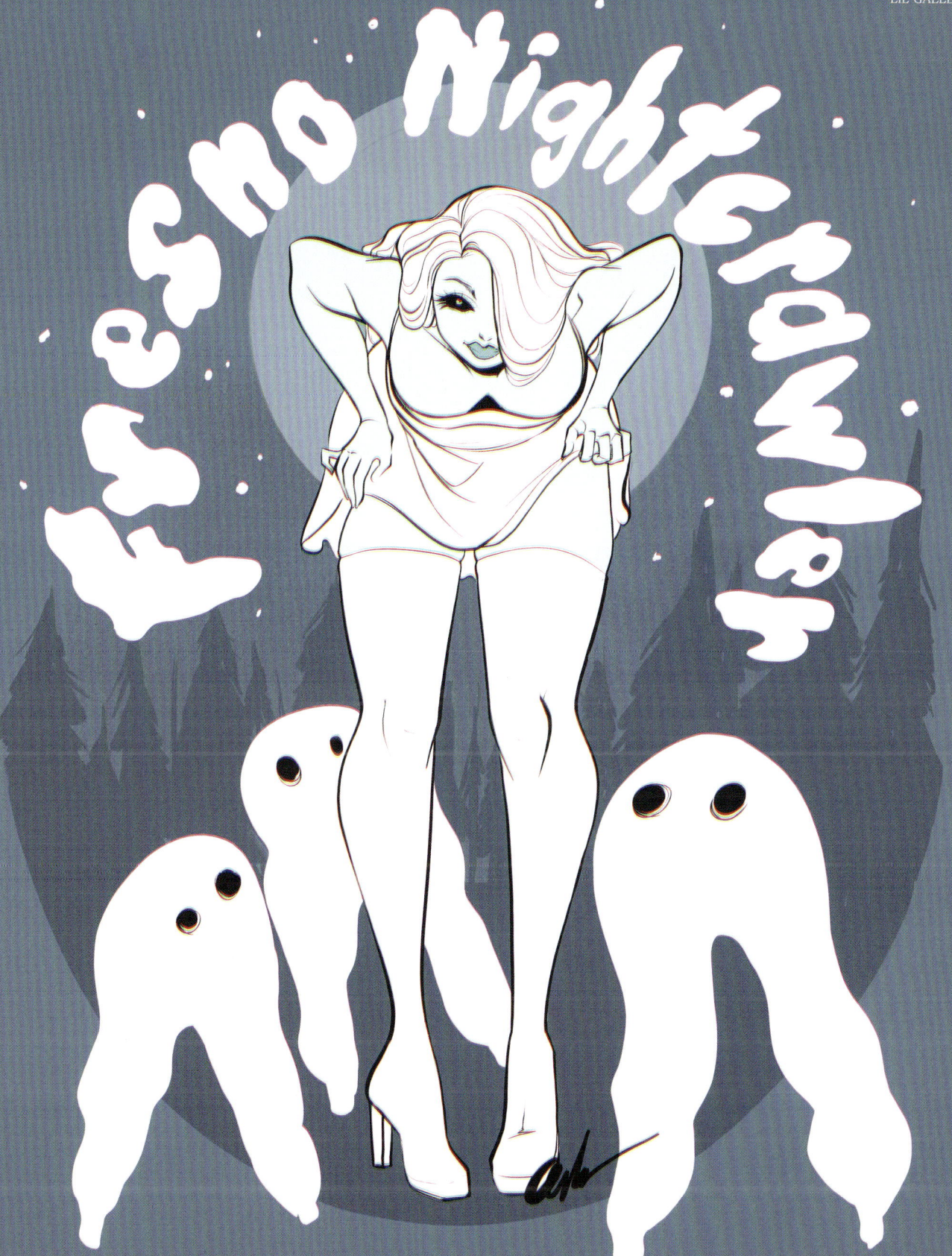

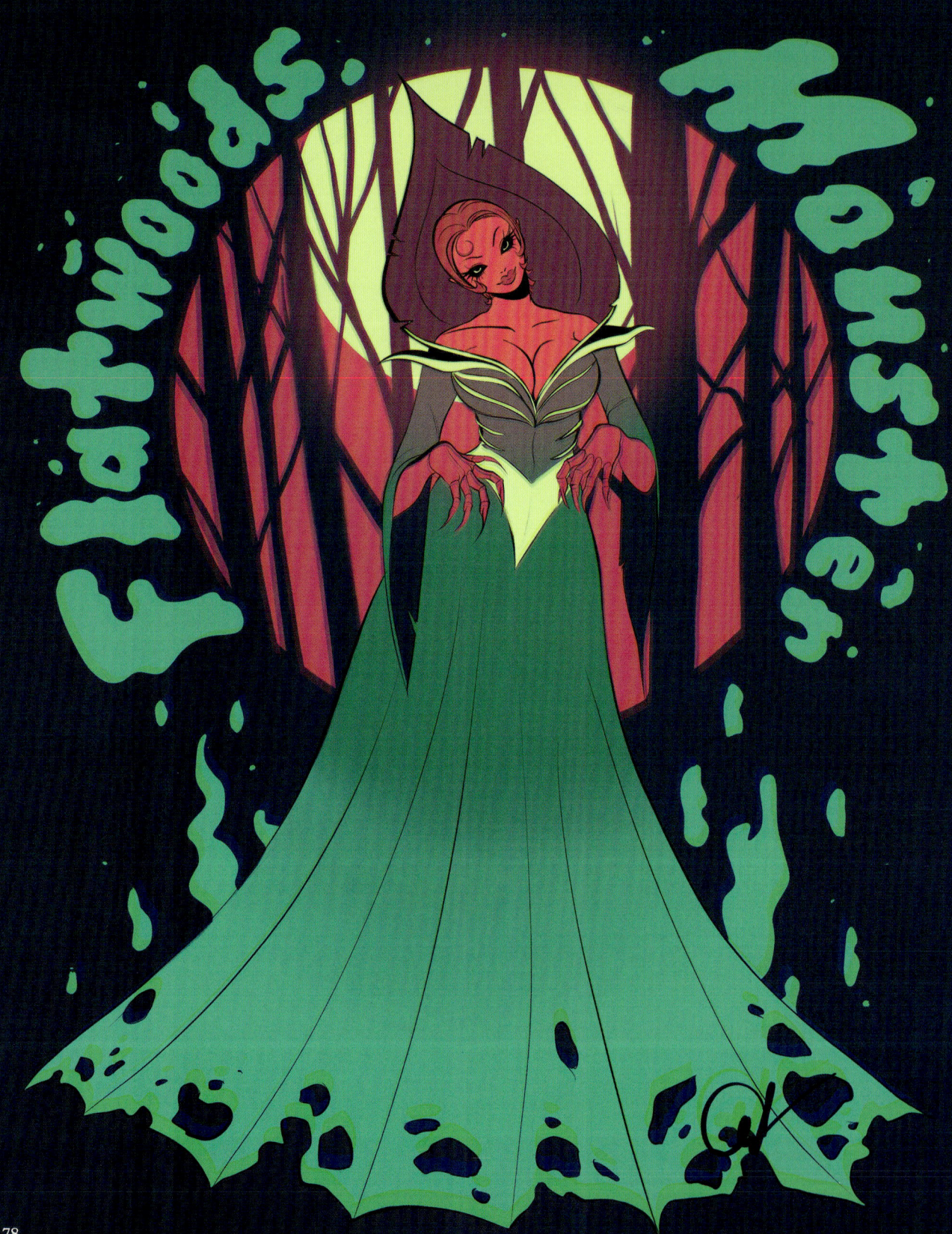

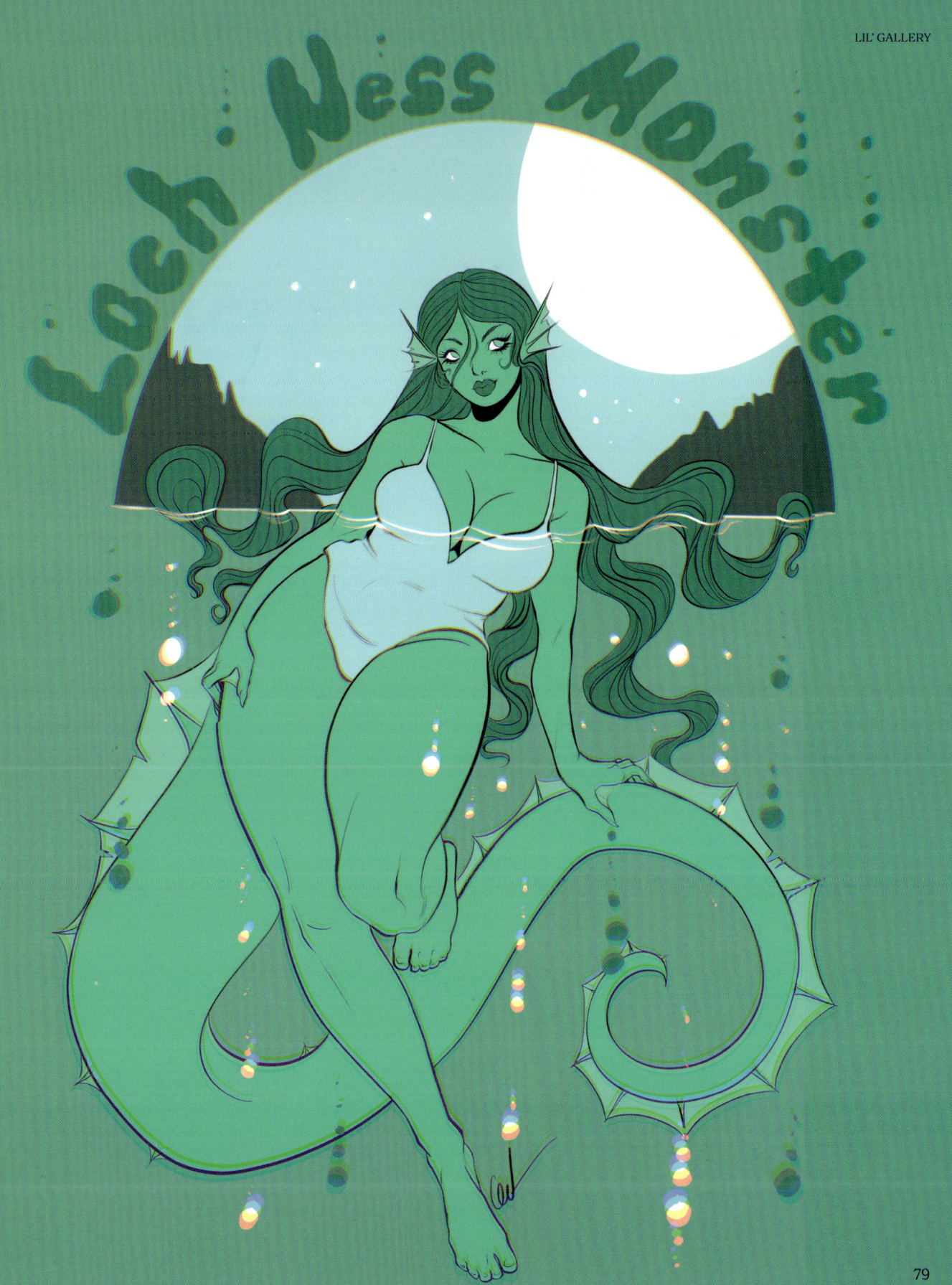

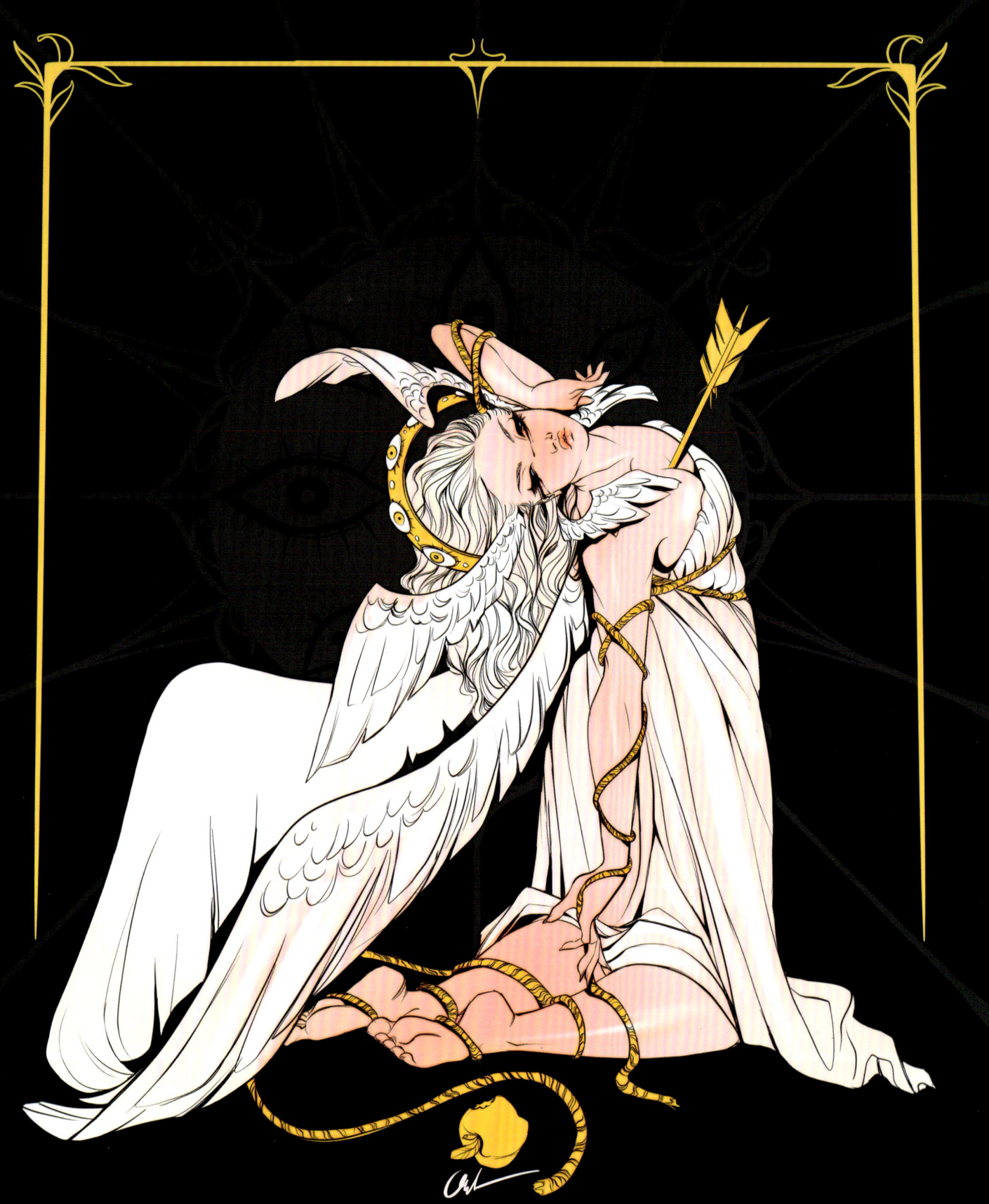

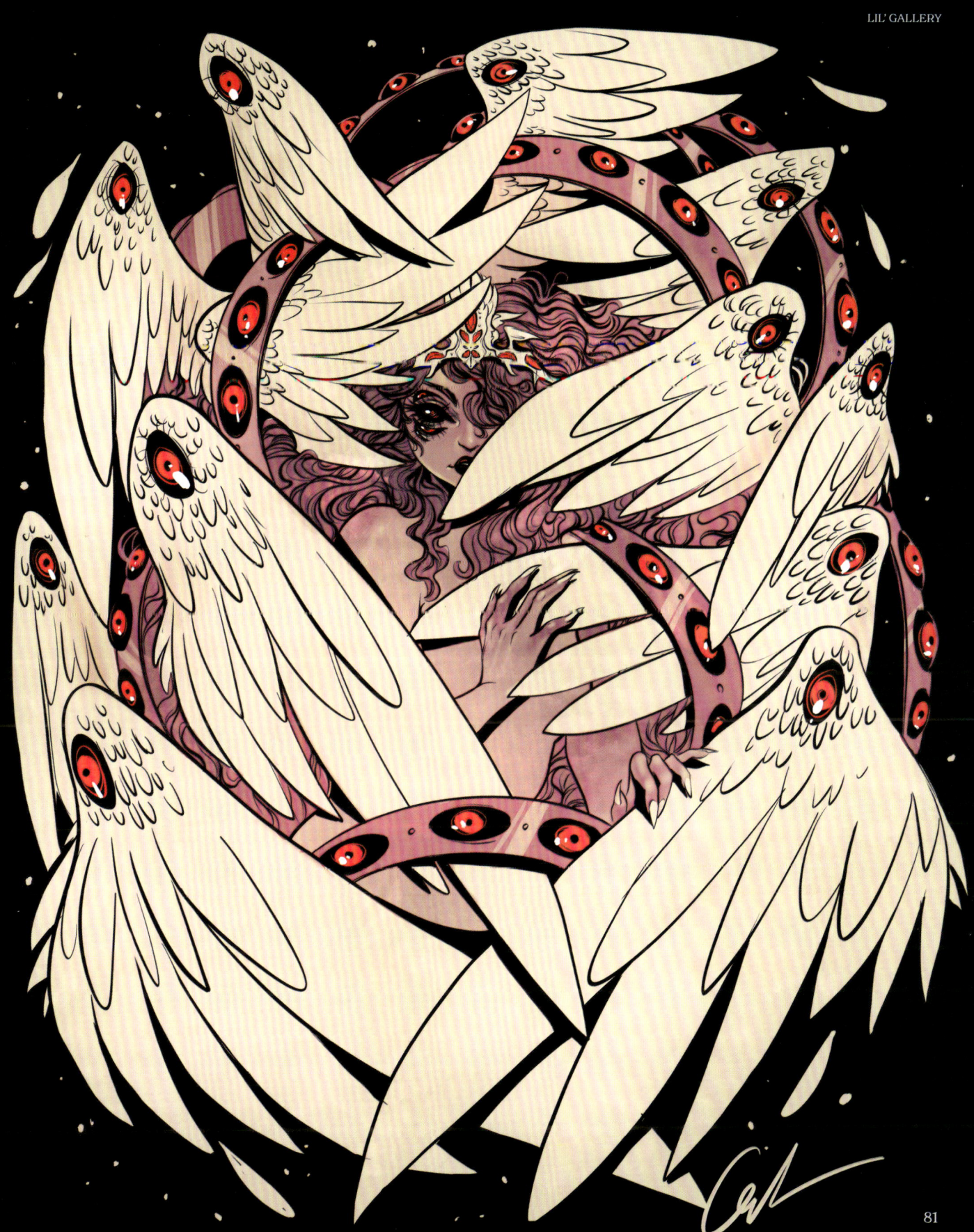

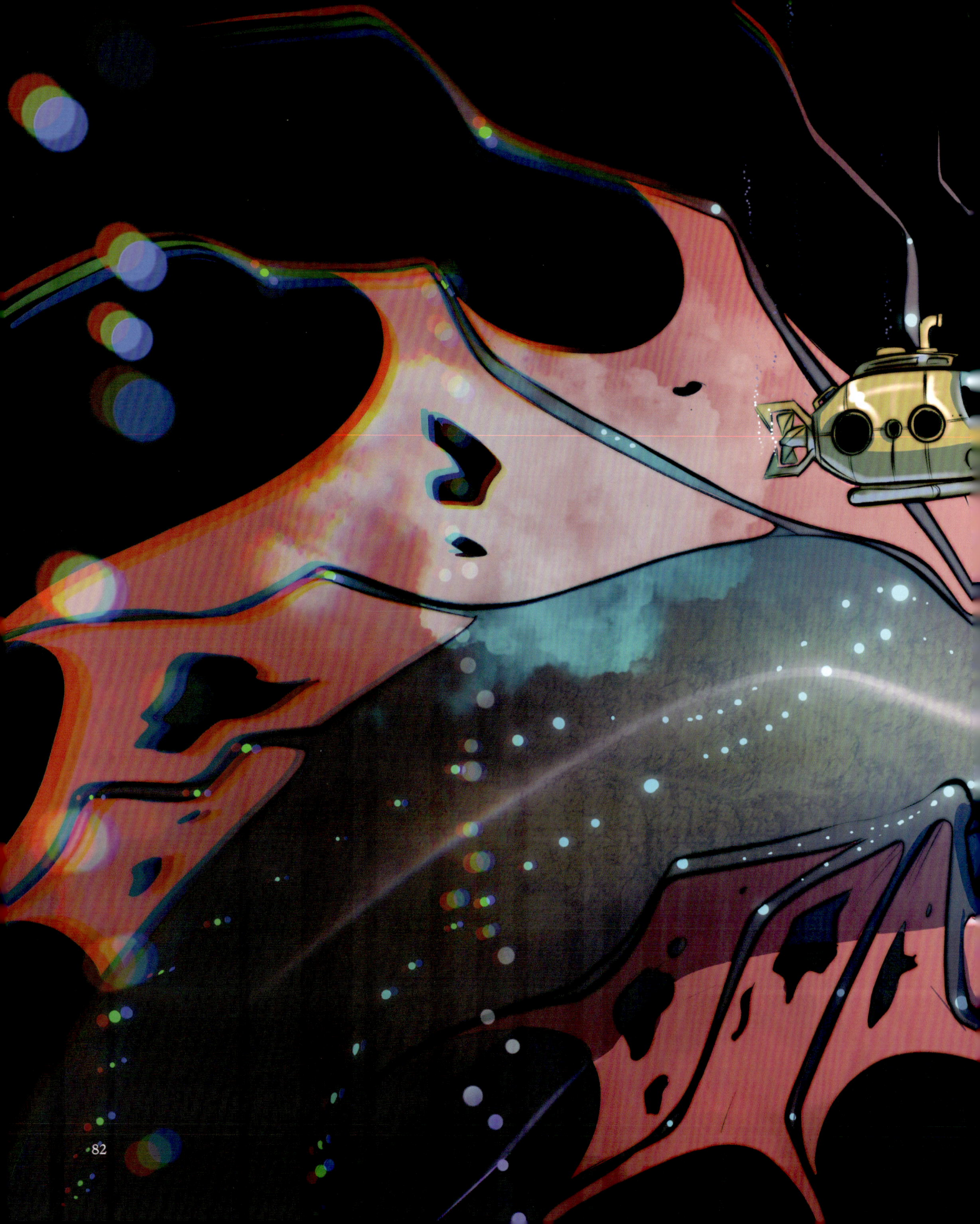

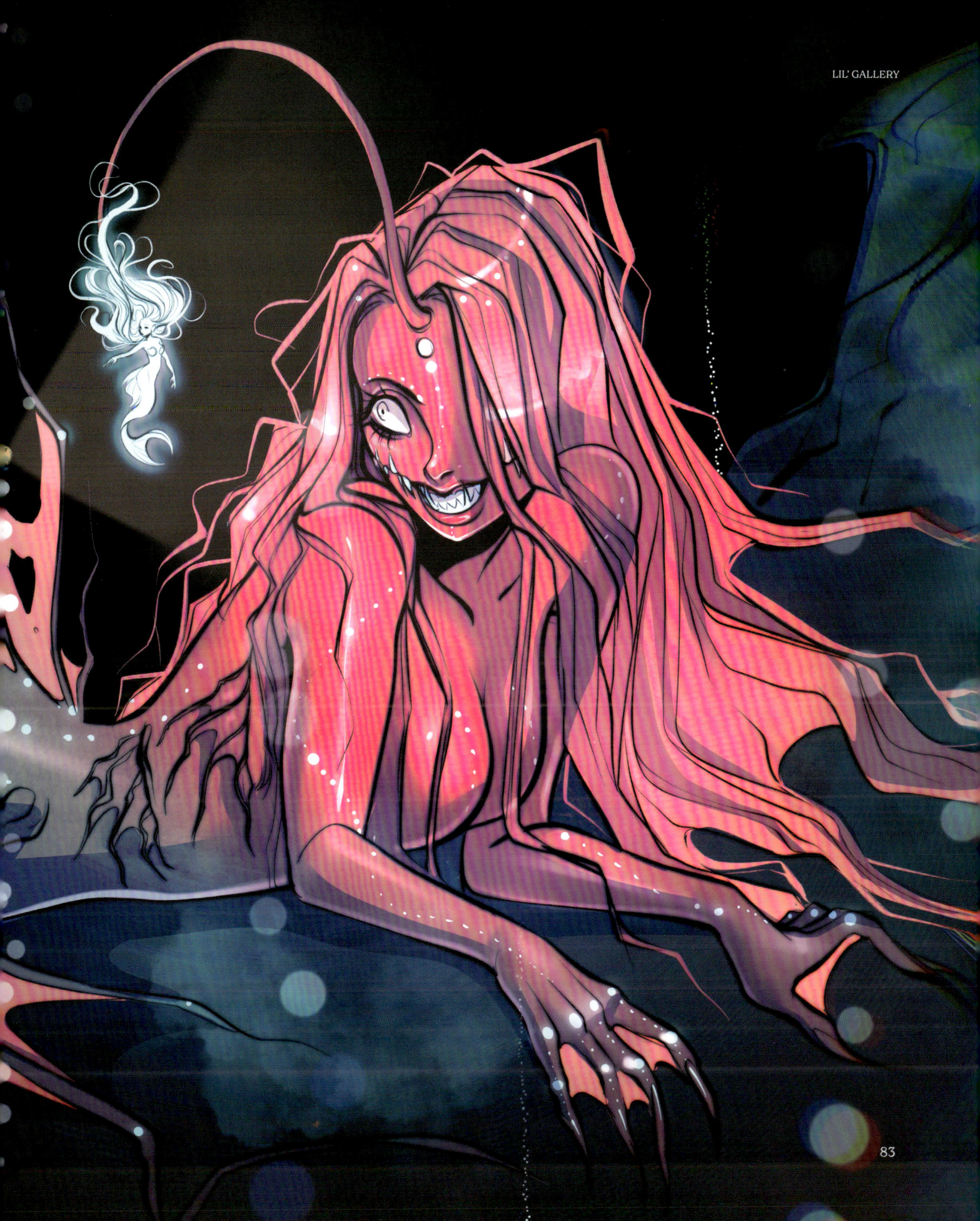

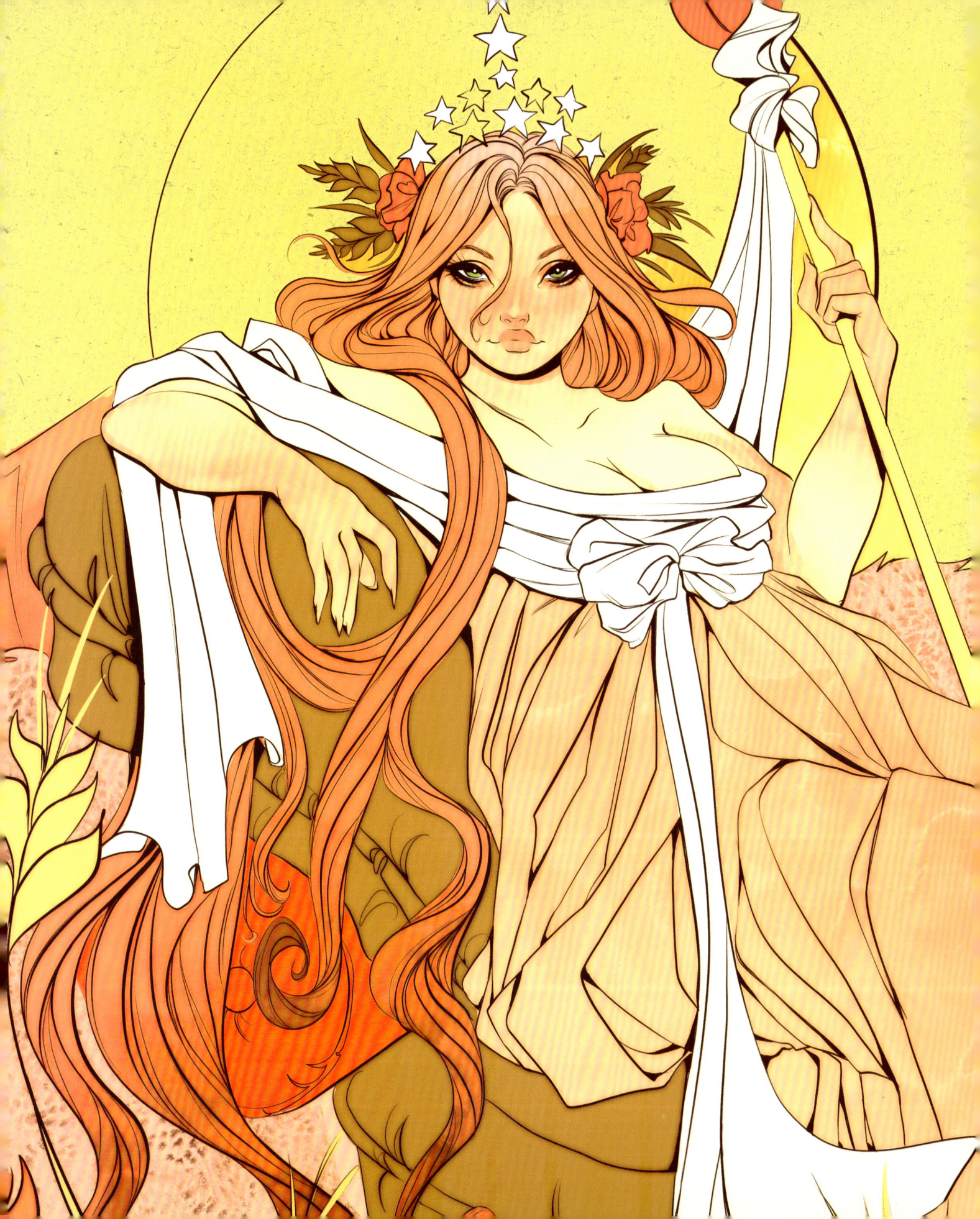

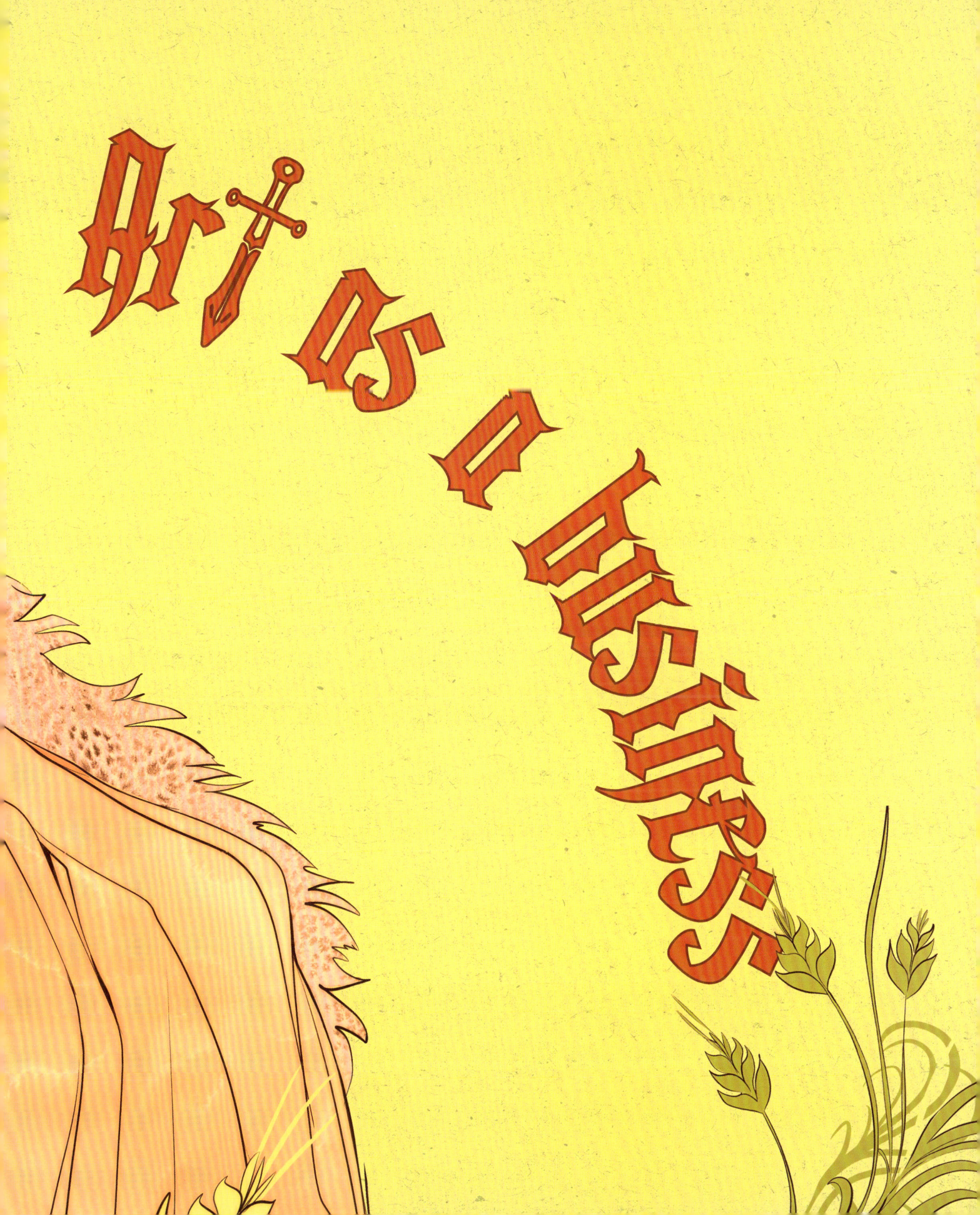

Art as a business

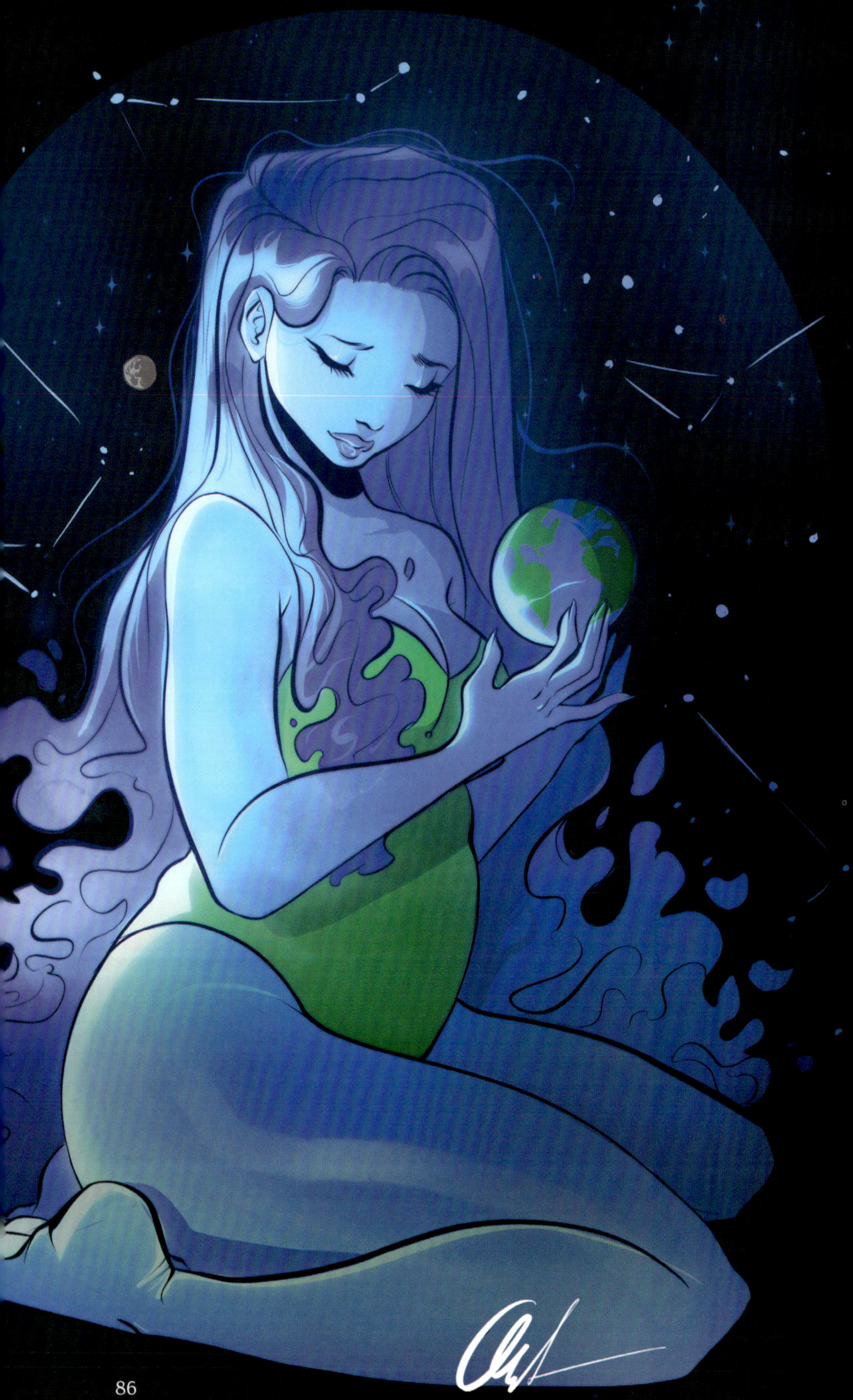

Online shop

As an artist, one of the most important things to tick off your list is creating your own online shop. It lets you take control of your art in a way that wasn't quite accessible in the past. Once you get your social-media presence up and running, it's important for your shop to be ready as well. Many artists think it's better to wait until they are well known or have nicer products, but I think that holds you back from ever really getting started.

When I first opened my shop, I used to do my own prints and cut my own stickers. You can always start small and work your way up to larger, higher-quality prints and products. As soon as you start getting enough sales, you can move into outsourcing your products. In time, this might get to be a lot for one person to handle, and you will either have to look into fulfilment centres or hire someone to manage your shop.

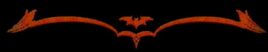

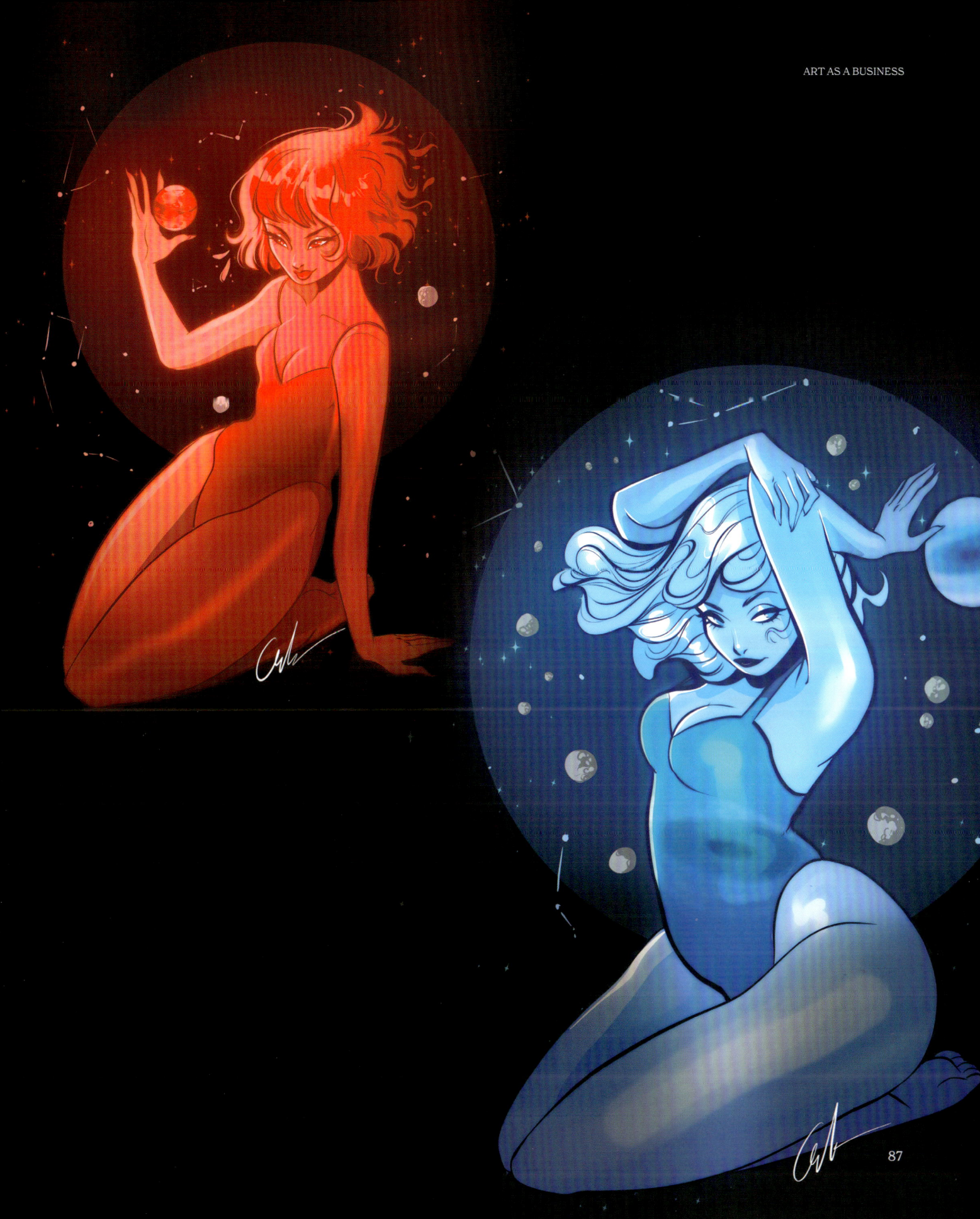

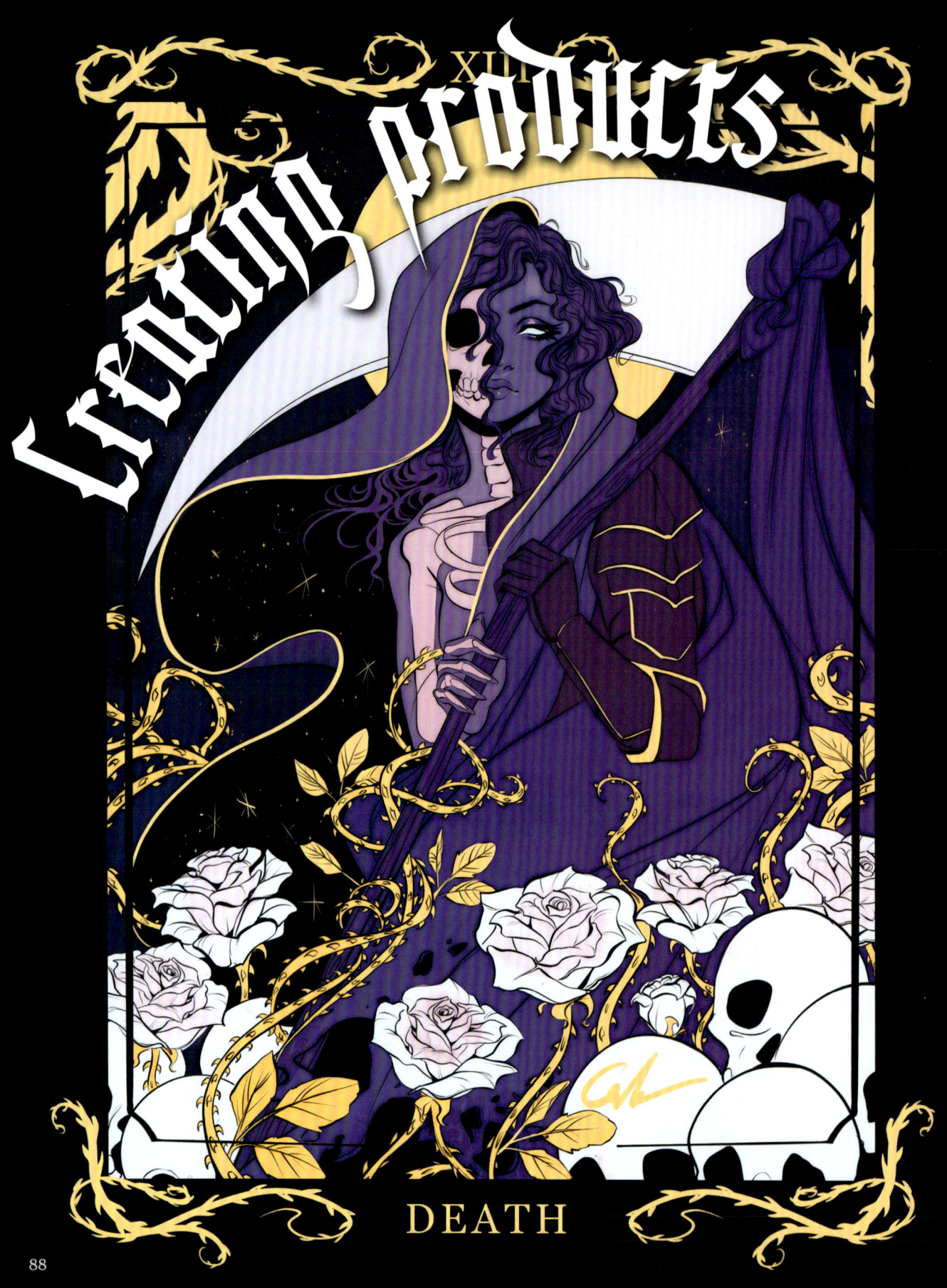

Creating products

DEATH

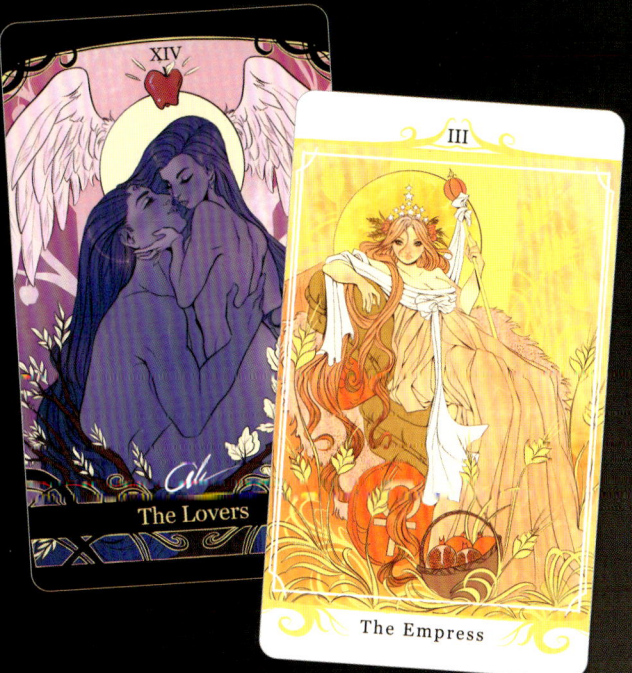

One of my favourite parts about being an artist is getting to create products! Of course, like I previously said, it's always good to start with prints and stickers, but there are endless possibilities when it comes to new merchandise. I highly recommend creating items that you would actually want yourself. That could be key rings, apparel, or stationery. Stick to stuff you want to make instead of making things just for the sake of having it.

Once you've got some ideas, then it's time to research. You can ask other artists how they make their own products or what production companies they use, but this can be tricky as many artists hold that information close to their chests. So, do the deep diving yourself. Production companies are super easy to find and there are a bunch of different options to choose from.

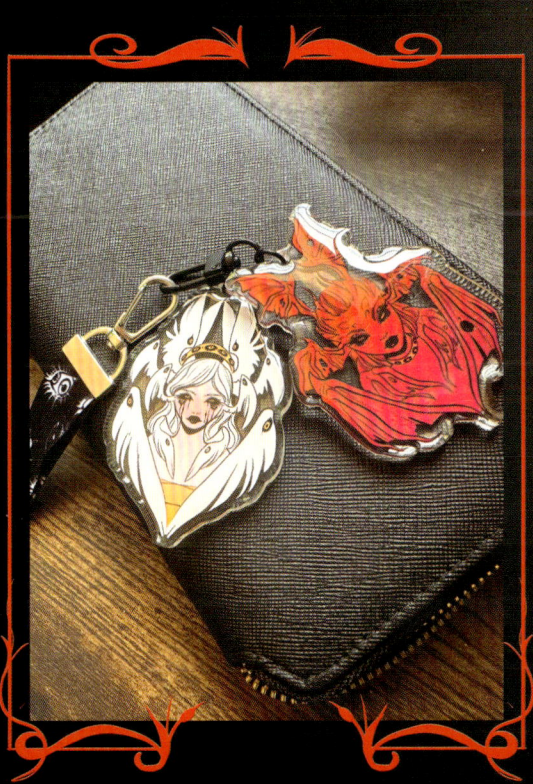

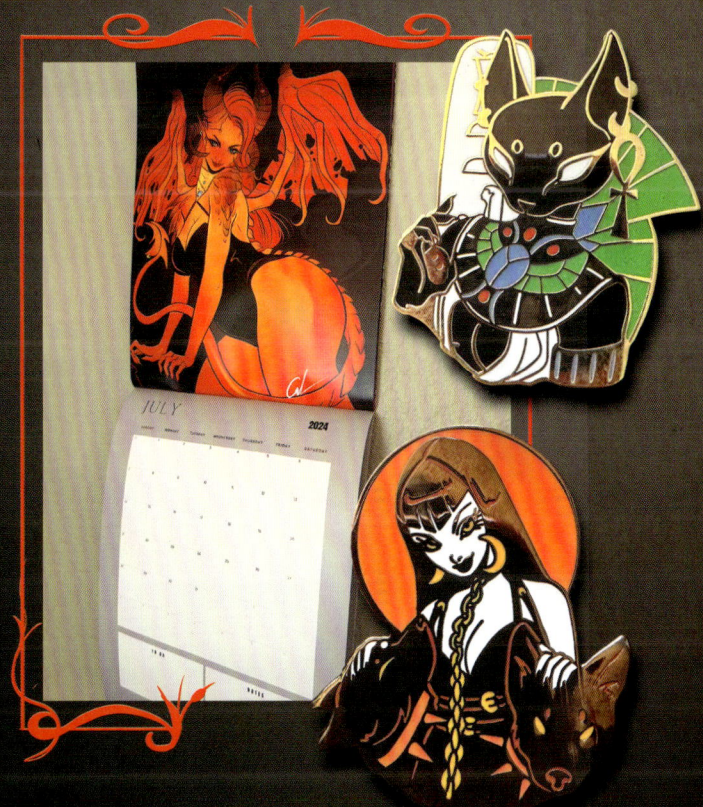

Freelancing

It took me a while to get my first freelance job. Social media was great for allowing companies to find me and reach out about working together on projects. In particular, Instagram made it really easy to have an accessible portfolio for everyone to see. If you want to get into freelancing, it's important to have your portfolio on a website *and* on social-media accounts. Companies need a place to see your art in one place to figure out if you're the perfect fit for the job. You can also go about getting a freelance agent, but you will still need an online portfolio for that.

Freelance is the basis of my career, but it's not something I heavily rely on. Some months, there will be a bunch of jobs and other months there won't be any. It's important to find multiple sources of income as an artist. Make sure you try out as many options as possible to see what jobs work best for you. It does start off as a bit of a balancing act, but you will get into the swing of things. It's important to be flexible and interested in exploring because sometimes you land a job you didn't even know you would love! I never thought I would get into apparel design but, after my first freelance job, I fell in love with it and I still design apparel for my own personal brand.

Patreon

I love Patreon, Kickstarter, and other similar platforms. They give so much freedom to artists. When it comes to creating monthly subscriptions for your audience, be sure to include them in some way. I let my patrons choose monthly themes, which means they get to choose what I draw. Patreon also gives me the chance to dive into those themes without worrying about income. Having that sort of freedom as an artist is amazing and really gives me the chance to have fun with art and try new things.

I also use platforms like these to experiment with other products, especially stickers and pins. It helps me get a good idea of what is popular. It also goes back to just simply creating a connection with people who love your art. They're not following you at arm's length like they do on Instagram – they are choosing to support you so that you can create more work!

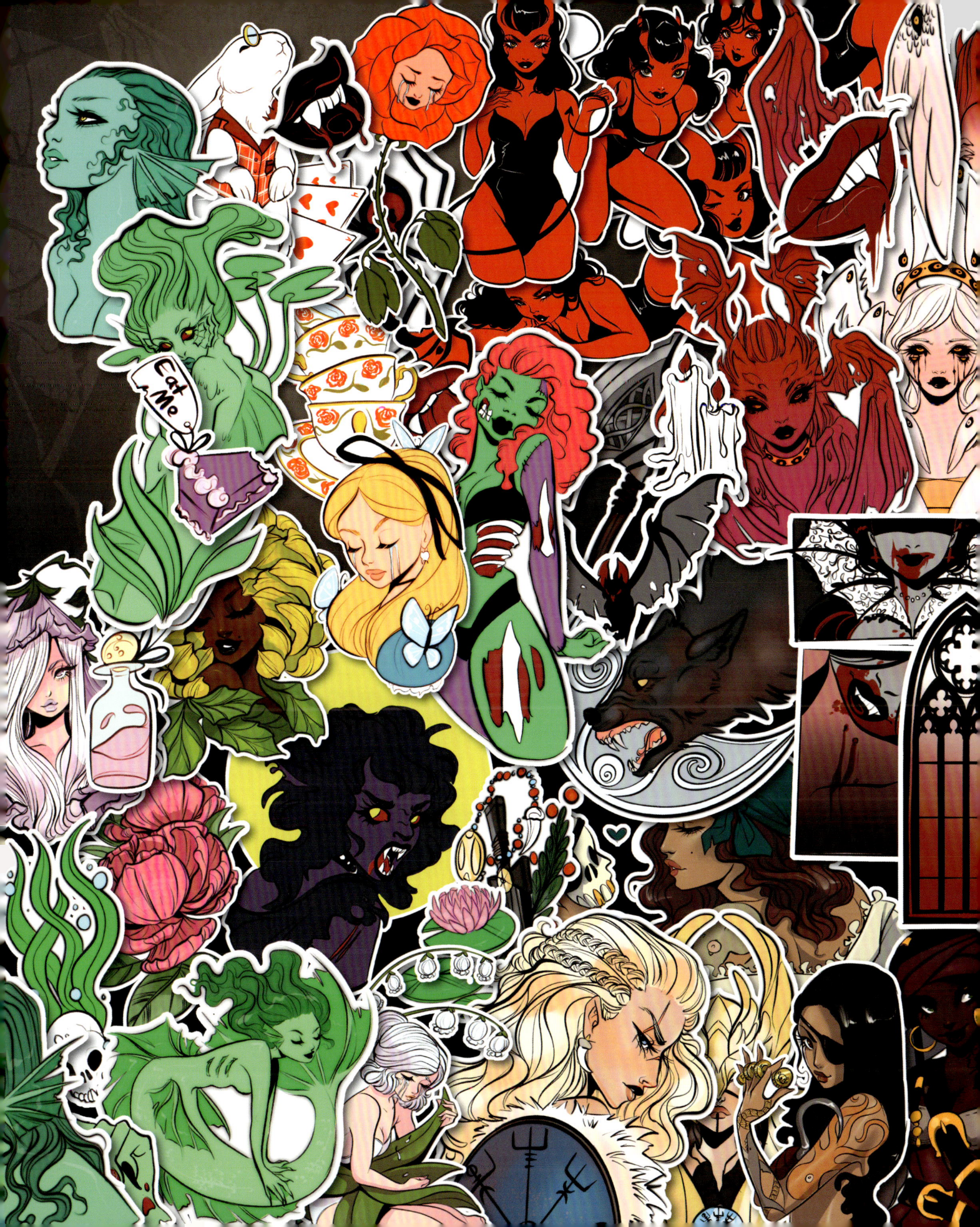

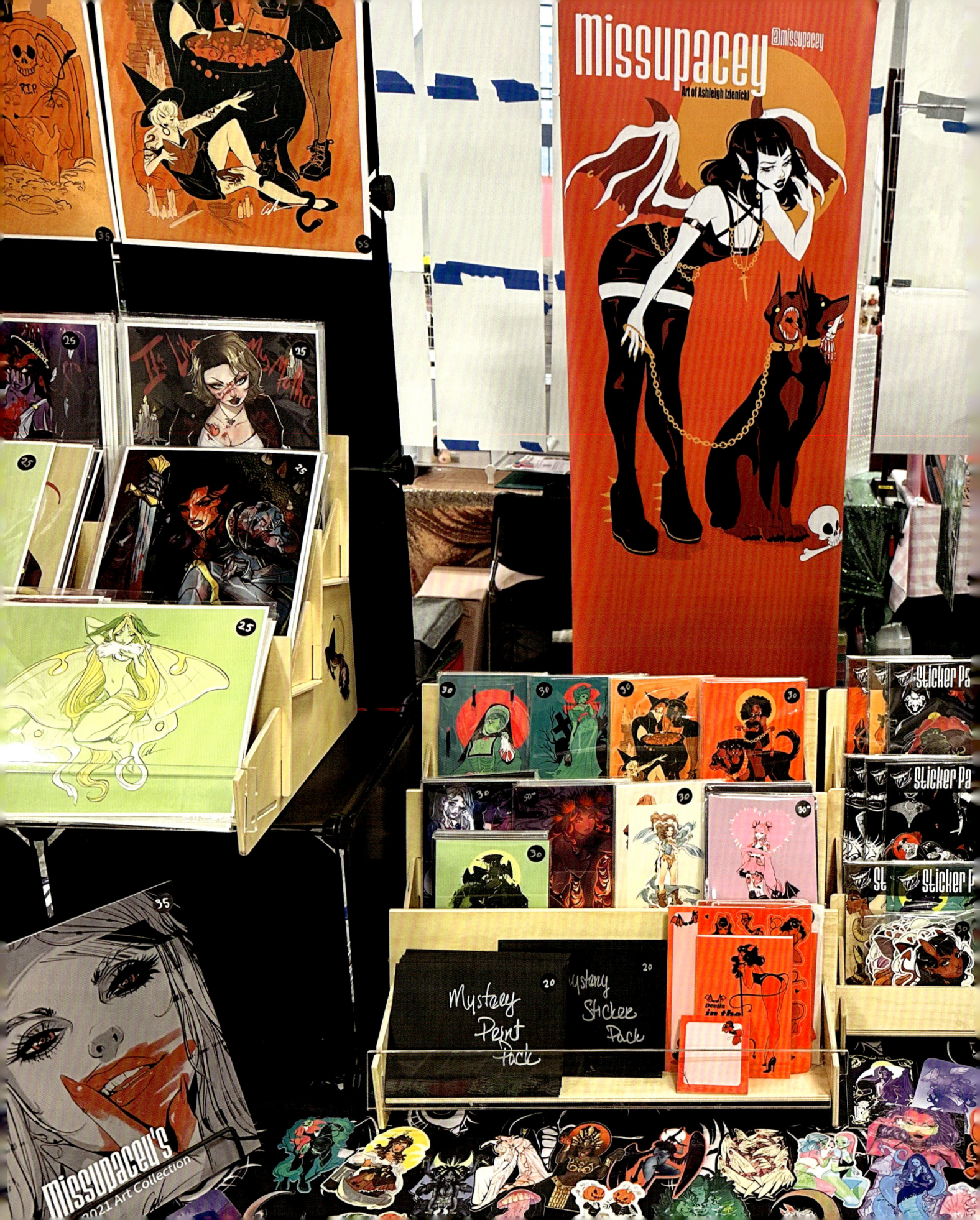

Conventions

I love attending conventions. They've not only given me the opportunity to travel, but also to meet the many artists I've looked up to over the years. I've made so many friends through conventions, and of course, it gets your name out there and you get to sell your work in person. You're just surrounded by so much art and inspiration. I always feel so energized afterwards, and I walk away with many new ideas for illustrations and products. As a new artist, it's also a good chance to establish yourself, not to mention the networking opportunities.

Think about finding conventions that really fit with your style or what you're trying to achieve with your art. For example, if you want to work in comics, then Comic Con is a perfect place to go. I also attend horror conventions, since horror is a genre I love to watch and dark art is what I love to create. That way, I have a chance to connect with people who like the same things as me and what I tend to draw.

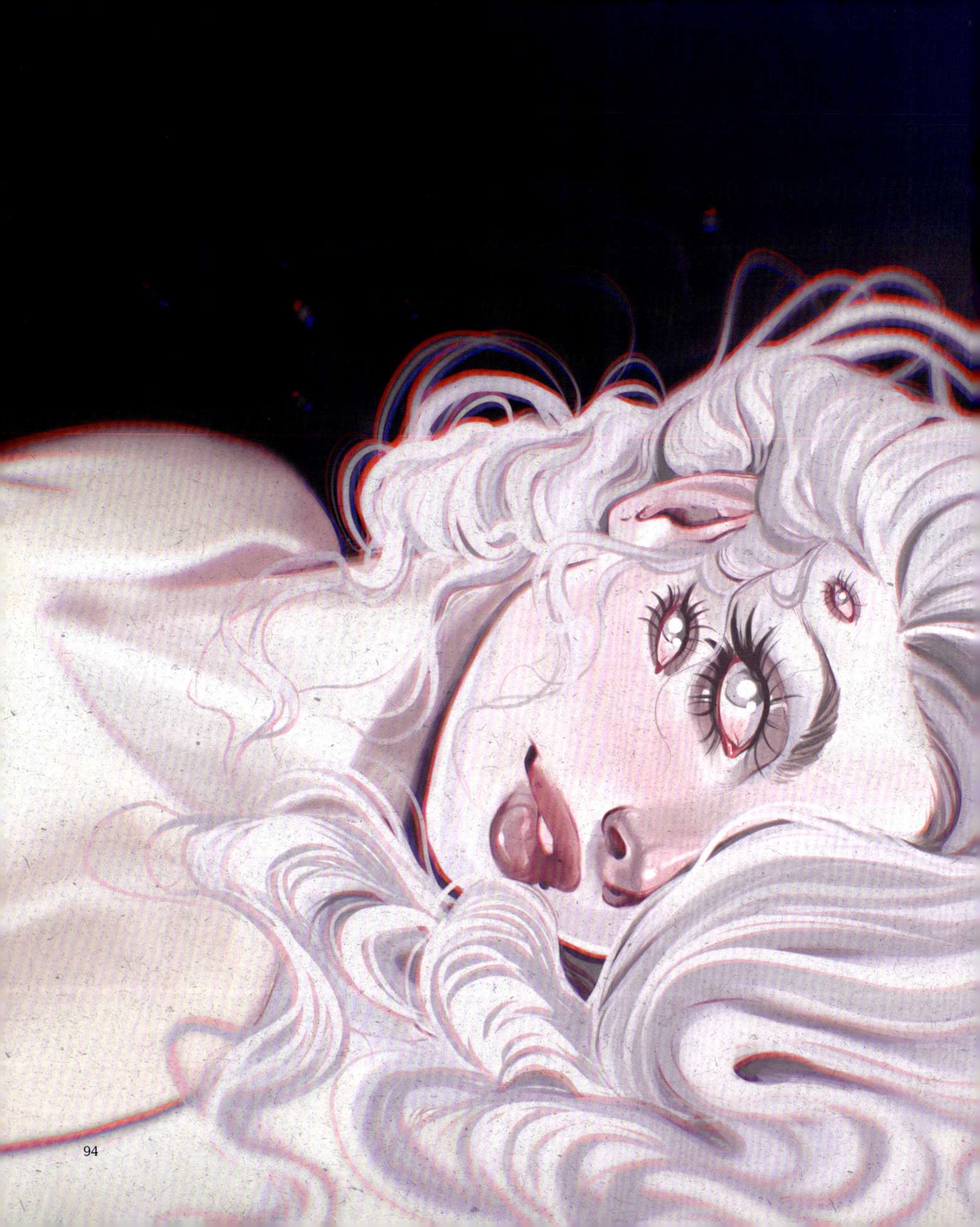

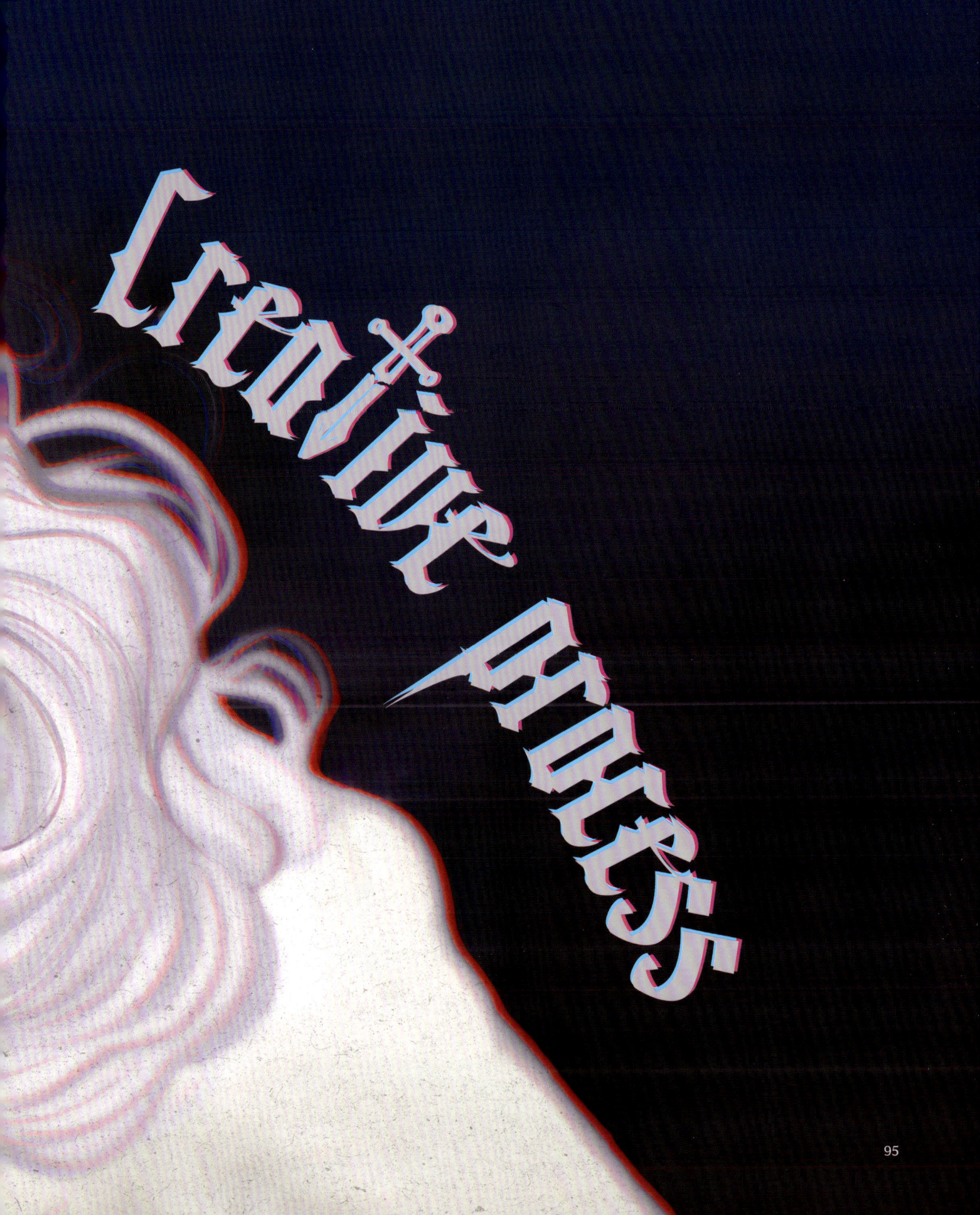

Creative Process

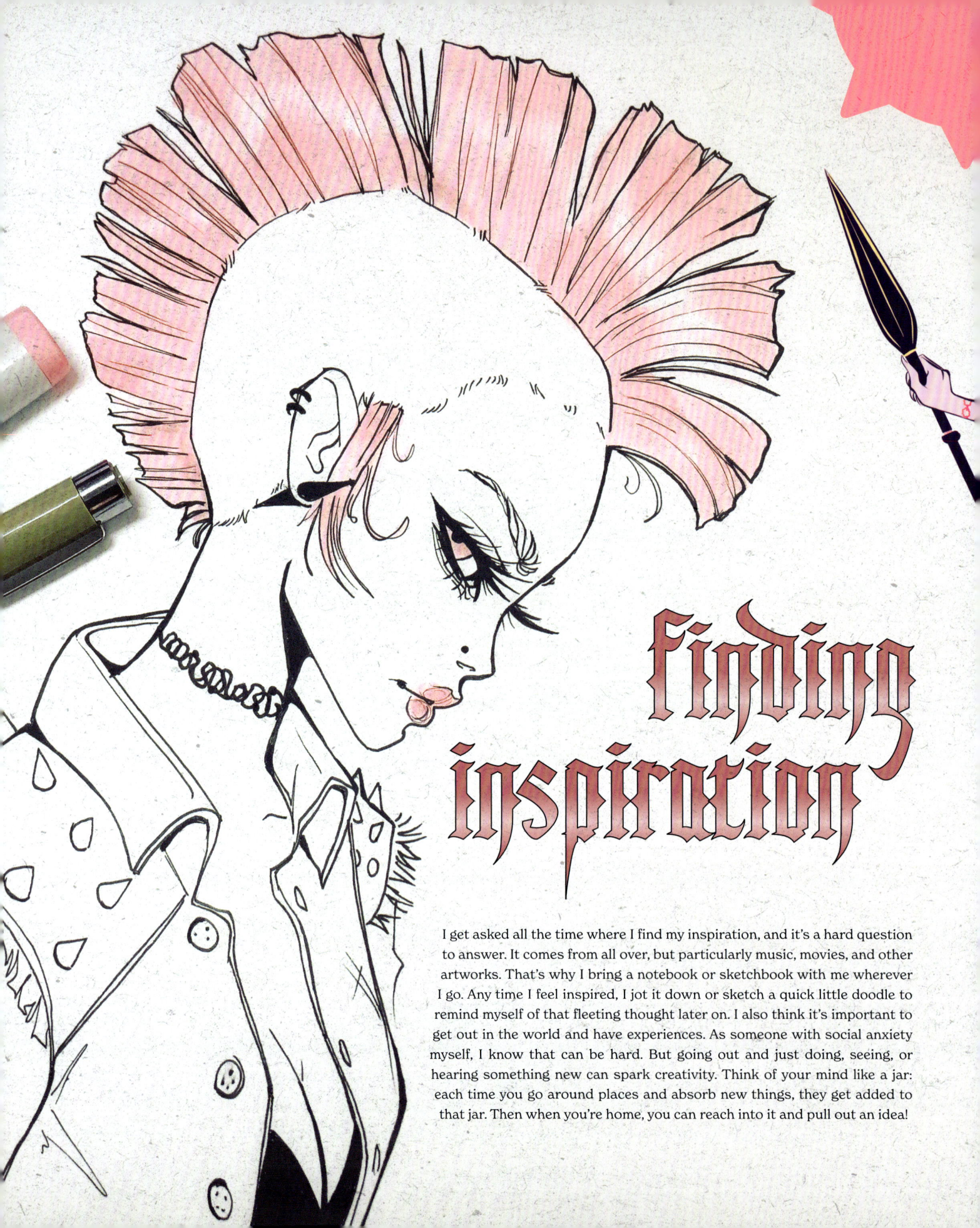

finding inspiration

I get asked all the time where I find my inspiration, and it's a hard question to answer. It comes from all over, but particularly music, movies, and other artworks. That's why I bring a notebook or sketchbook with me wherever I go. Any time I feel inspired, I jot it down or sketch a quick little doodle to remind myself of that fleeting thought later on. I also think it's important to get out in the world and have experiences. As someone with social anxiety myself, I know that can be hard. But going out and just doing, seeing, or hearing something new can spark creativity. Think of your mind like a jar: each time you go around places and absorb new things, they get added to that jar. Then when you're home, you can reach into it and pull out an idea!

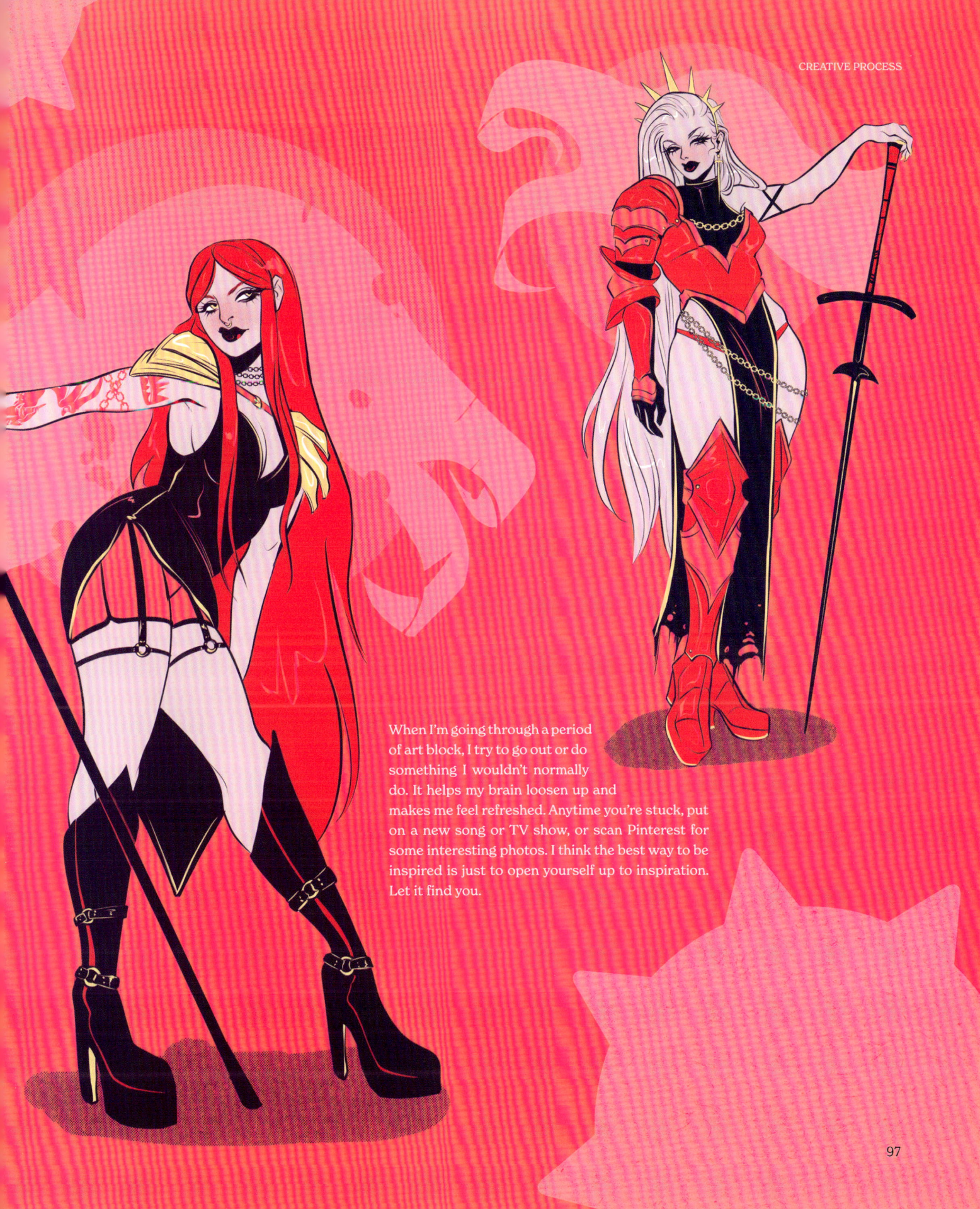

When I'm going through a period of art block, I try to go out or do something I wouldn't normally do. It helps my brain loosen up and makes me feel refreshed. Anytime you're stuck, put on a new song or TV show, or scan Pinterest for some interesting photos. I think the best way to be inspired is just to open yourself up to inspiration. Let it find you.

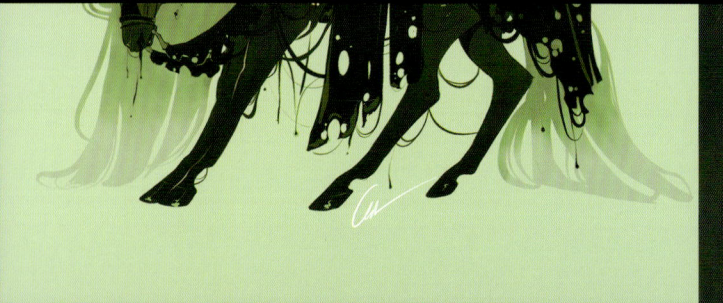
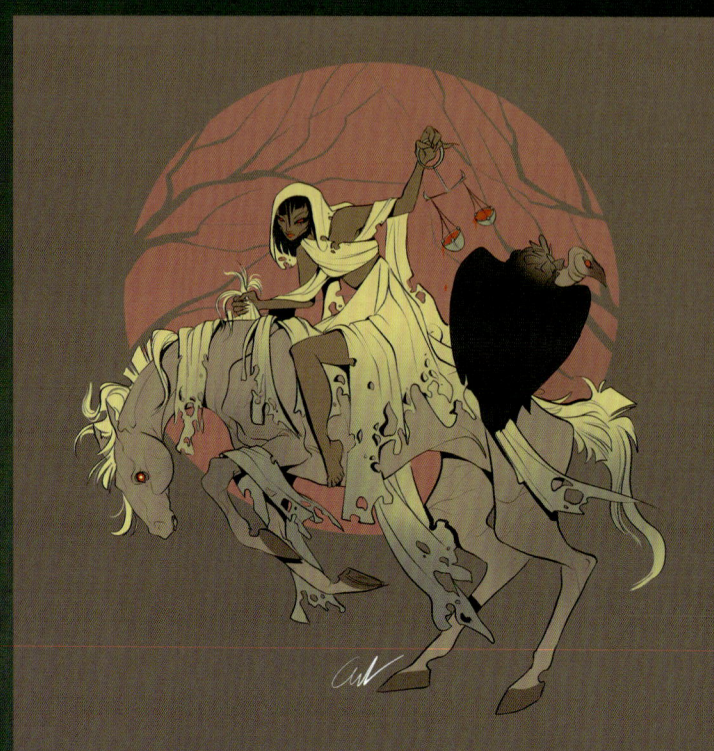
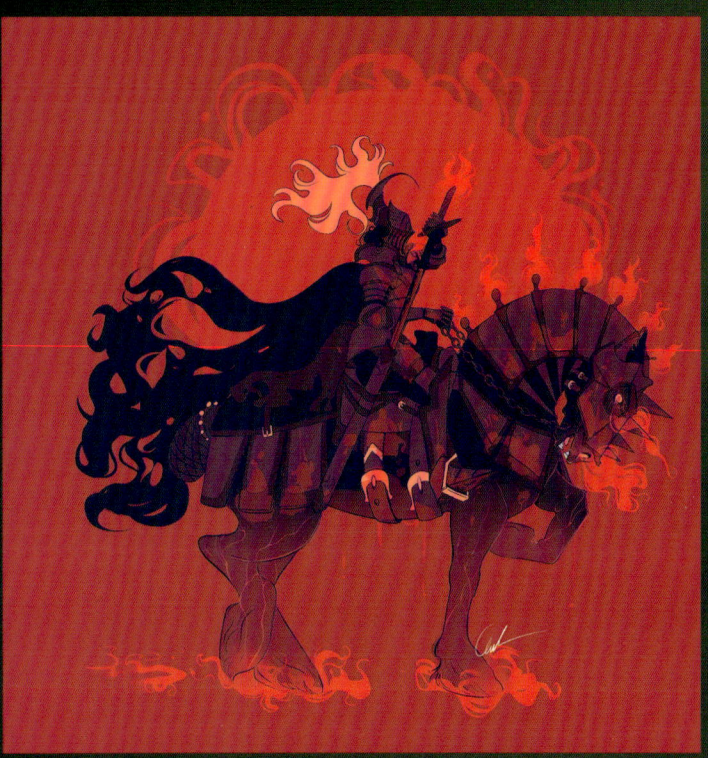
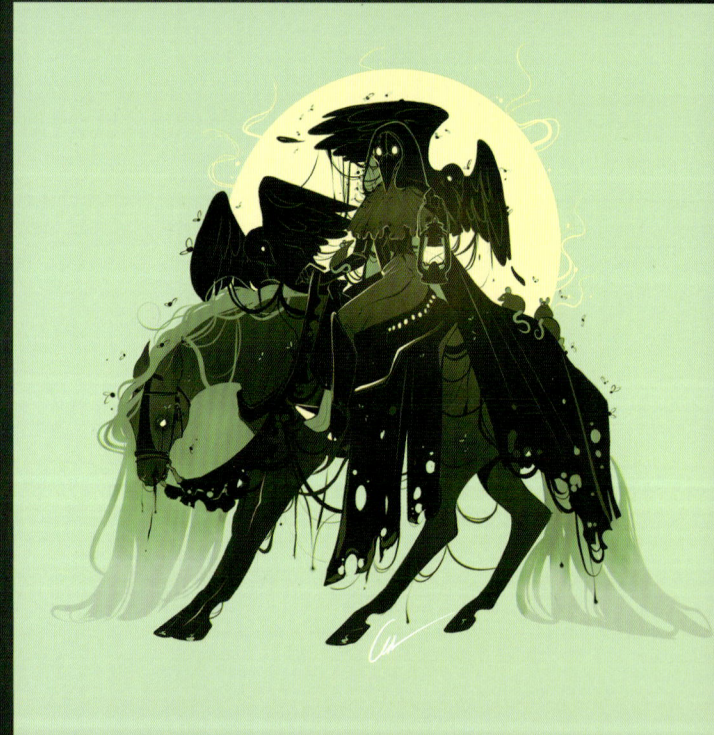
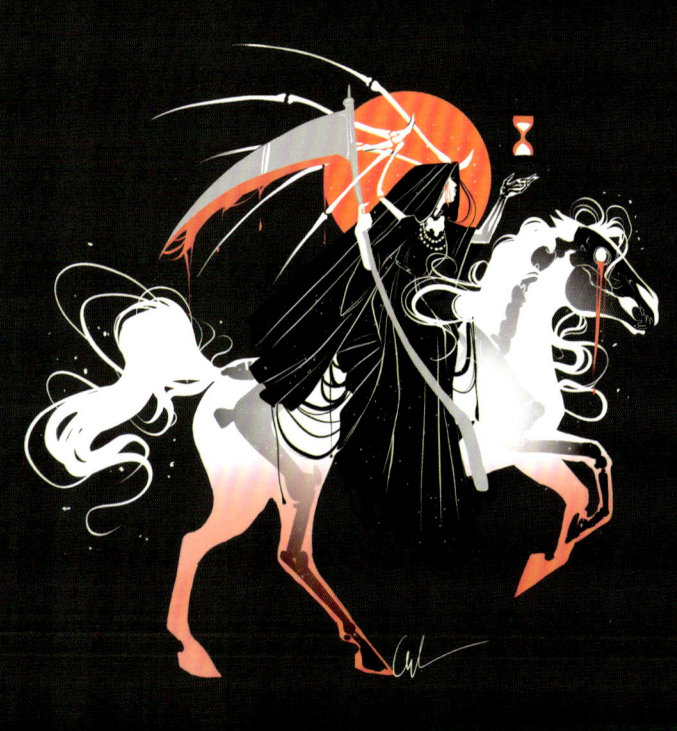
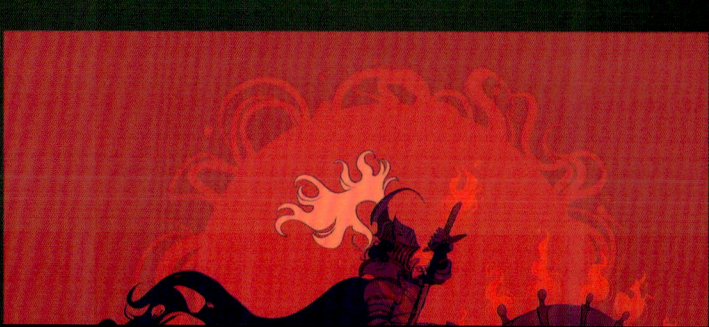

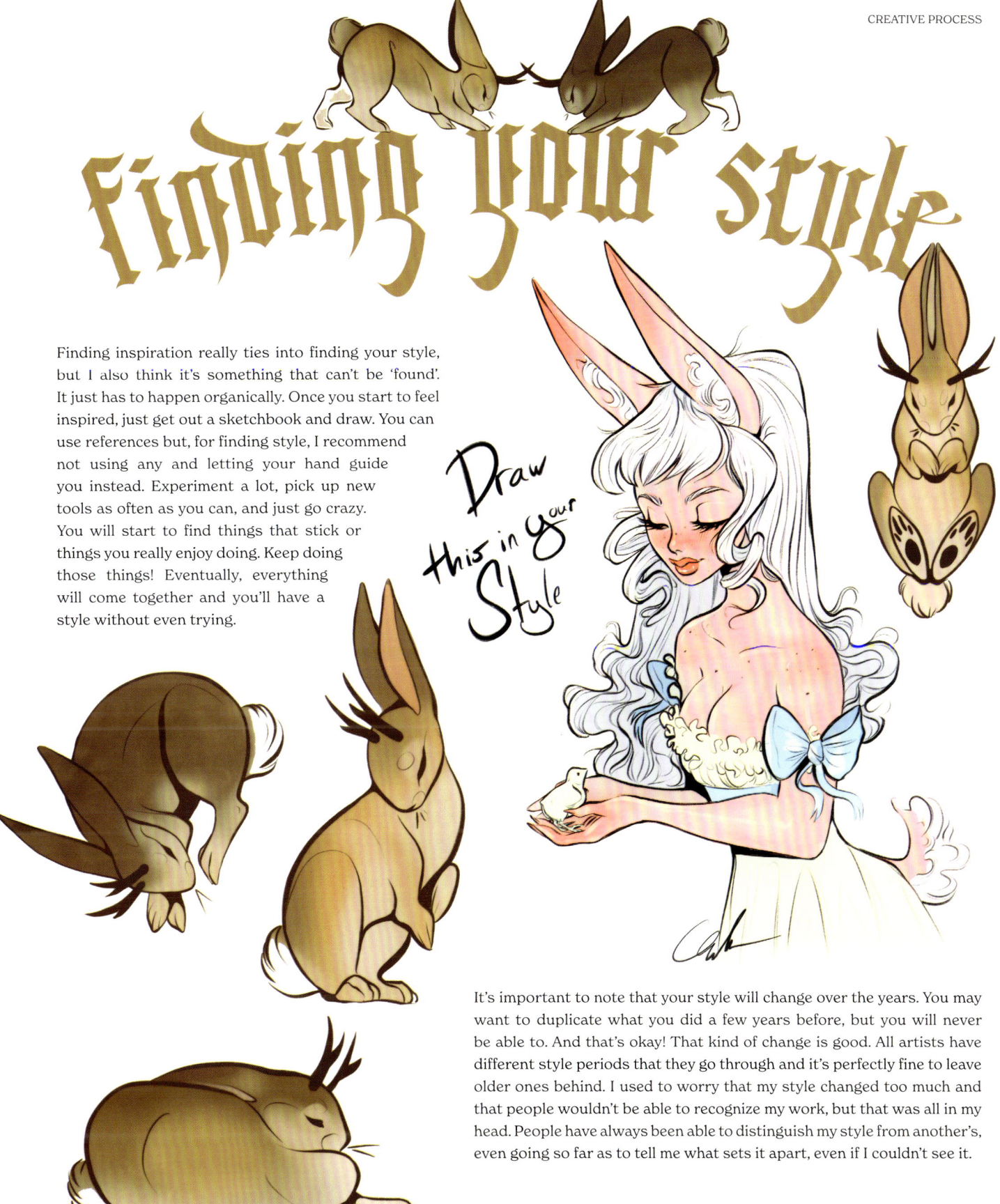

finding your style

Finding inspiration really ties into finding your style, but I also think it's something that can't be 'found'. It just has to happen organically. Once you start to feel inspired, just get out a sketchbook and draw. You can use references but, for finding style, I recommend not using any and letting your hand guide you instead. Experiment a lot, pick up new tools as often as you can, and just go crazy. You will start to find things that stick or things you really enjoy doing. Keep doing those things! Eventually, everything will come together and you'll have a style without even trying.

Draw this in your Style

It's important to note that your style will change over the years. You may want to duplicate what you did a few years before, but you will never be able to. And that's okay! That kind of change is good. All artists have different style periods that they go through and it's perfectly fine to leave older ones behind. I used to worry that my style changed too much and that people wouldn't be able to recognize my work, but that was all in my head. People have always been able to distinguish my style from another's, even going so far as to tell me what sets it apart, even if I couldn't see it.

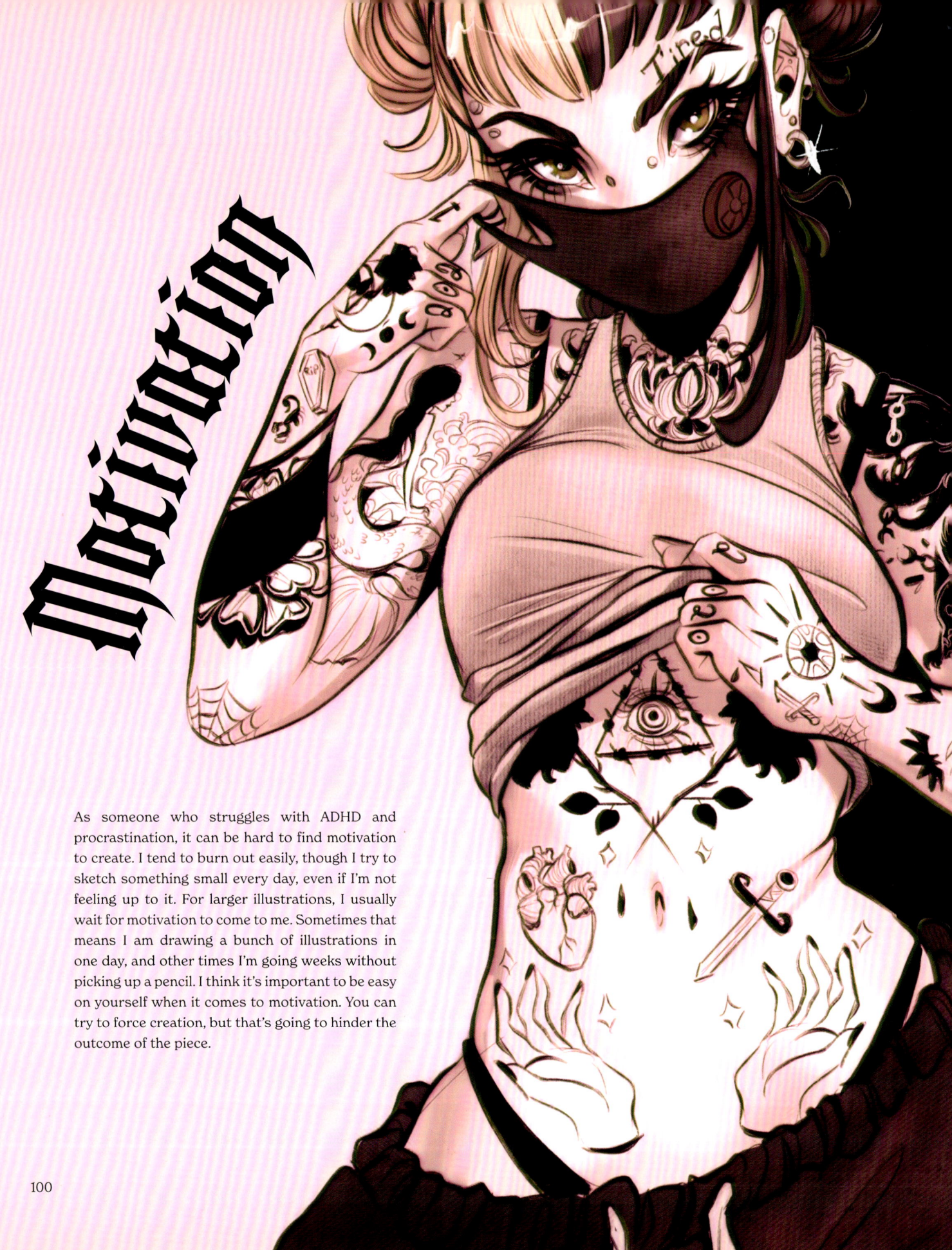

Motivation

As someone who struggles with ADHD and procrastination, it can be hard to find motivation to create. I tend to burn out easily, though I try to sketch something small every day, even if I'm not feeling up to it. For larger illustrations, I usually wait for motivation to come to me. Sometimes that means I am drawing a bunch of illustrations in one day, and other times I'm going weeks without picking up a pencil. I think it's important to be easy on yourself when it comes to motivation. You can try to force creation, but that's going to hinder the outcome of the piece.

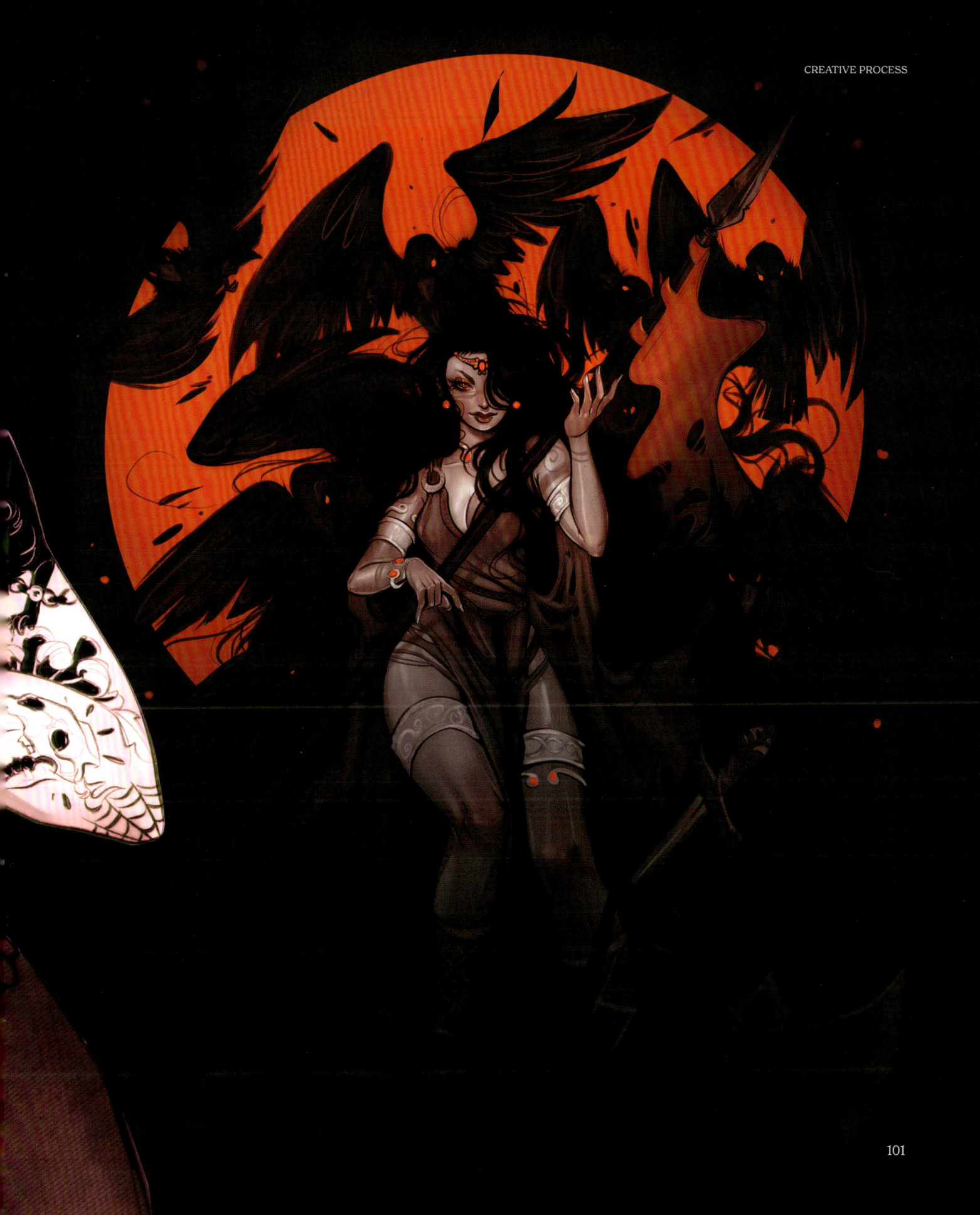

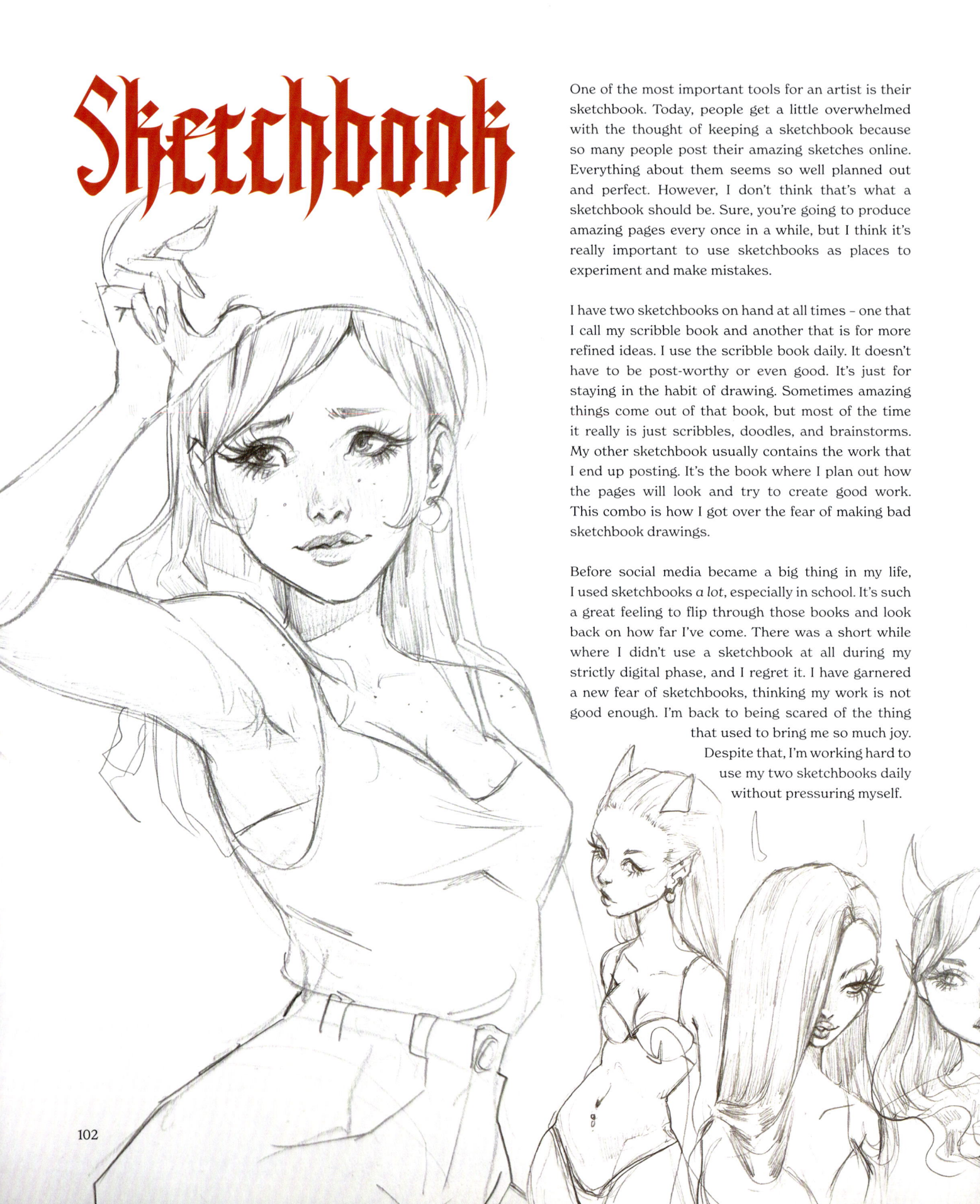

Sketchbook

One of the most important tools for an artist is their sketchbook. Today, people get a little overwhelmed with the thought of keeping a sketchbook because so many people post their amazing sketches online. Everything about them seems so well planned out and perfect. However, I don't think that's what a sketchbook should be. Sure, you're going to produce amazing pages every once in a while, but I think it's really important to use sketchbooks as places to experiment and make mistakes.

I have two sketchbooks on hand at all times – one that I call my scribble book and another that is for more refined ideas. I use the scribble book daily. It doesn't have to be post-worthy or even good. It's just for staying in the habit of drawing. Sometimes amazing things come out of that book, but most of the time it really is just scribbles, doodles, and brainstorms. My other sketchbook usually contains the work that I end up posting. It's the book where I plan out how the pages will look and try to create good work. This combo is how I got over the fear of making bad sketchbook drawings.

Before social media became a big thing in my life, I used sketchbooks *a lot*, especially in school. It's such a great feeling to flip through those books and look back on how far I've come. There was a short while where I didn't use a sketchbook at all during my strictly digital phase, and I regret it. I have garnered a new fear of sketchbooks, thinking my work is not good enough. I'm back to being scared of the thing that used to bring me so much joy. Despite that, I'm working hard to use my two sketchbooks daily without pressuring myself.

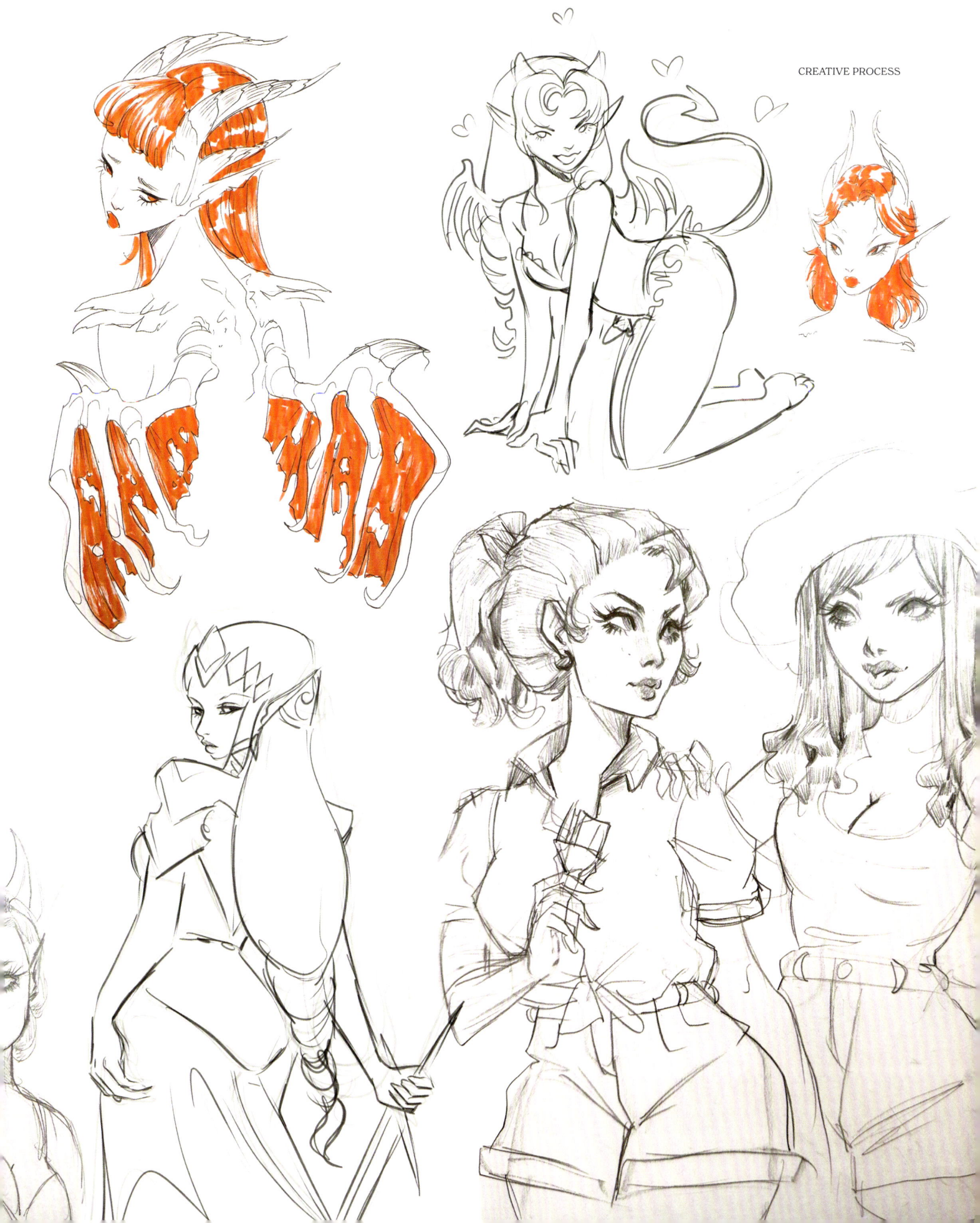

Inking

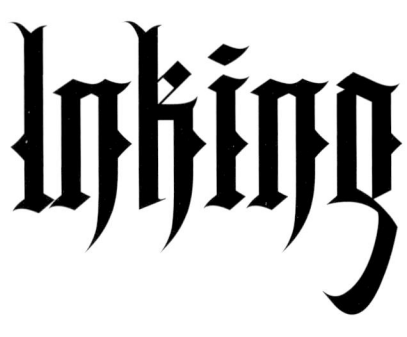

I love inking – it's my favourite part of the process! The ability to add life to a drawing with just the use of lines still amazes me. I think many people overlook the inking stage and just move on to painting, which is fine, but I love to take my time with it.

One of the main things I keep in mind while inking is light and shadow. Where there is shadow, the line will be thicker, and where there is more light, the line will be thinner. It's also important to understand the subject. For example, when drawing clothing, super-thin material needs a thin line to suggest the weight, and other heavier and blockier fabrics need straighter and thicker lines. Try this out by drawing one distinct line with different variations in pressure (don't cheat by sketching more than one line!).

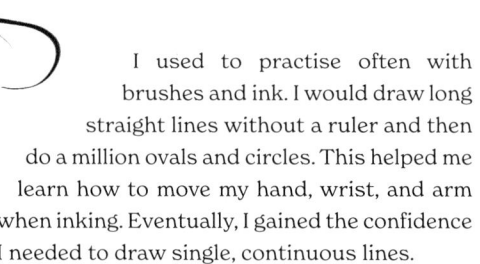

I used to practise often with brushes and ink. I would draw long straight lines without a ruler and then do a million ovals and circles. This helped me learn how to move my hand, wrist, and arm when inking. Eventually, I gained the confidence I needed to draw single, continuous lines.

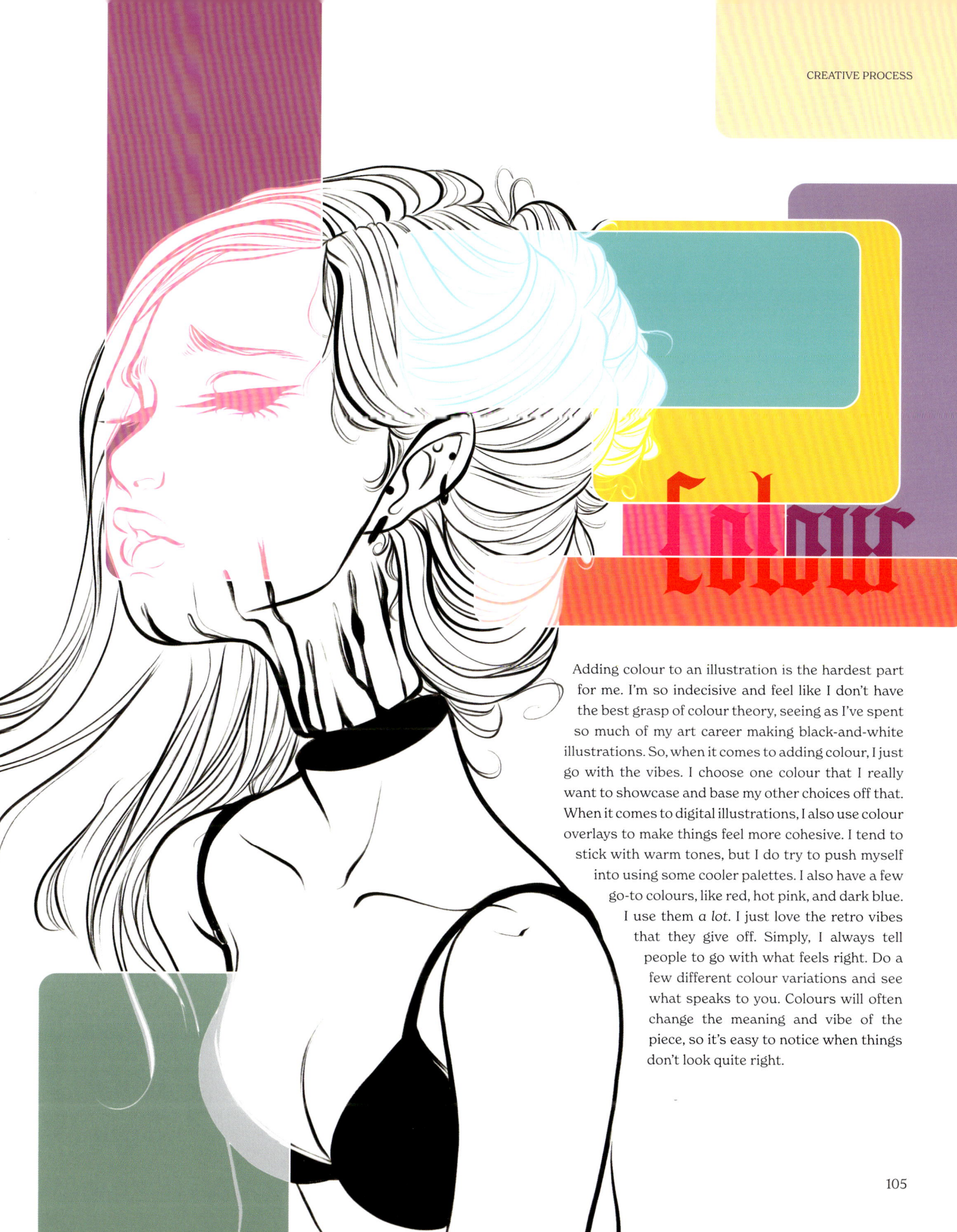

Colour

Adding colour to an illustration is the hardest part for me. I'm so indecisive and feel like I don't have the best grasp of colour theory, seeing as I've spent so much of my art career making black-and-white illustrations. So, when it comes to adding colour, I just go with the vibes. I choose one colour that I really want to showcase and base my other choices off that. When it comes to digital illustrations, I also use colour overlays to make things feel more cohesive. I tend to stick with warm tones, but I do try to push myself into using some cooler palettes. I also have a few go-to colours, like red, hot pink, and dark blue. I use them *a lot*. I just love the retro vibes that they give off. Simply, I always tell people to go with what feels right. Do a few different colour variations and see what speaks to you. Colours will often change the meaning and vibe of the piece, so it's easy to notice when things don't look quite right.

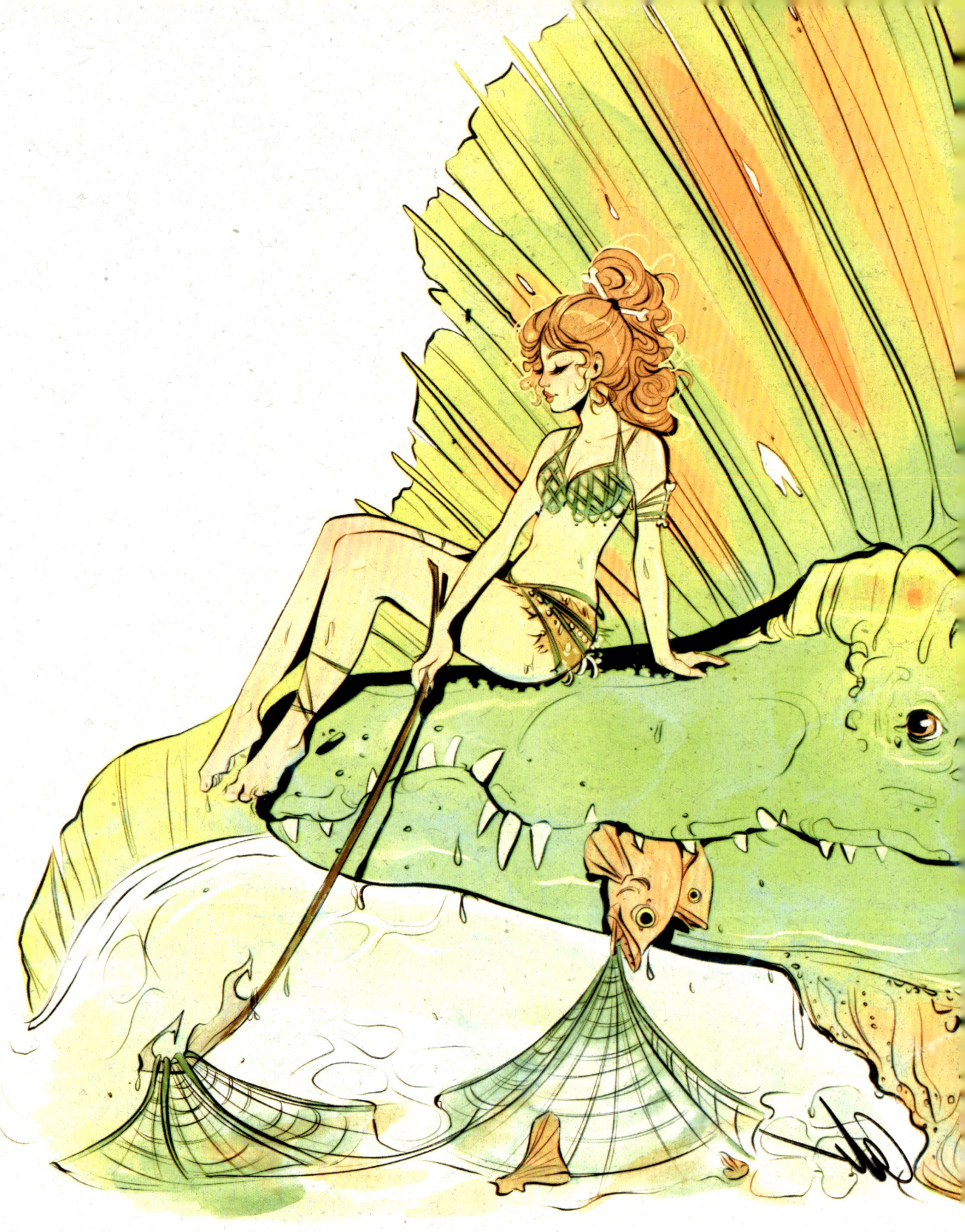

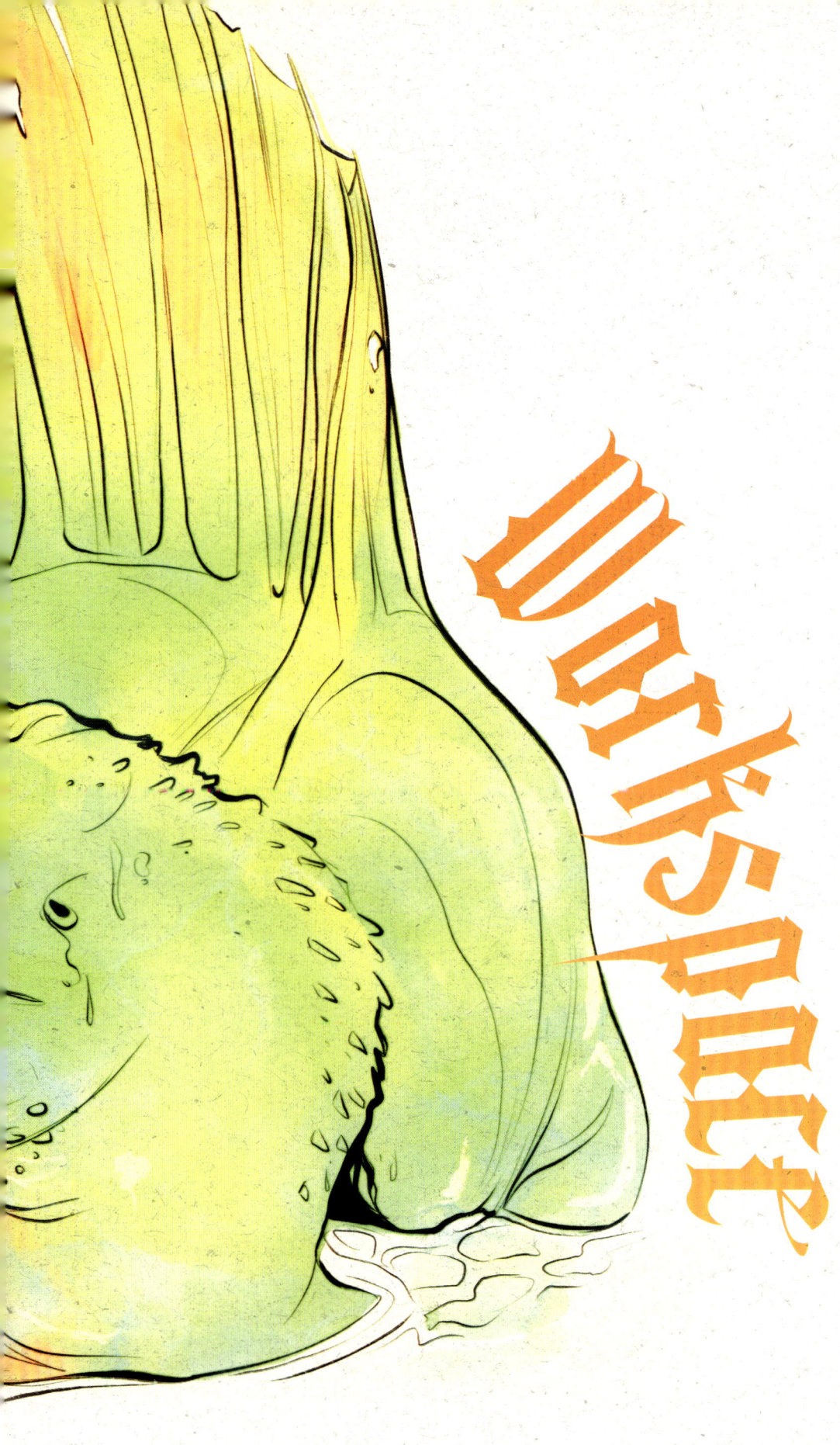

Workspace

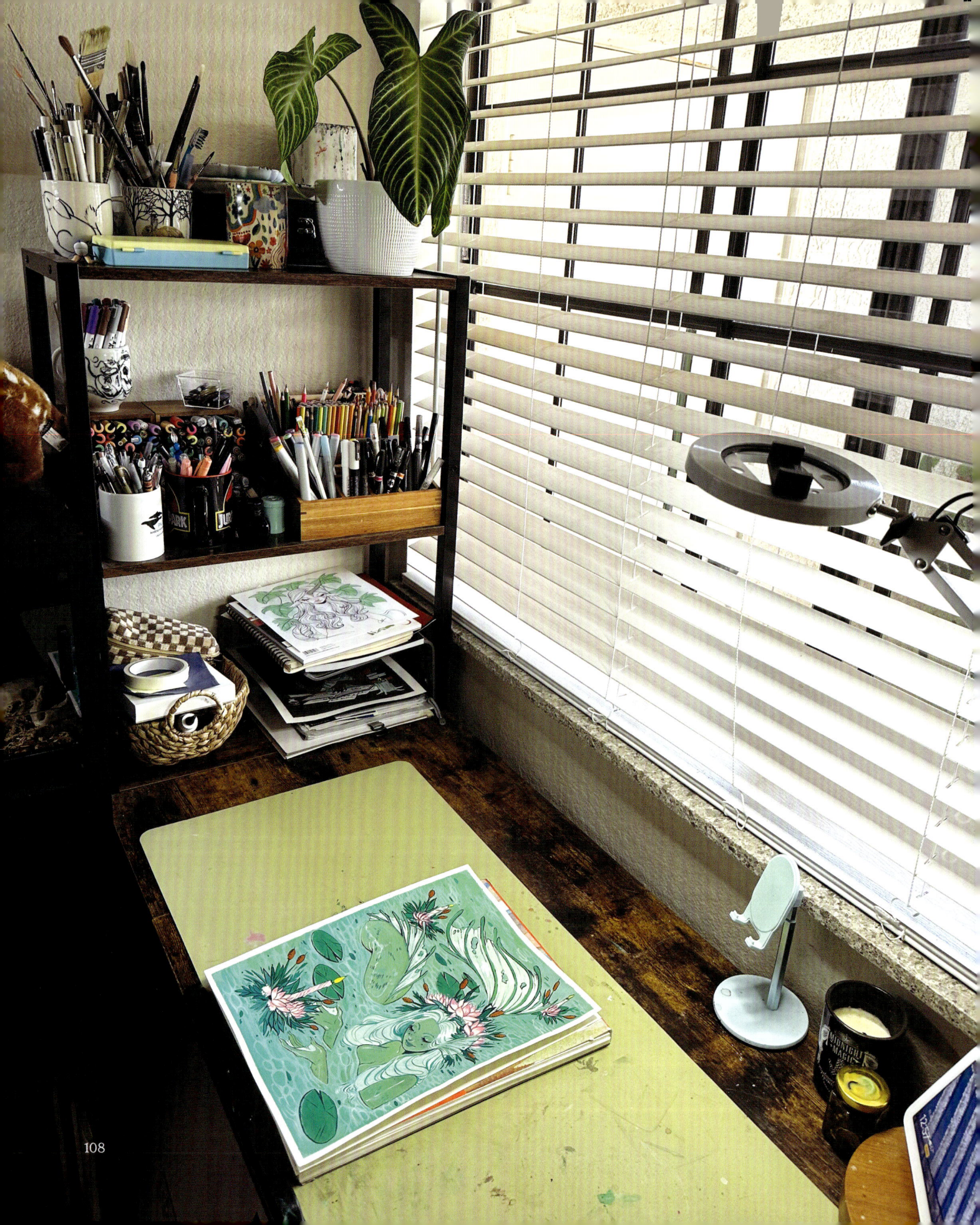

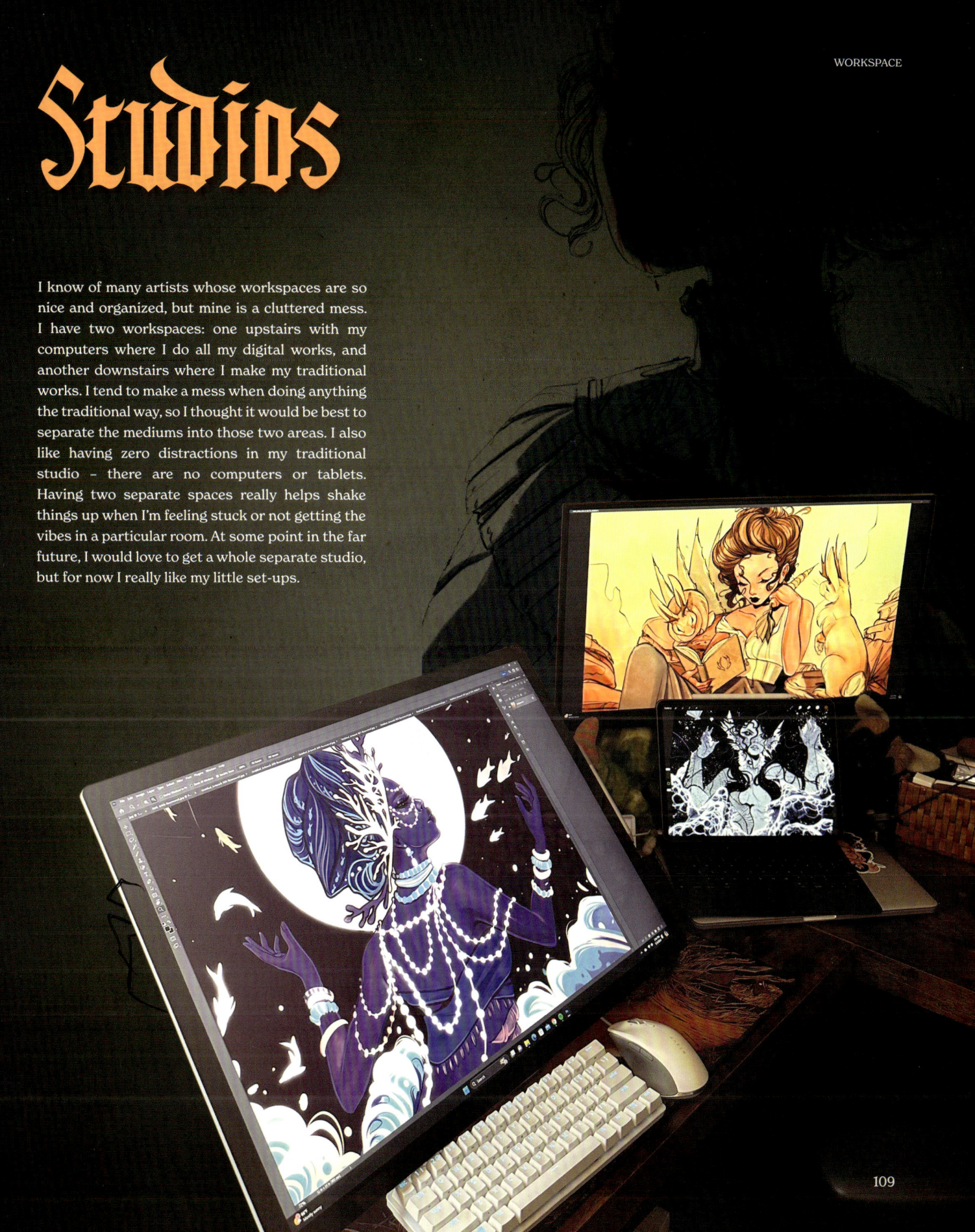

Studios

I know of many artists whose workspaces are so nice and organized, but mine is a cluttered mess. I have two workspaces: one upstairs with my computers where I do all my digital works, and another downstairs where I make my traditional works. I tend to make a mess when doing anything the traditional way, so I thought it would be best to separate the mediums into those two areas. I also like having zero distractions in my traditional studio – there are no computers or tablets. Having two separate spaces really helps shake things up when I'm feeling stuck or not getting the vibes in a particular room. At some point in the far future, I would love to get a whole separate studio, but for now I really like my little set-ups.

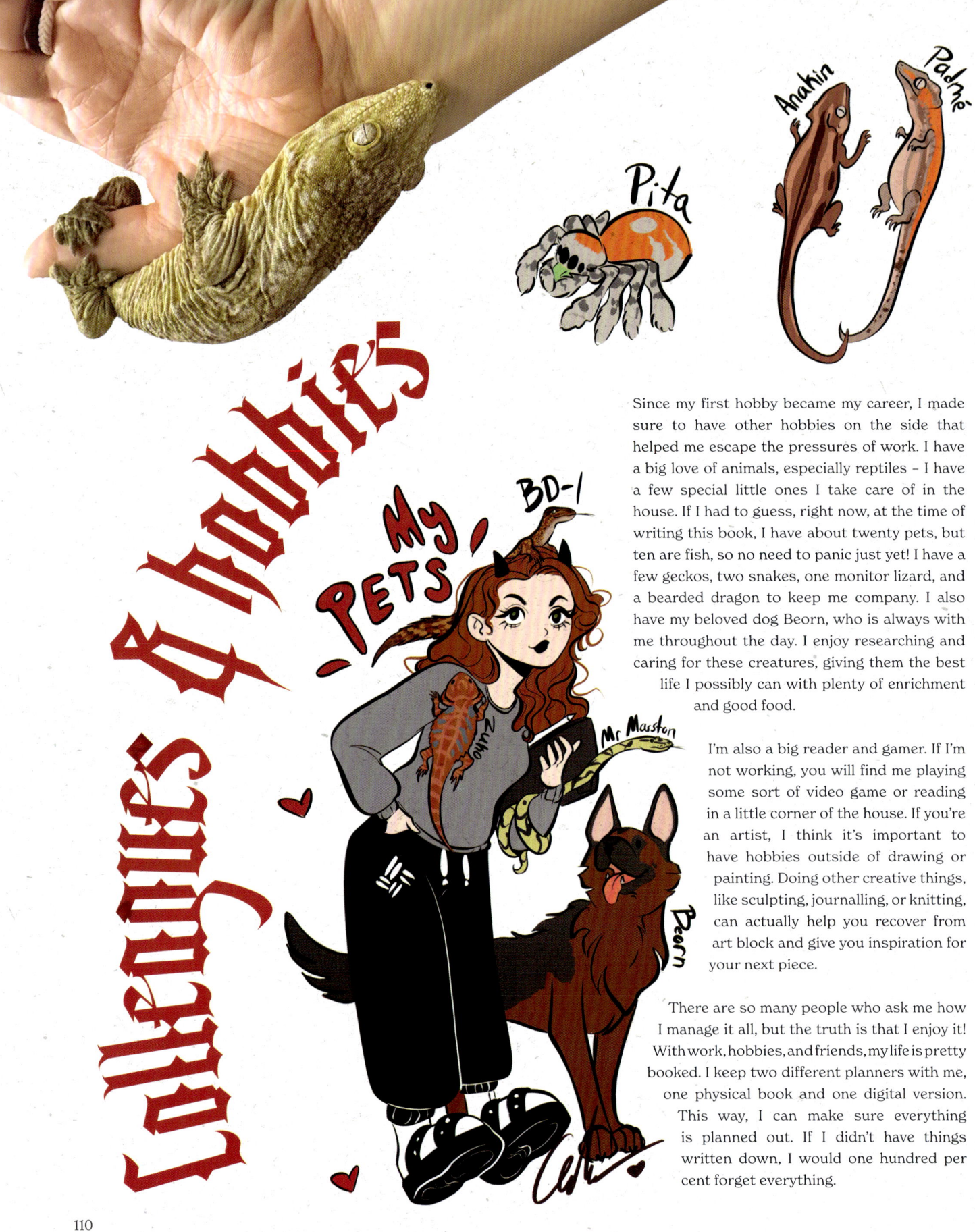

Pita

Anakin

Padmé

BD-1

MY PETS

Mr Marston

Beorn

Colleagues & hobbies

Since my first hobby became my career, I made sure to have other hobbies on the side that helped me escape the pressures of work. I have a big love of animals, especially reptiles – I have a few special little ones I take care of in the house. If I had to guess, right now, at the time of writing this book, I have about twenty pets, but ten are fish, so no need to panic just yet! I have a few geckos, two snakes, one monitor lizard, and a bearded dragon to keep me company. I also have my beloved dog Beorn, who is always with me throughout the day. I enjoy researching and caring for these creatures, giving them the best life I possibly can with plenty of enrichment and good food.

I'm also a big reader and gamer. If I'm not working, you will find me playing some sort of video game or reading in a little corner of the house. If you're an artist, I think it's important to have hobbies outside of drawing or painting. Doing other creative things, like sculpting, journalling, or knitting, can actually help you recover from art block and give you inspiration for your next piece.

There are so many people who ask me how I manage it all, but the truth is that I enjoy it! With work, hobbies, and friends, my life is pretty booked. I keep two different planners with me, one physical book and one digital version. This way, I can make sure everything is planned out. If I didn't have things written down, I would one hundred per cent forget everything.

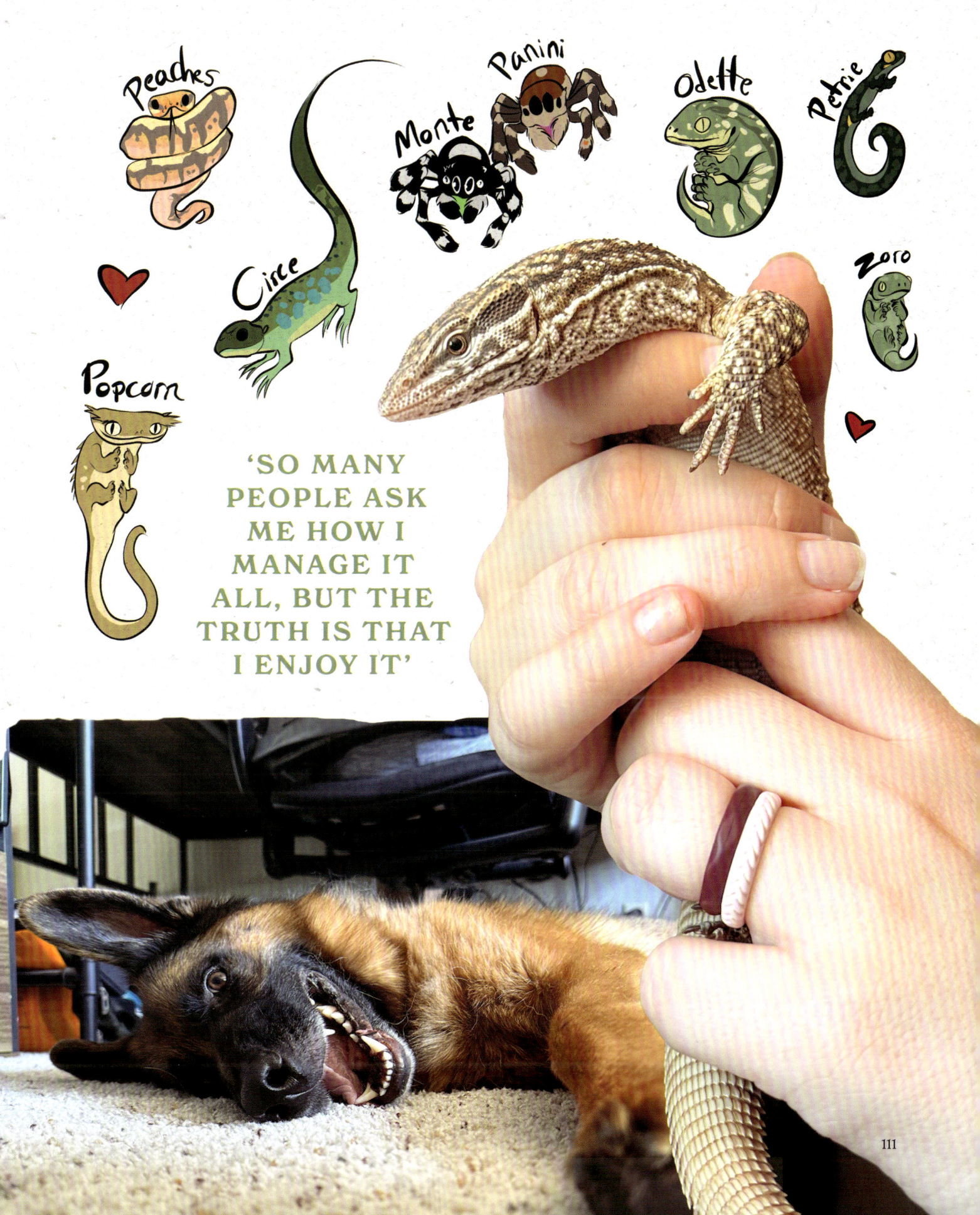

Peaches

Circe

Monte

Panini

Odette

Petrie

Zoro

Popcorn

'SO MANY PEOPLE ASK ME HOW I MANAGE IT ALL, BUT THE TRUTH IS THAT I ENJOY IT'

111

Traditional tools

I have really stuck to digital art for the past few years, which is funny because I was super strict at the beginning of my career and only made traditional art. Now it feels a bit foreign to me, but I have been pushing myself to dive back into traditional mediums.

Of course, pen and ink is my go-to, but I also really like using a mix of alcohol markers and coloured pencils. This is usually what I use for sketching and smaller illustrations, but for my larger illustrations, gouache is my preference. In my opinion, it is the easiest way to mimic digital art compared to most other mediums. I love how it dries matt but still keeps its colour. It's also nice that I can rework it when I need to, whereas I couldn't with acrylic. I used to use watercolours, but I feel like they're a little hard for me to control, or at least for my process. I tend to want to work fast, and watercolour just doesn't allow for that.

In the future, I would definitely like to jump into acrylics more, so be sure to stay tuned for that!

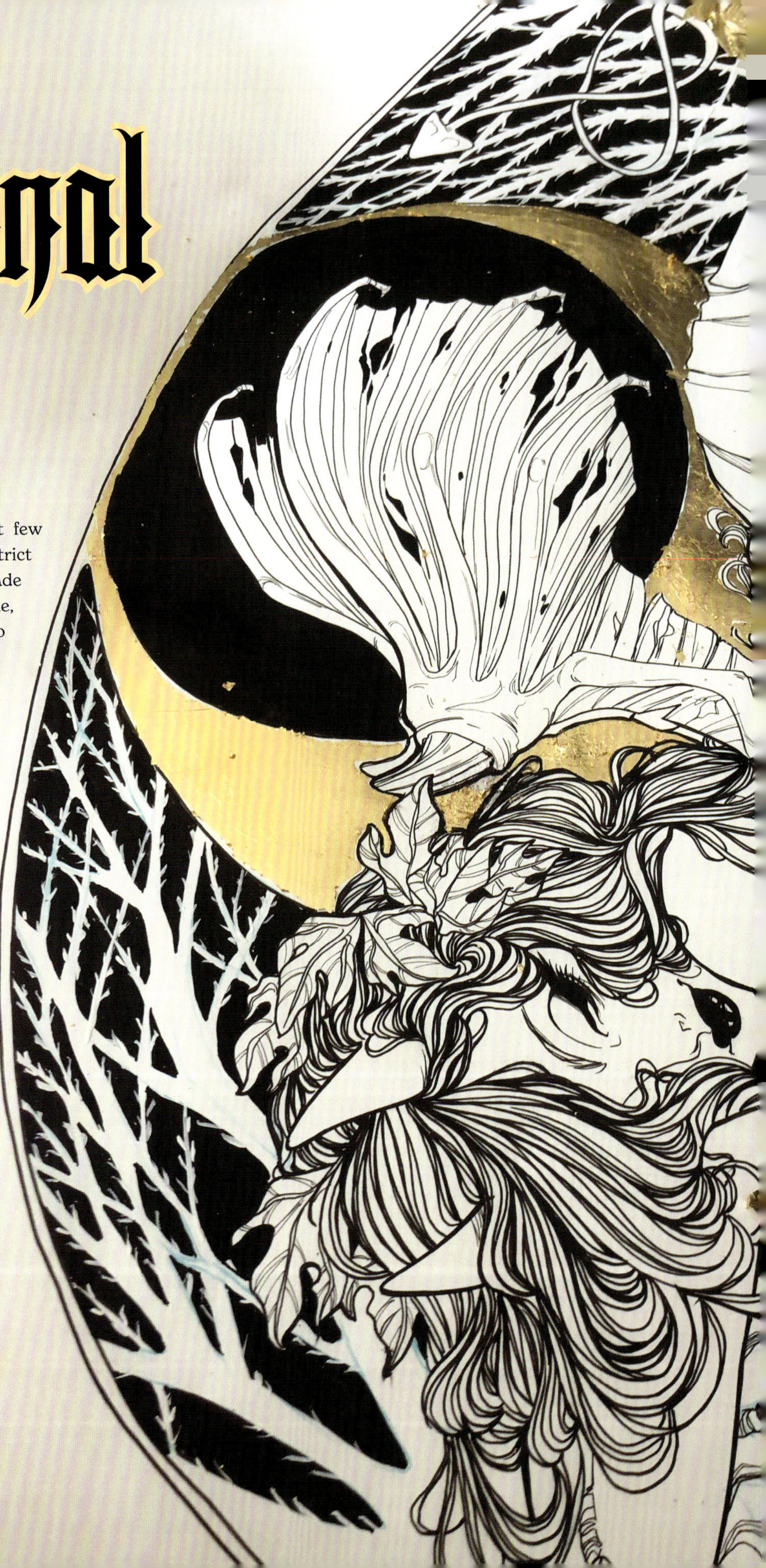

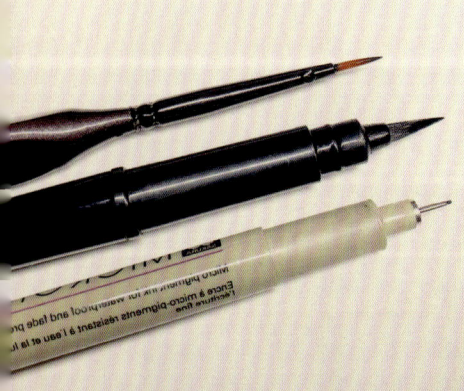

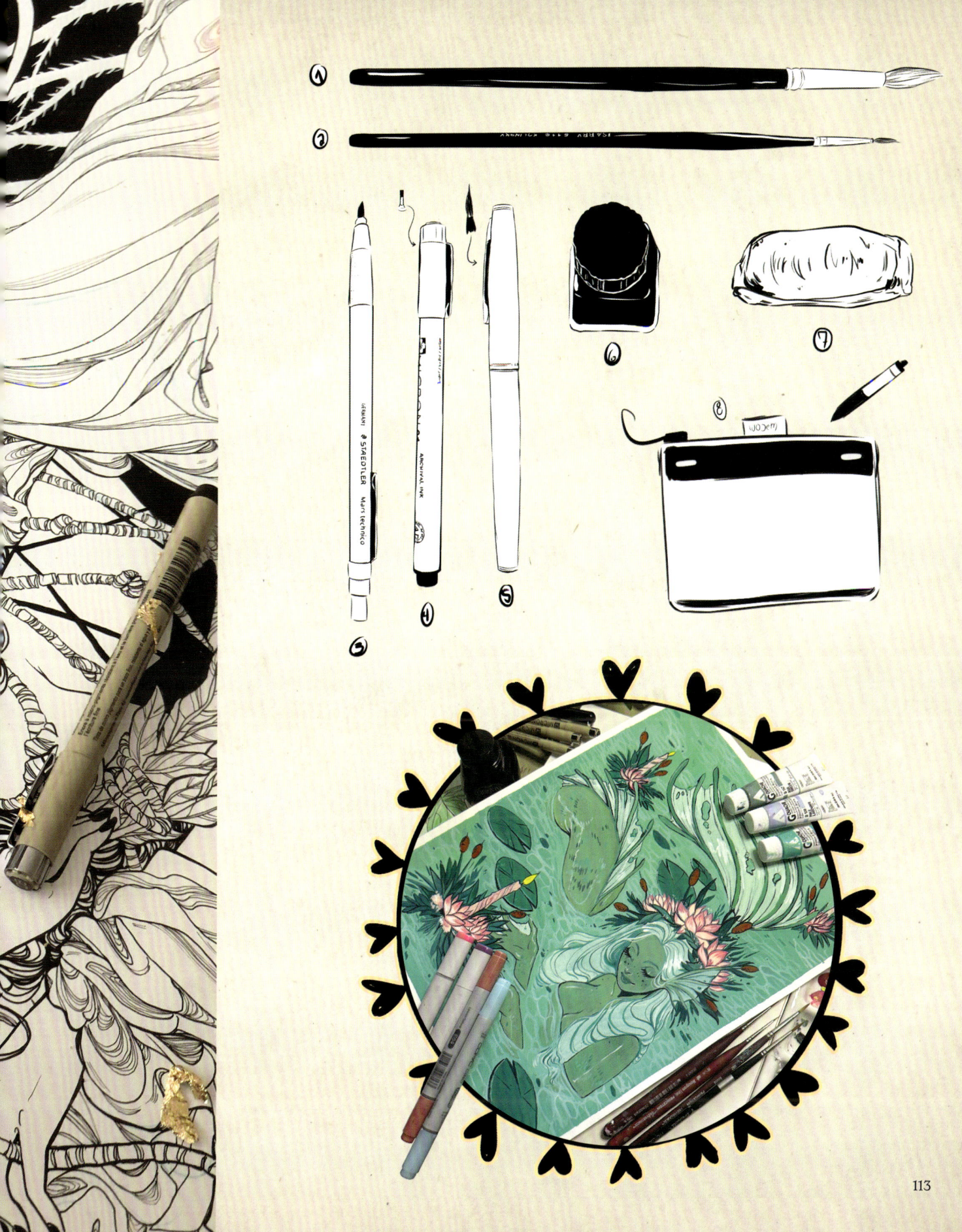

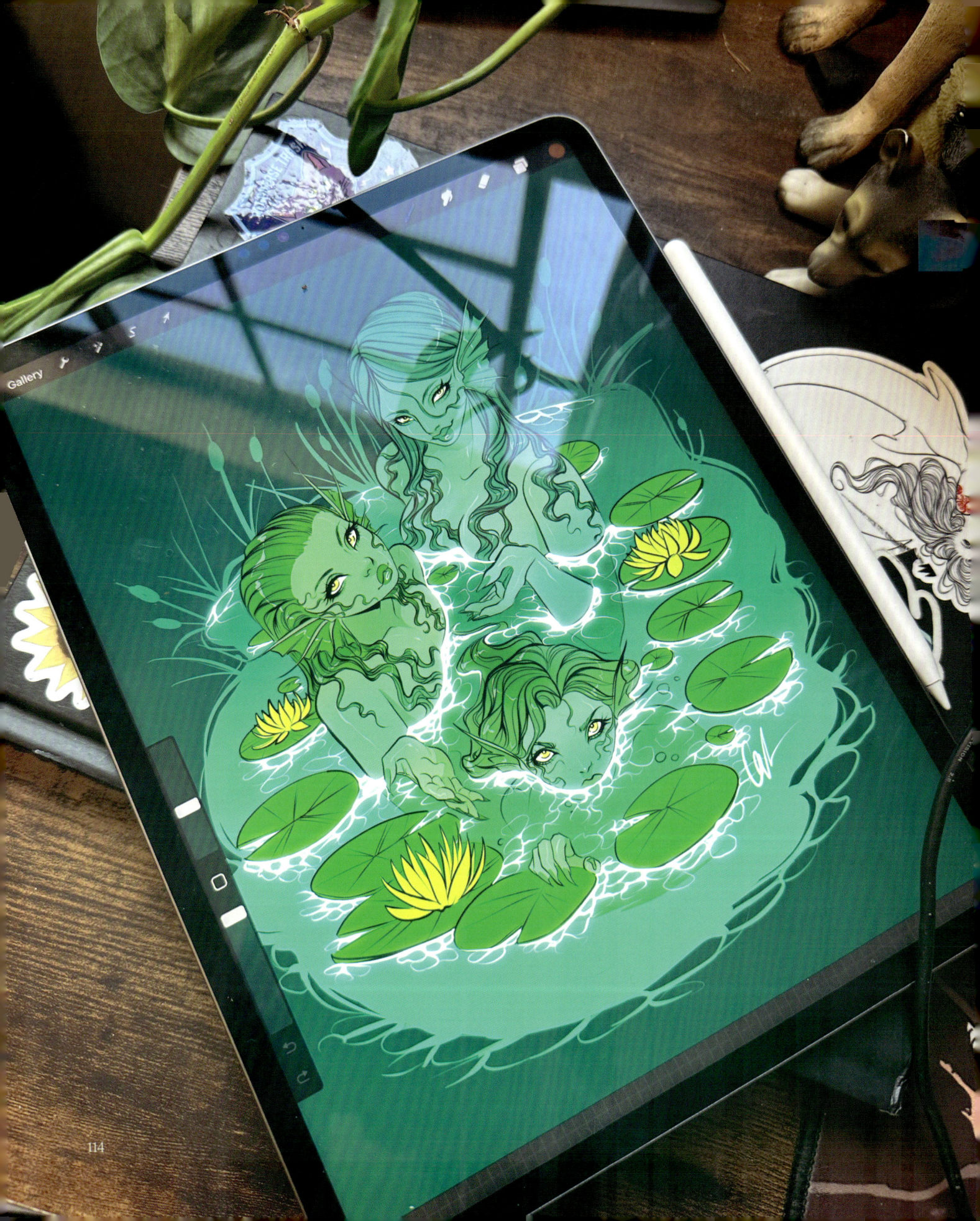

Digital tools

My most-used digital tool is, of course, my iPad Pro with an Apple Pencil. I mostly just use Procreate, but I have dived into other programs as well. Before I had an iPad, I only used Adobe Photoshop and a tablet. I now have a giant computer where the monitor can be used as a tablet, which I use all the time.

I think I just enjoy the freedom the iPad allows, being able to move around and sit wherever I want to work. I tend to get a little stir-crazy if I sit in one spot for too long. However, the big con about using an iPad is that it doesn't have the processing power of a computer, so I can't make huge illustrations with hundreds of layers. Luckily, I don't need to make huge files too often, so it isn't so much of an issue. I also still use Photoshop and Adobe Illustrator for product design and such.

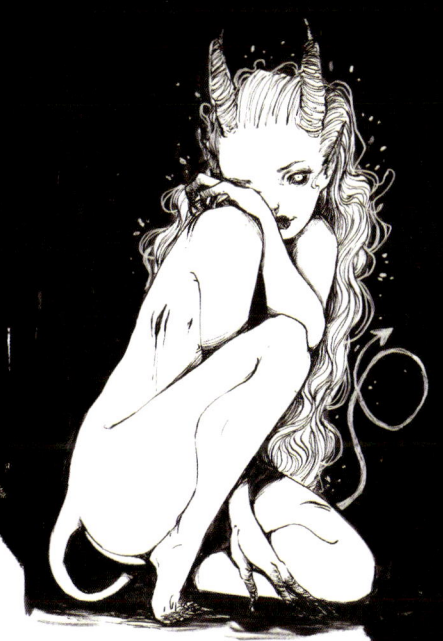

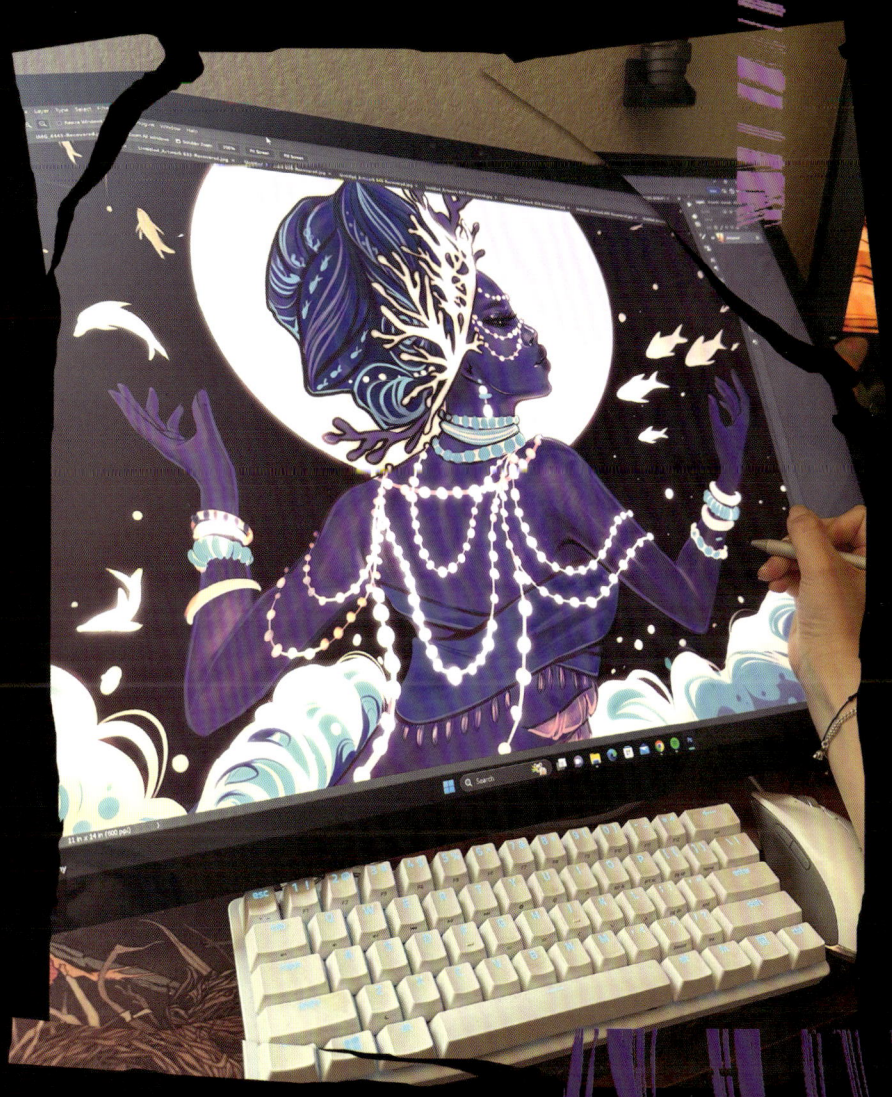

115

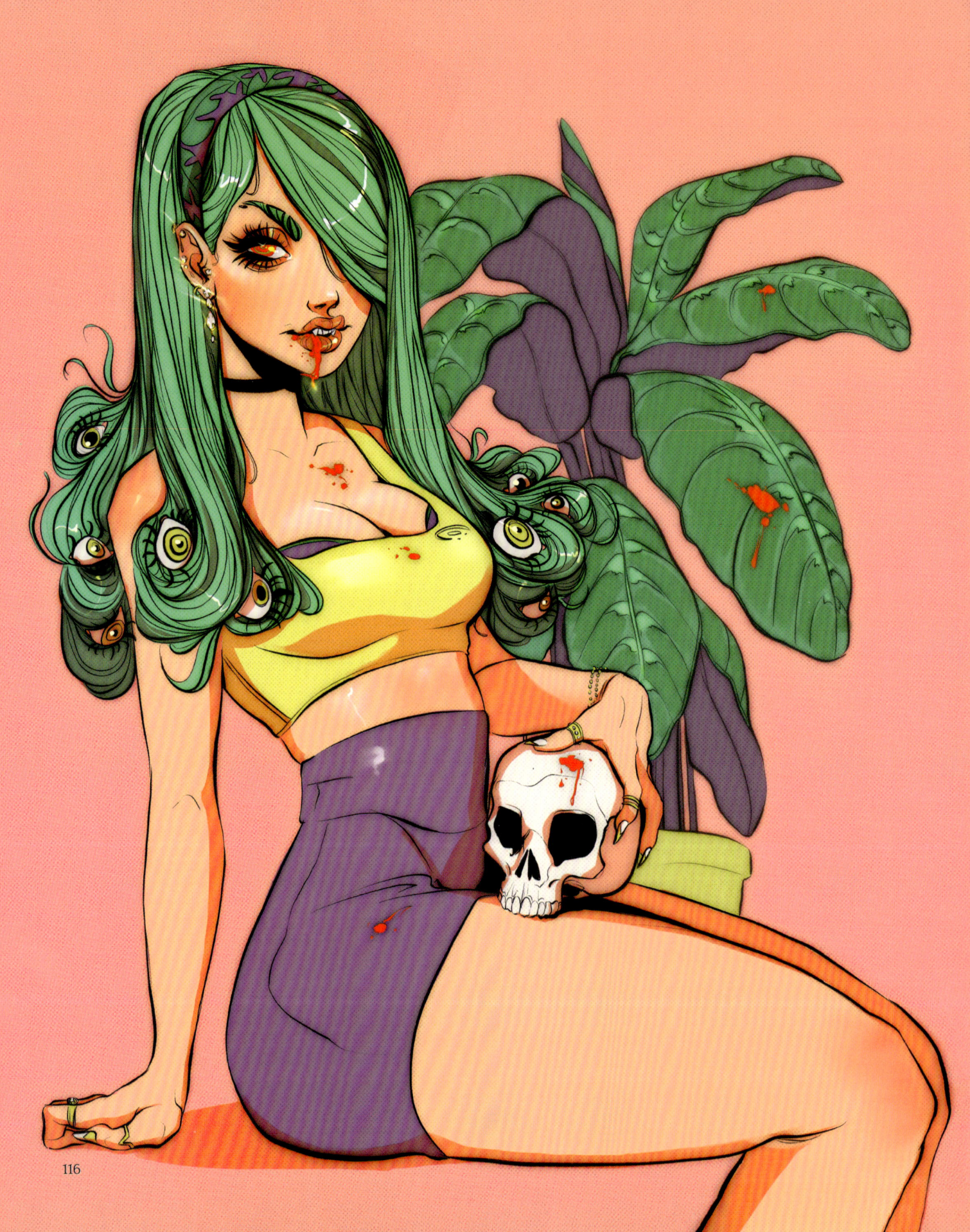

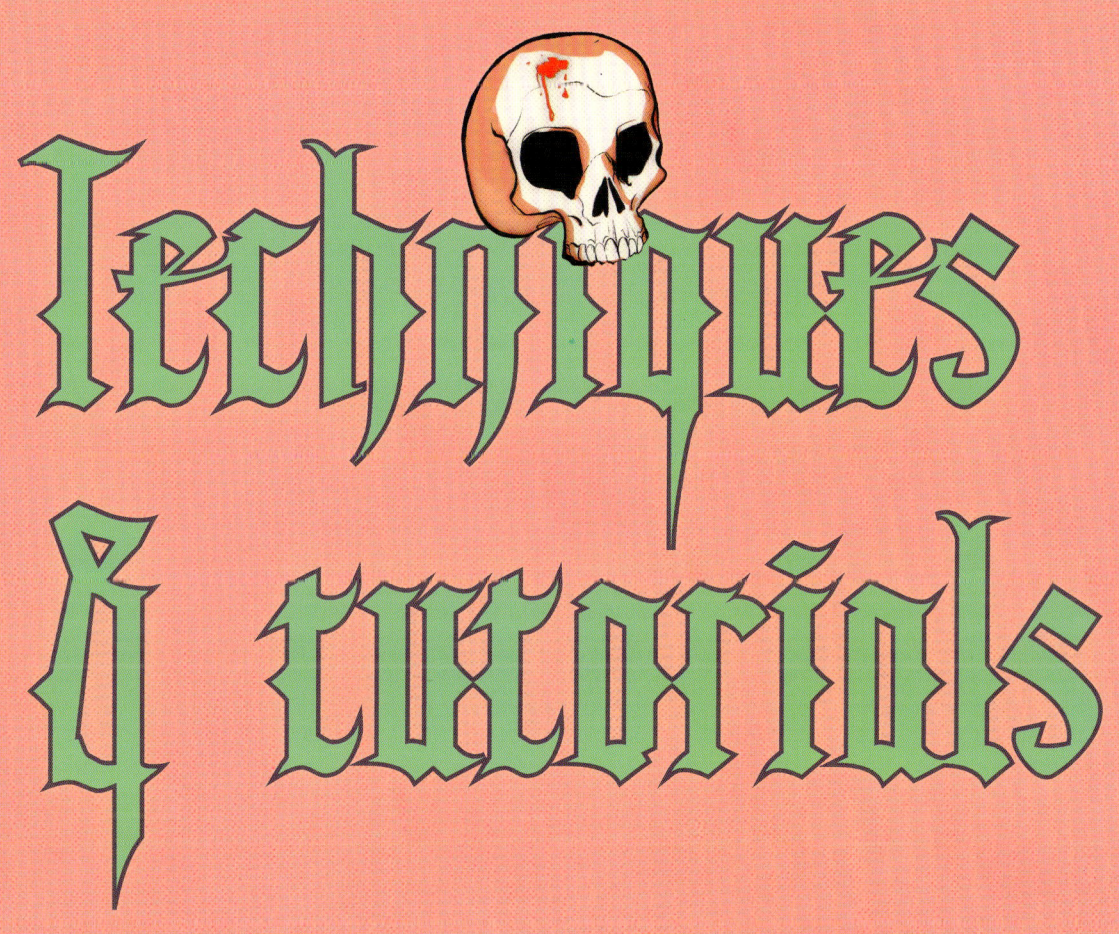

Techniques & tutorials

Loving your line work

When it comes to art, I think the best overall advice I could give is to be confident with your lines and brushstrokes. I see so many newer artists scribble and redo line after line when sketching or inking. They take each line extra slow and once they are done, you can see every shaky breath in that line. Be confident with them! Do your best with that one line and move on. Don't slowly try to work it out or scratch in multiple lines.

Practise drawing straight lines and circles. Do that over and over again until it feels like second nature. Build that confidence up in your wrist and arm. It will really make a difference. I can look at any sketch I've drawn and tell you if I was nervous about it or just not confident with what I was doing. I can also tell when I loved what I was making and knew it would turn out great. And you know what? So can everyone else. A big part of art is just pouring your own heart and soul out on paper, and if your fear is holding you back, you will be able to see it in every little line and brushstroke. So, my advice is to work on your conviction, scribble constantly in your sketchbook – your safe place – and when you're ready, go make some amazing art!

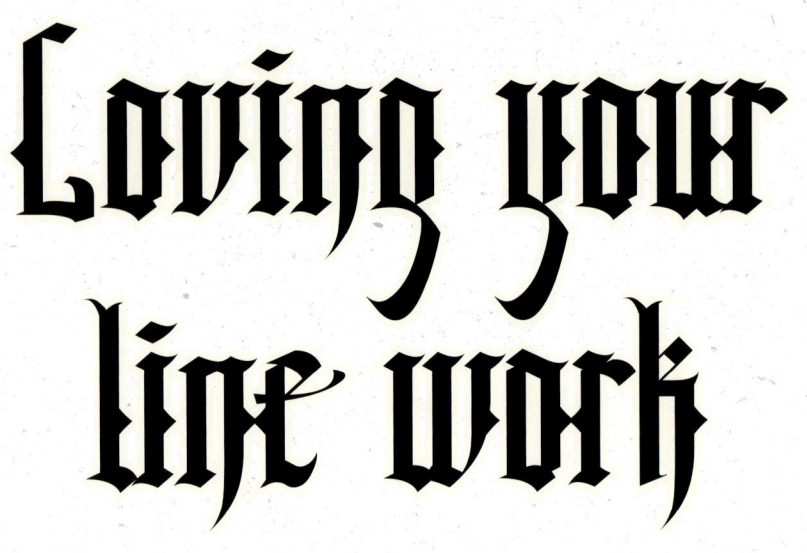

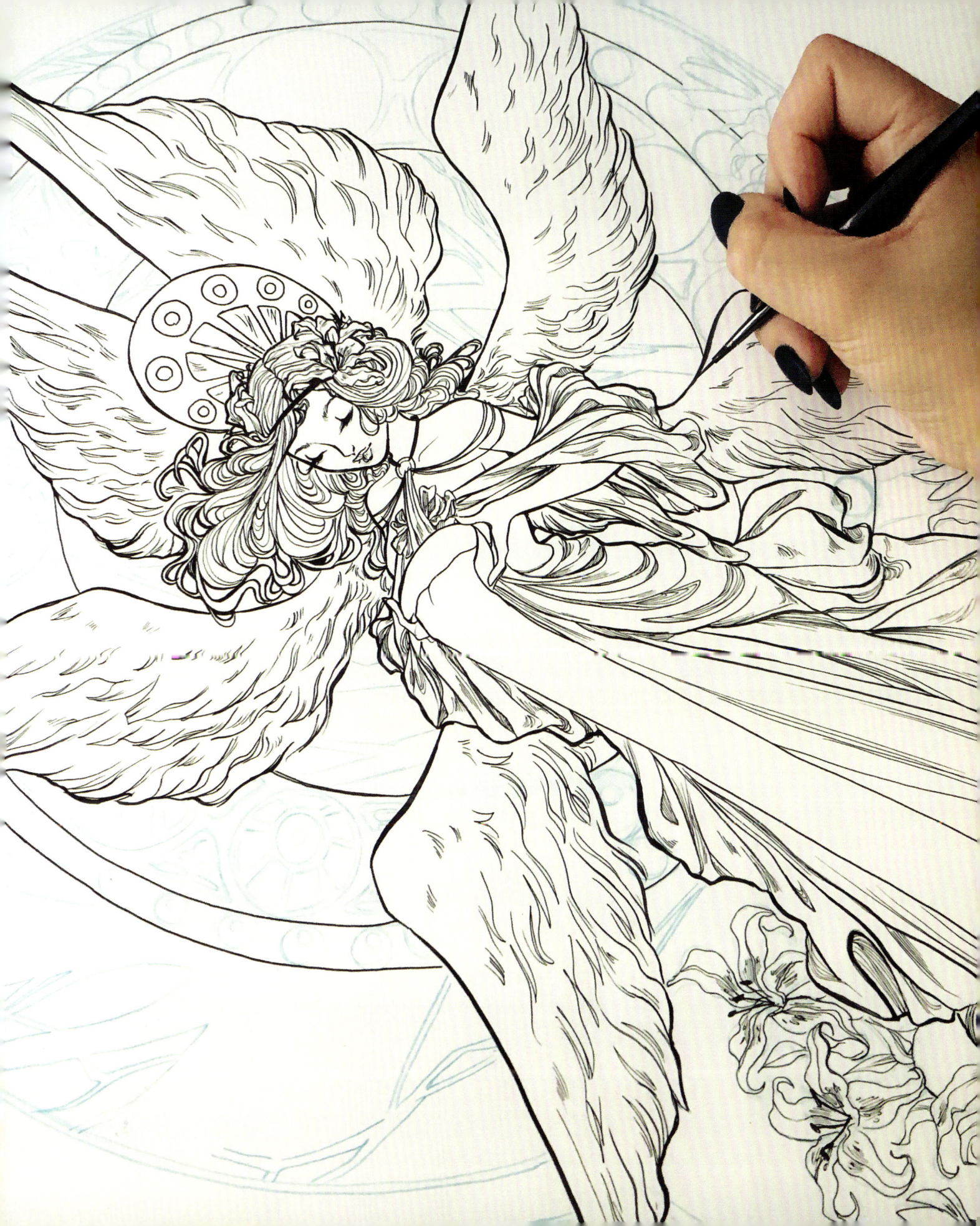

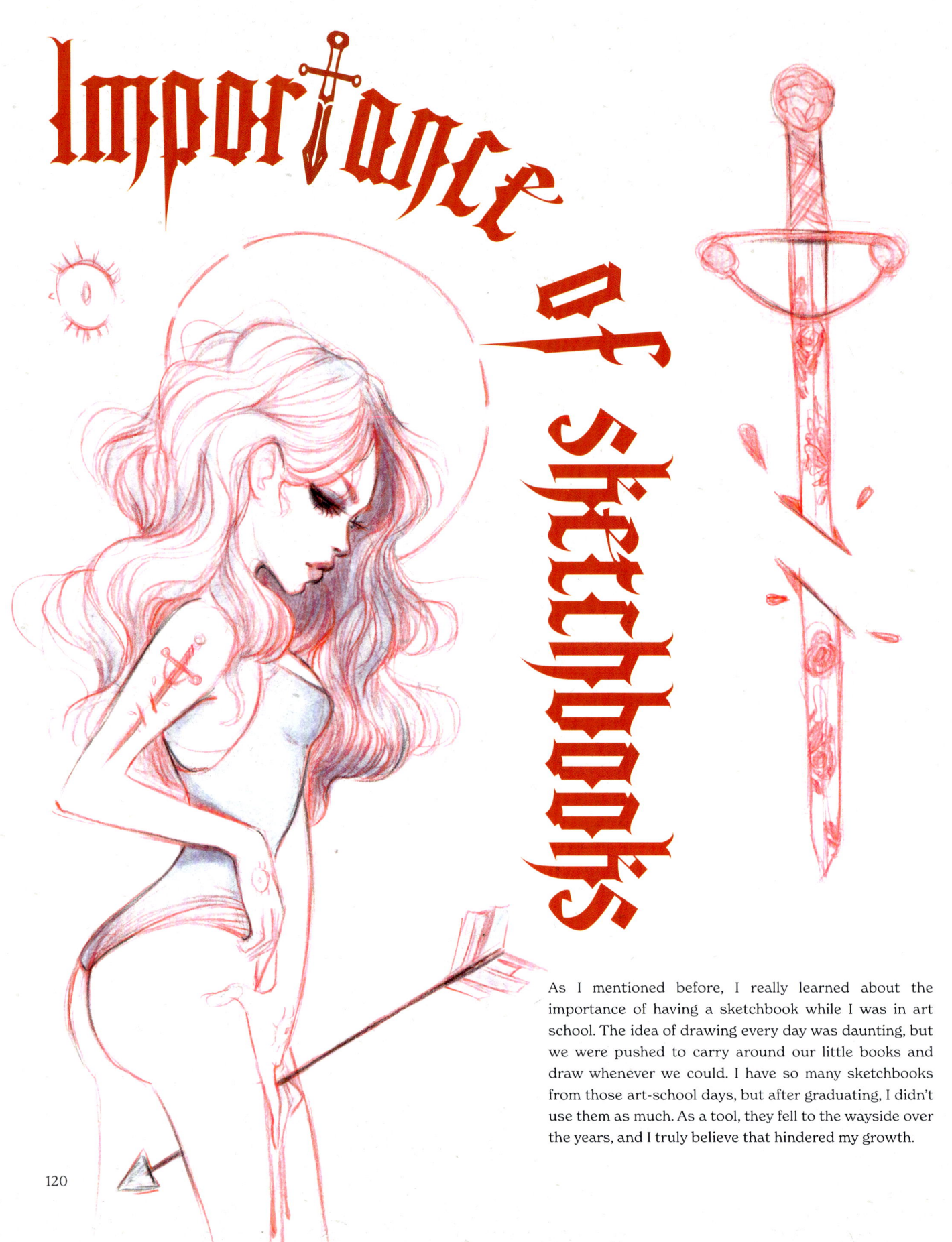

Importance of sketchbooks

As I mentioned before, I really learned about the importance of having a sketchbook while I was in art school. The idea of drawing every day was daunting, but we were pushed to carry around our little books and draw whenever we could. I have so many sketchbooks from those art-school days, but after graduating, I didn't use them as much. As a tool, they fell to the wayside over the years, and I truly believe that hindered my growth.

120

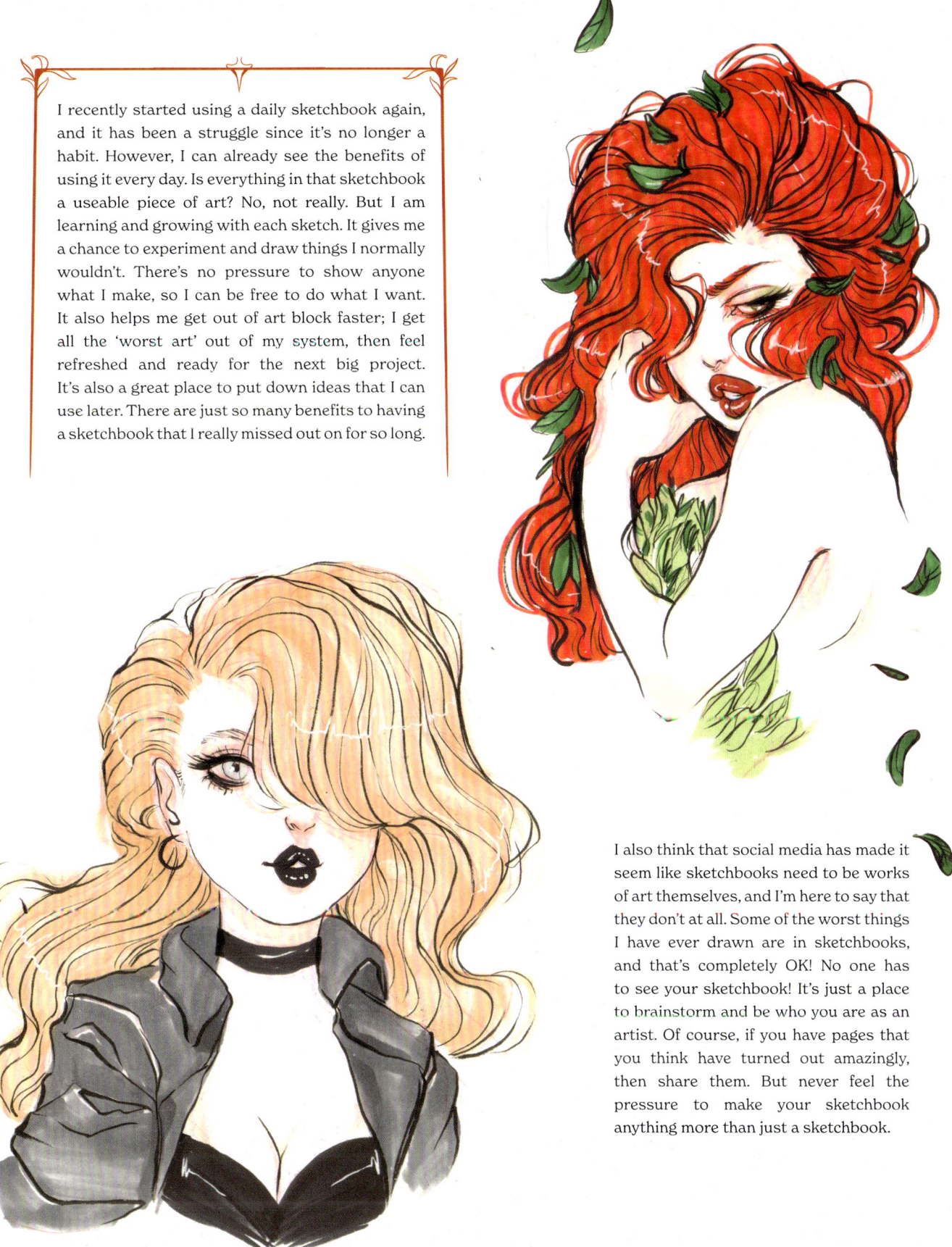

I recently started using a daily sketchbook again, and it has been a struggle since it's no longer a habit. However, I can already see the benefits of using it every day. Is everything in that sketchbook a useable piece of art? No, not really. But I am learning and growing with each sketch. It gives me a chance to experiment and draw things I normally wouldn't. There's no pressure to show anyone what I make, so I can be free to do what I want. It also helps me get out of art block faster; I get all the 'worst art' out of my system, then feel refreshed and ready for the next big project. It's also a great place to put down ideas that I can use later. There are just so many benefits to having a sketchbook that I really missed out on for so long.

I also think that social media has made it seem like sketchbooks need to be works of art themselves, and I'm here to say that they don't at all. Some of the worst things I have ever drawn are in sketchbooks, and that's completely OK! No one has to see your sketchbook! It's just a place to brainstorm and be who you are as an artist. Of course, if you have pages that you think have turned out amazingly, then share them. But never feel the pressure to make your sketchbook anything more than just a sketchbook.

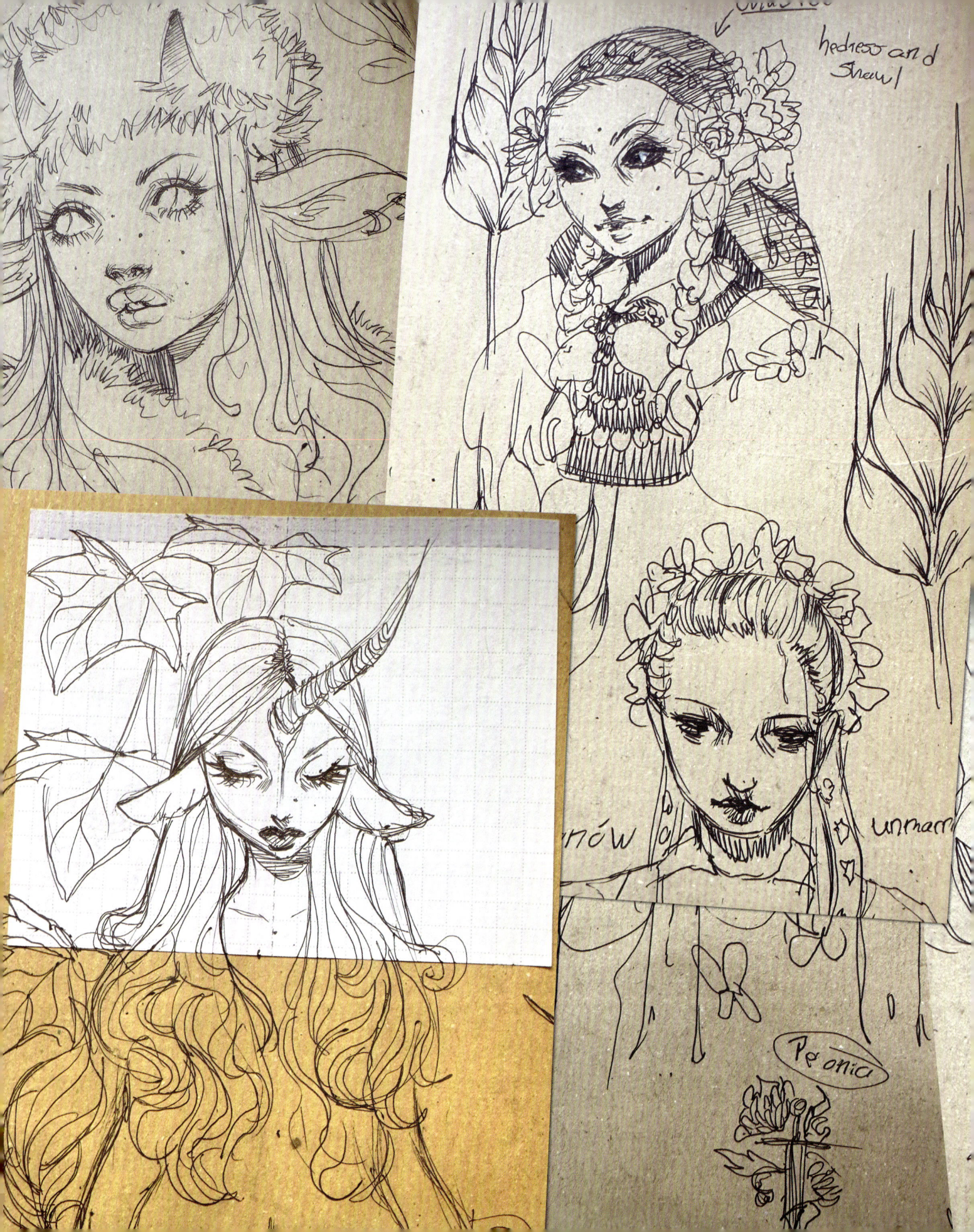

hedrew and
Shewl

nów

unman

Peonia

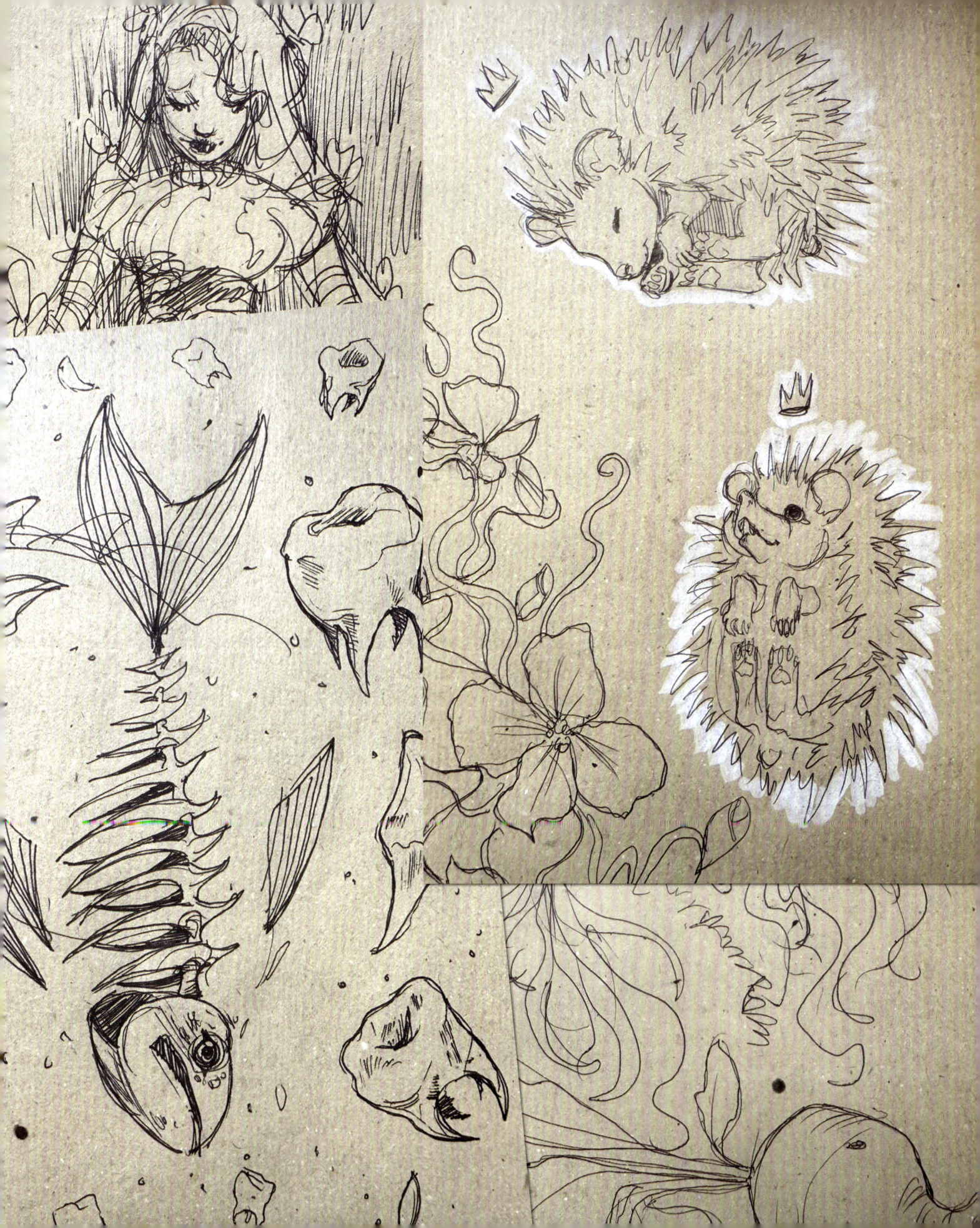

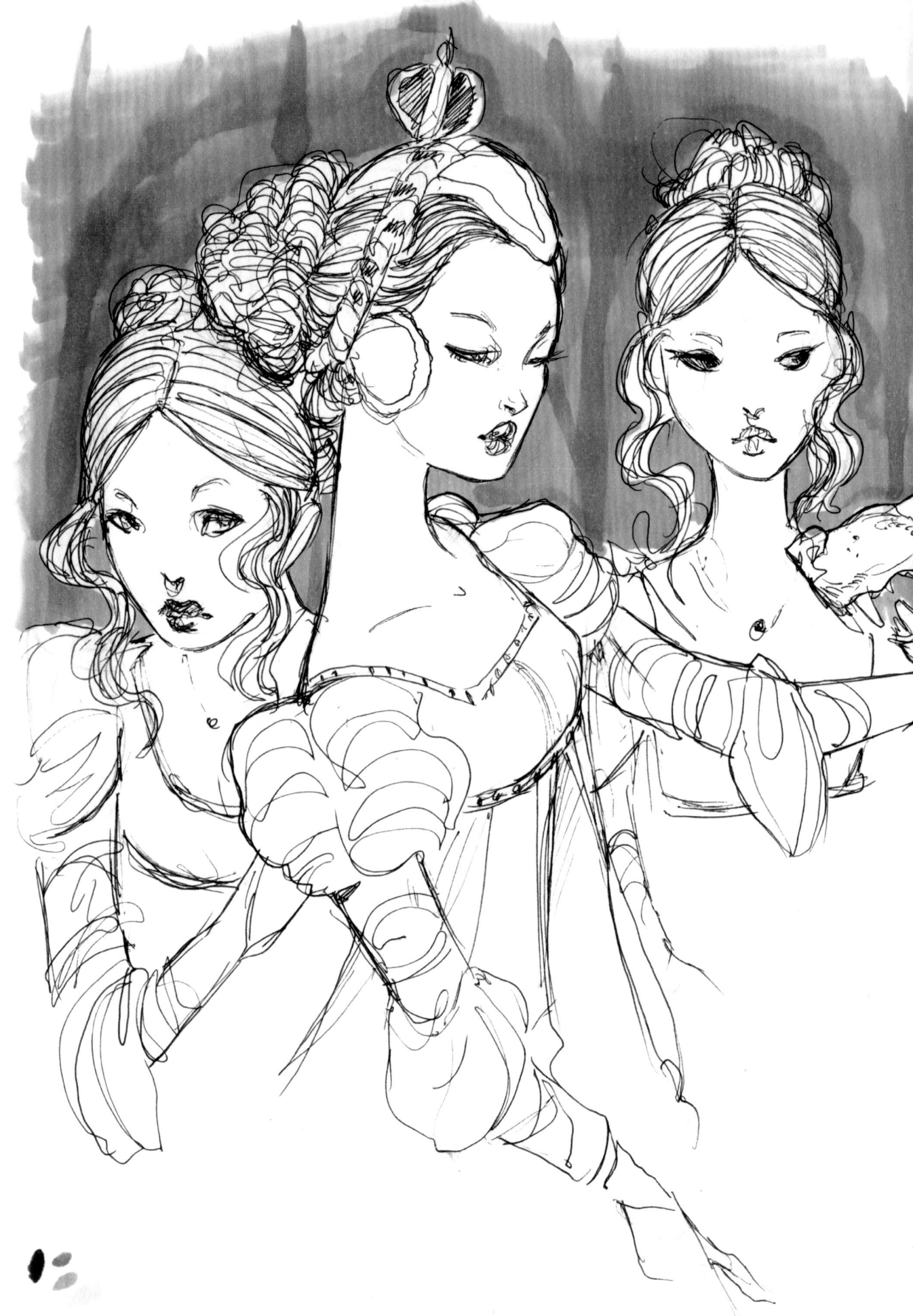

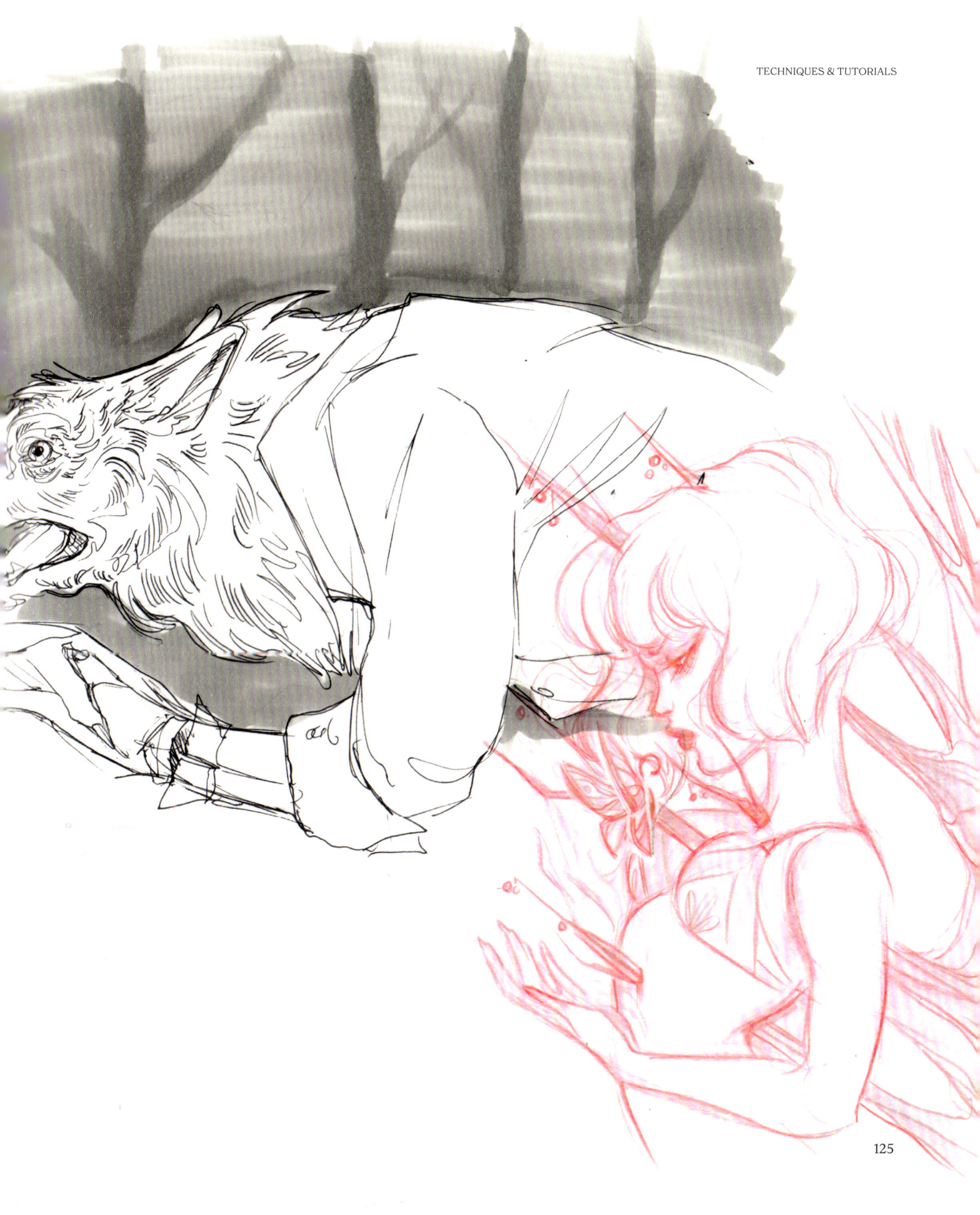

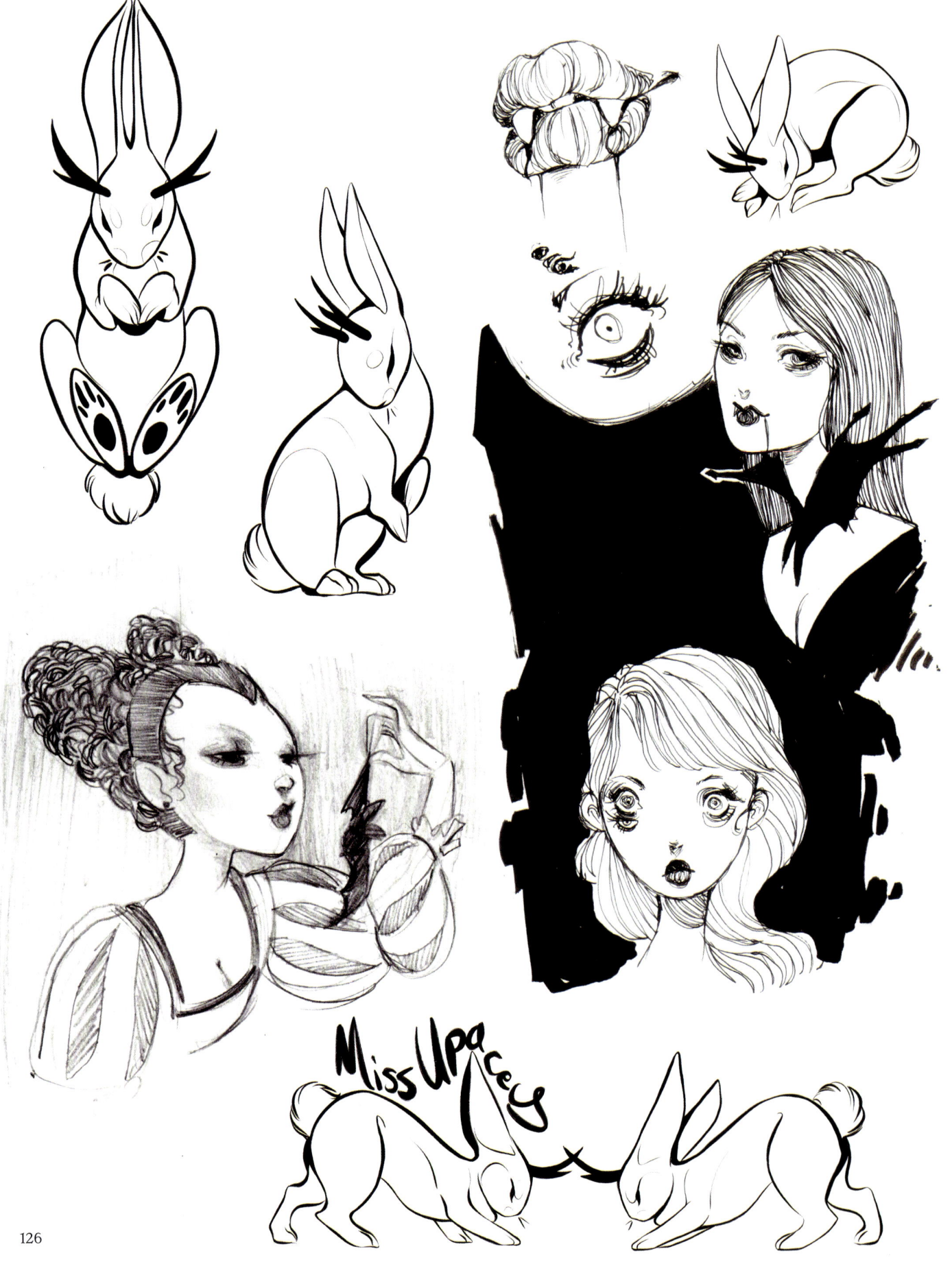

MissUpacey

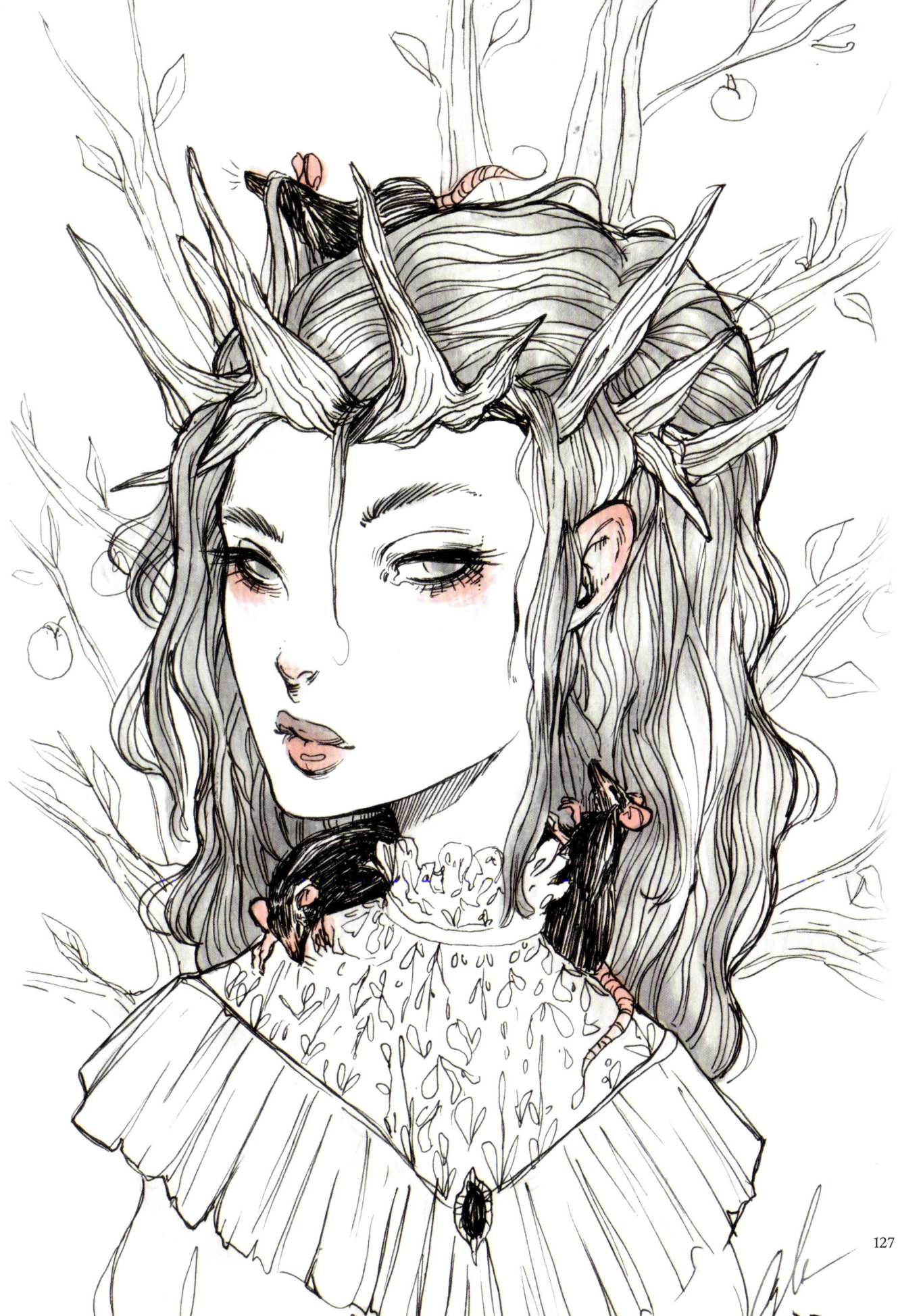

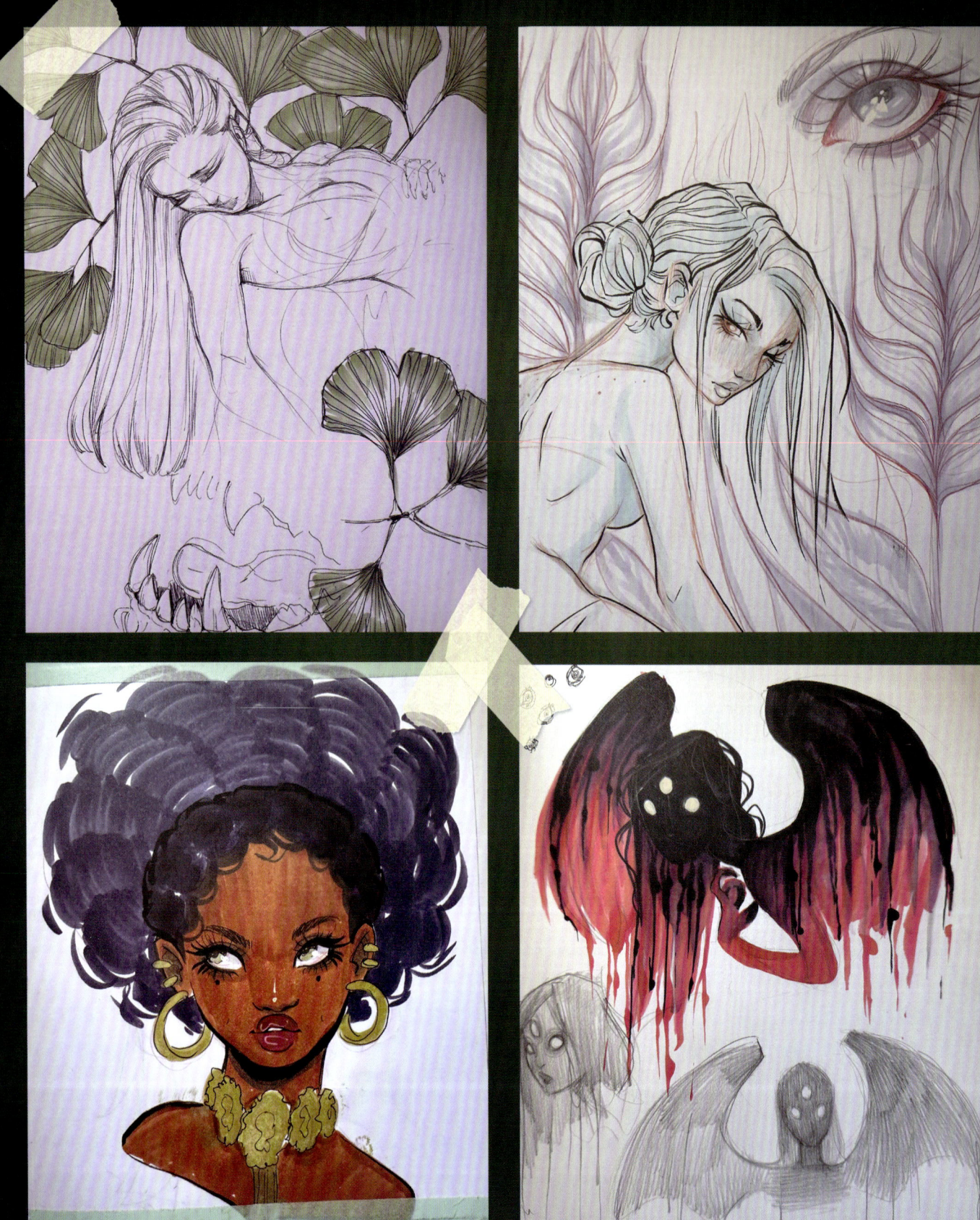

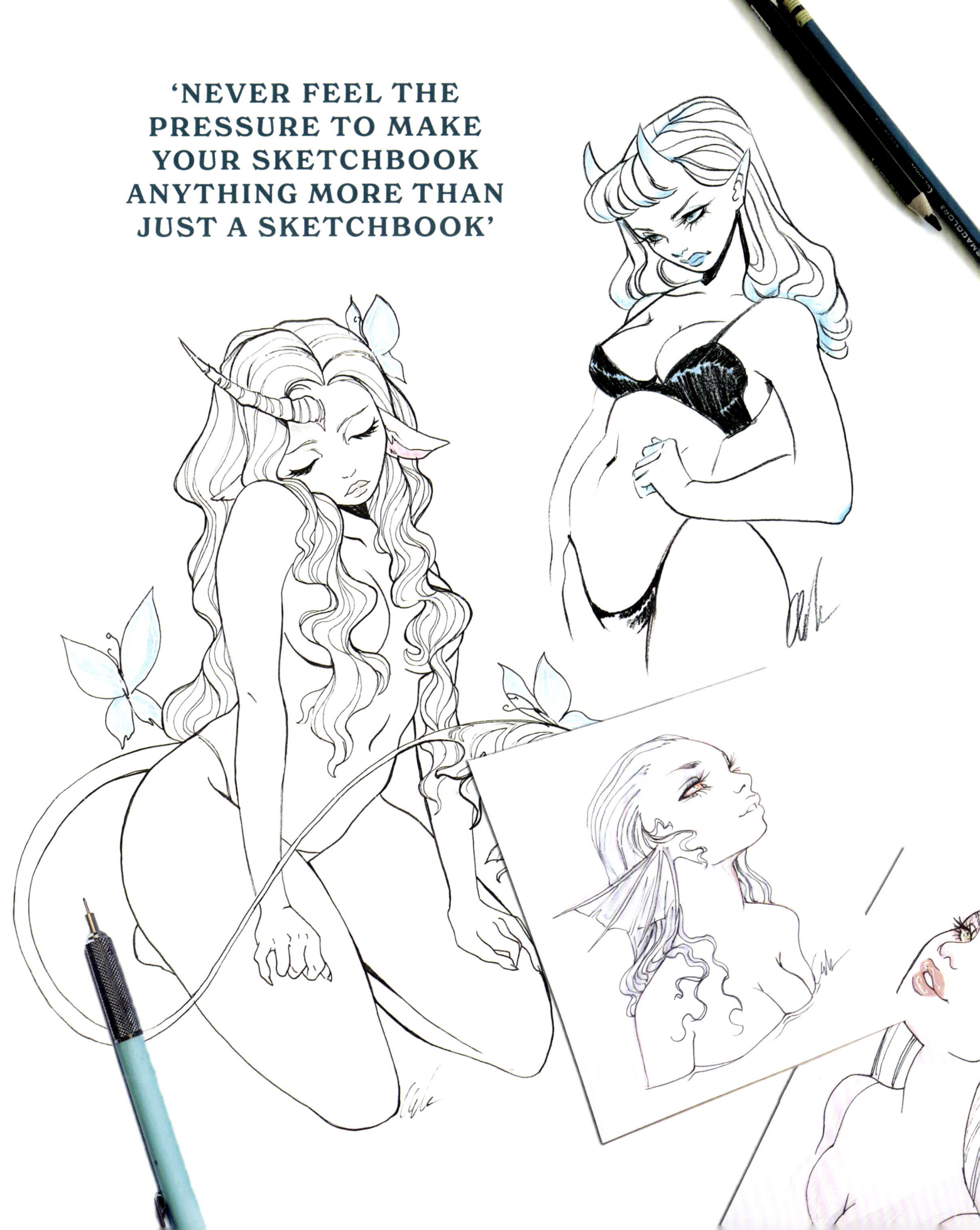

'NEVER FEEL THE PRESSURE TO MAKE YOUR SKETCHBOOK ANYTHING MORE THAN JUST A SKETCHBOOK'

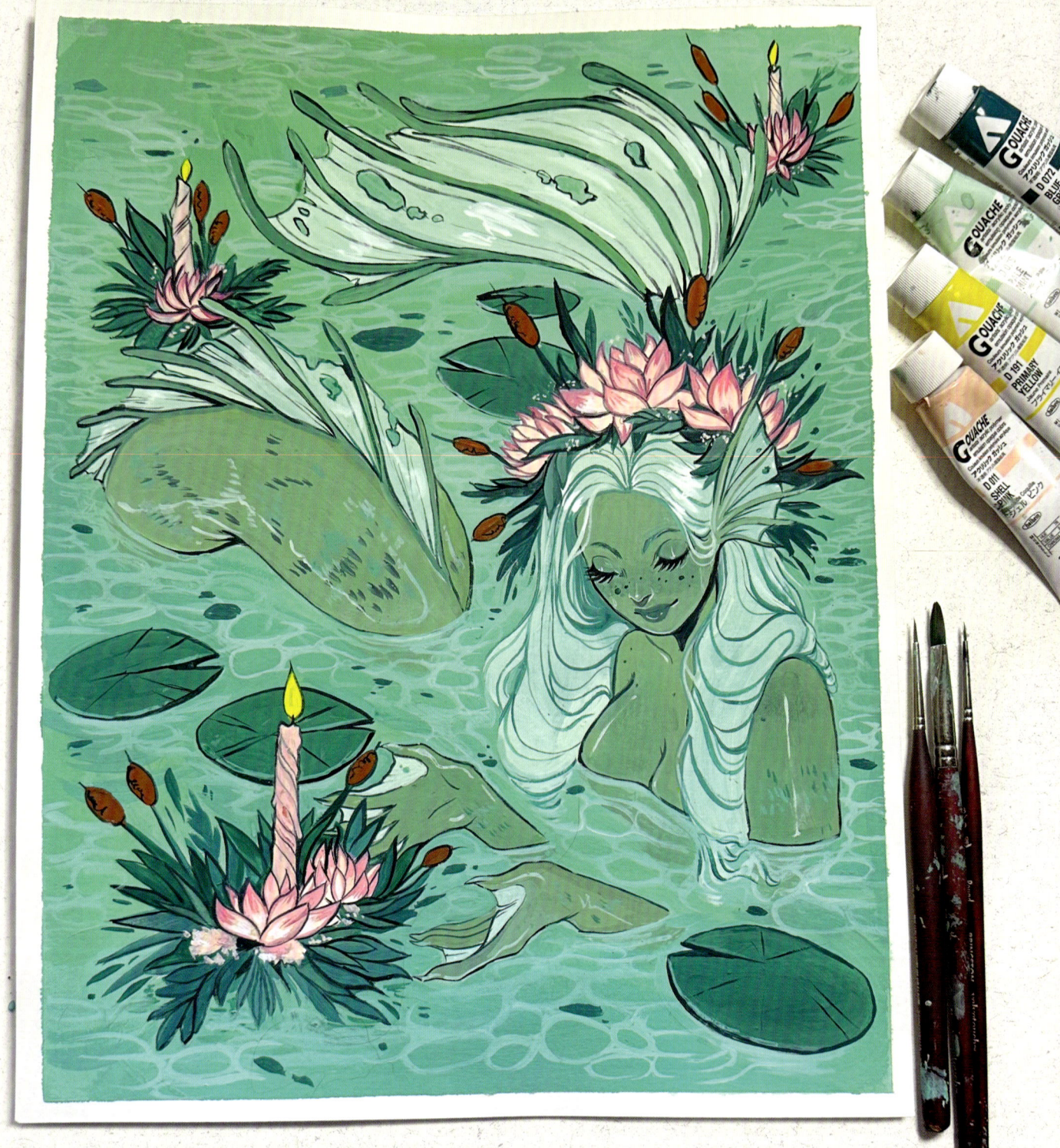

Traditional tutorial

In this tutorial, I'll go over my acrylic-gouache painting process. I try to make my traditional stuff look as close to my digital pieces as I can, so you will notice that I start off digitally. I also use other types of media, but the process is pretty much the same. I do tend to work a little all over the place when it comes to my traditional works, so don't mind me if I jump around while filling in the details!

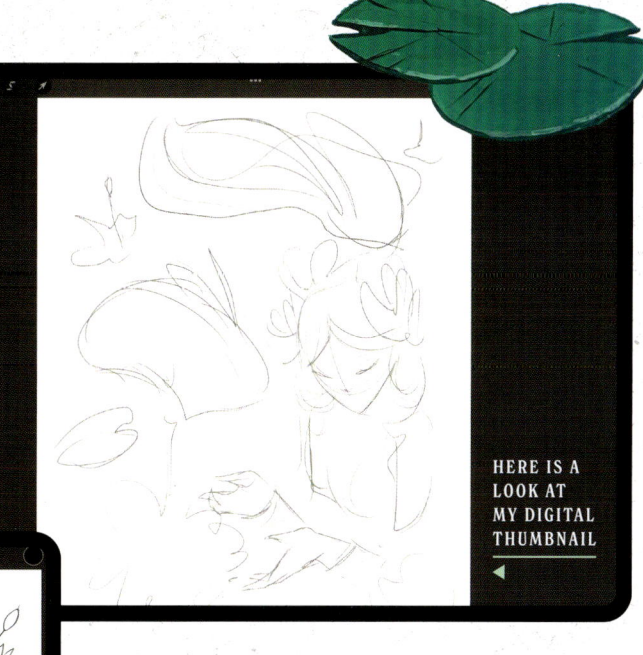

HERE IS A LOOK AT MY DIGITAL THUMBNAIL ◄

STEP 01: DIGITAL THUMBNAIL

Personally, it's easiest to start out digitally. This way, I can be really loose in the beginning and then edit things easily without the need to erase.

STEP 02: DIGITAL SKETCH

From here, I sketch everything out and complete a little bit of line art. I do this so I won't have to change anything once I trace it onto the watercolour paper.

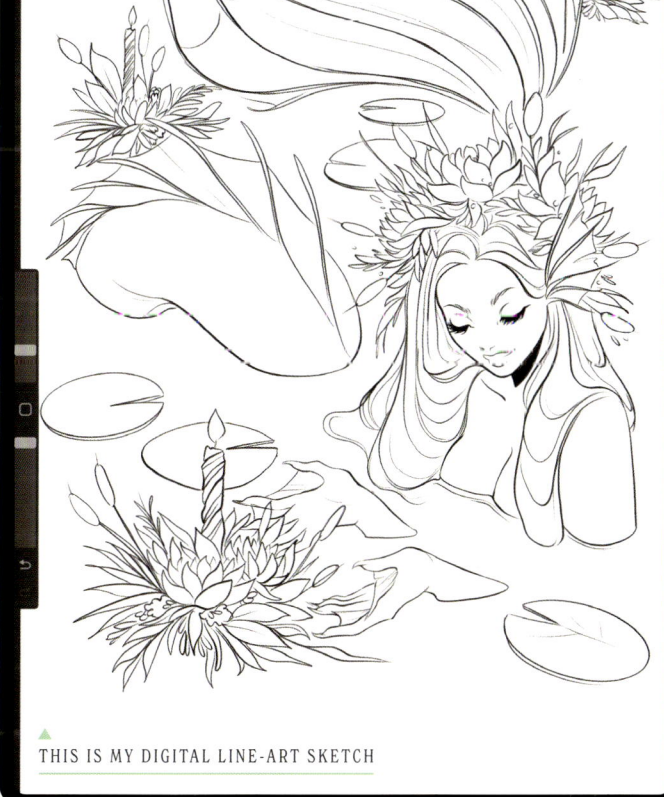

▲ THIS IS MY DIGITAL LINE-ART SKETCH

STEP 03: DIGITAL COLOUR PALETTE

I also take this time to complete a digital experiment with colour so that I can play around with combinations to see what works best. Once I'm ready to paint, I'll have this little reference handy!

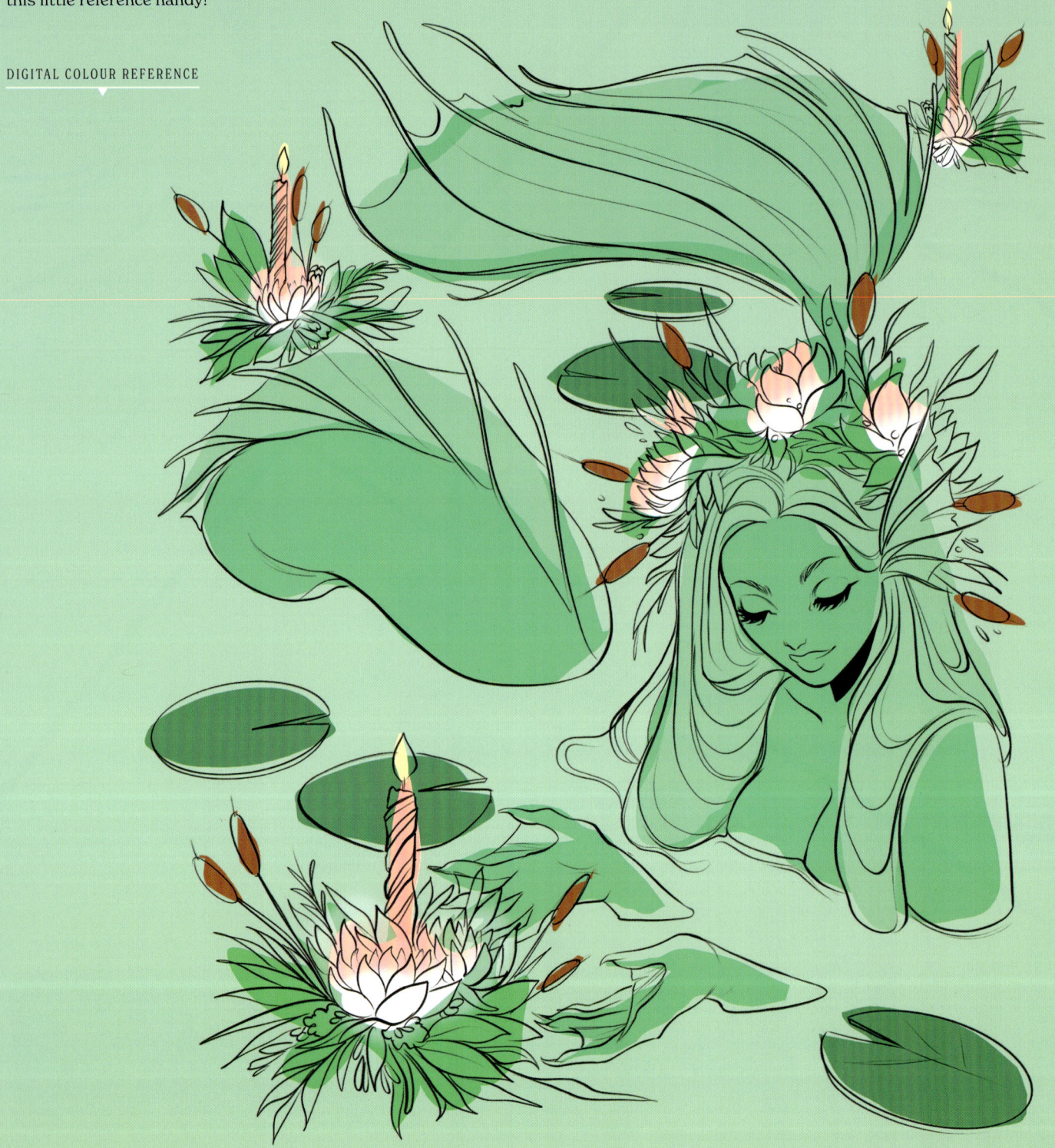

132

STEP 04: TRACING

Now to move into the traditional sphere. I get my big tracing board out and trace the digital sketch onto watercolour paper using a pencil. I make sure to not apply too much pressure when tracing so I don't leave an indent on the paper. If you want the painting to be quite large, you will most likely have to print multiple pages and piece them together like a puzzle.

YOU CAN SEE THAT I'VE TAPED TOGETHER THE PRINTED PAGES FOR TRACING AND THEN SKETCHED THEM ONTO WATERCOLOUR PAPER
►

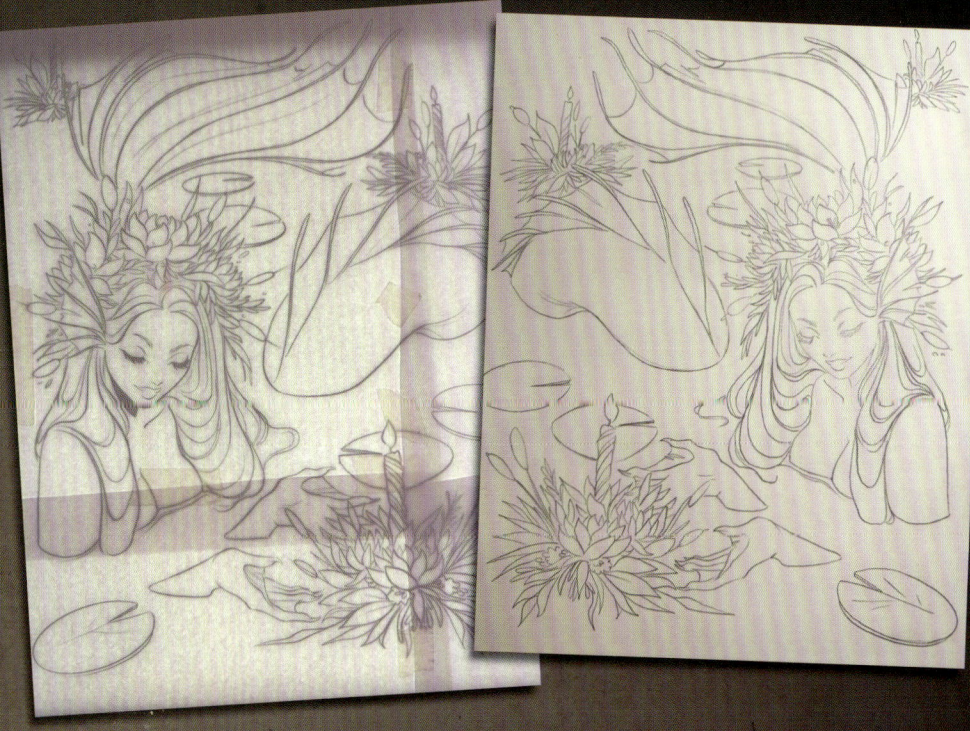

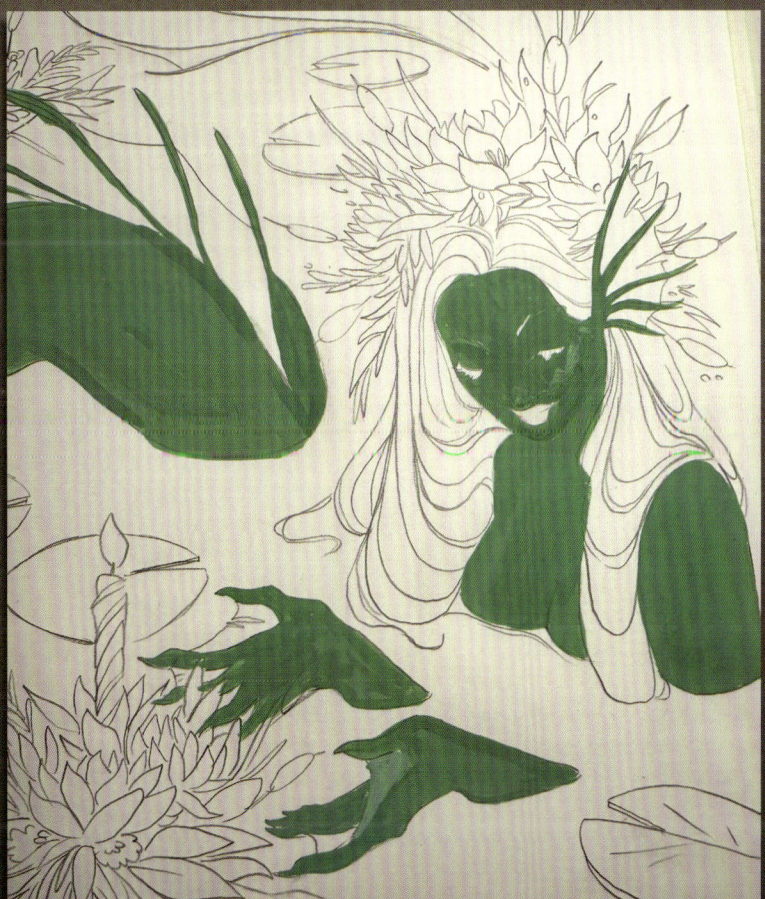

STEP 05: FIRST BASE LAYER

Here is where I begin painting! I add a base layer to the most important parts of the image.

◄ I USE GREEN AS MY FIRST BASE LAYER

133

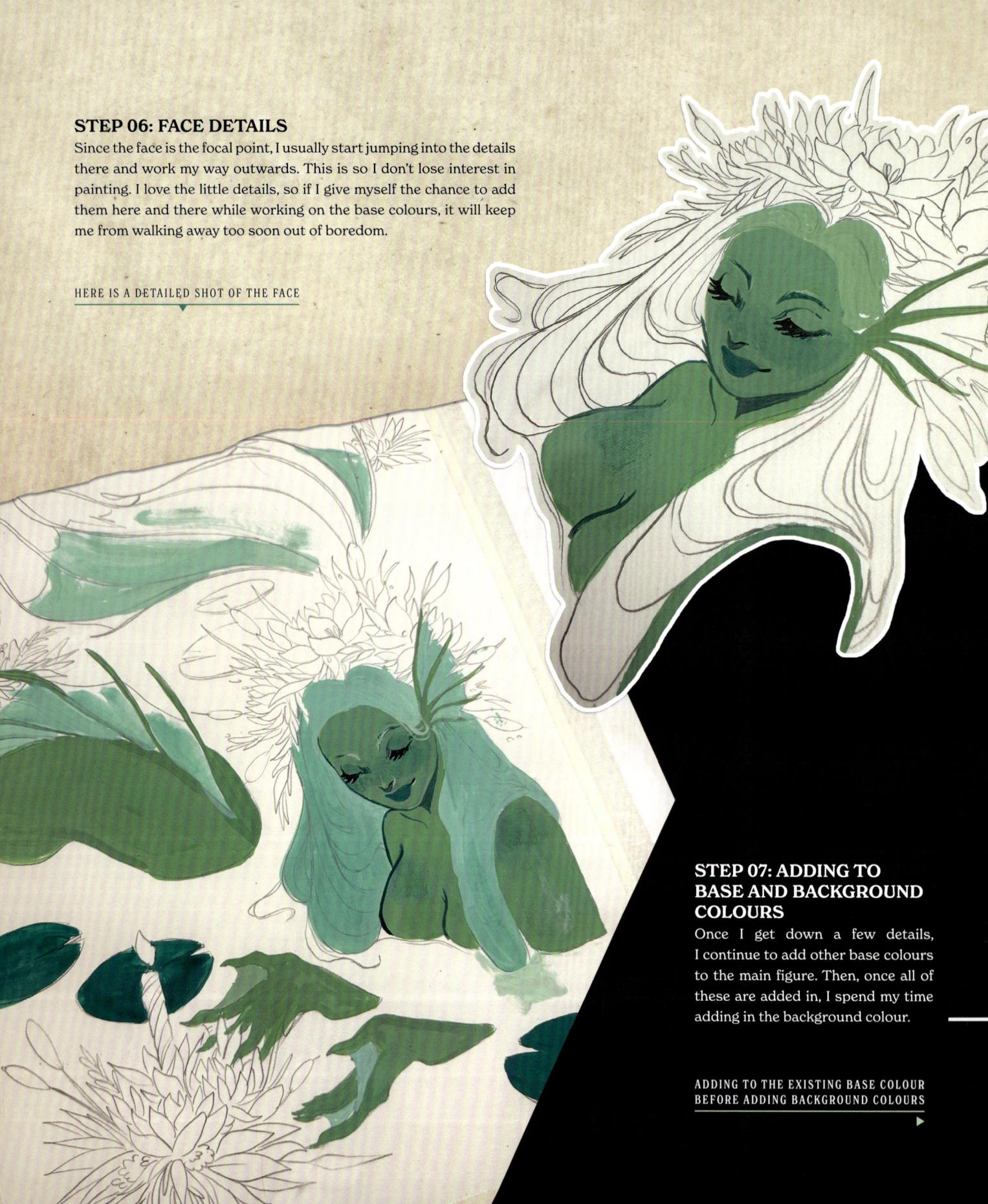

STEP 06: FACE DETAILS

Since the face is the focal point, I usually start jumping into the details there and work my way outwards. This is so I don't lose interest in painting. I love the little details, so if I give myself the chance to add them here and there while working on the base colours, it will keep me from walking away too soon out of boredom.

HERE IS A DETAILED SHOT OF THE FACE

STEP 07: ADDING TO BASE AND BACKGROUND COLOURS

Once I get down a few details, I continue to add other base colours to the main figure. Then, once all of these are added in, I spend my time adding in the background colour.

ADDING TO THE EXISTING BASE COLOUR
BEFORE ADDING BACKGROUND COLOURS

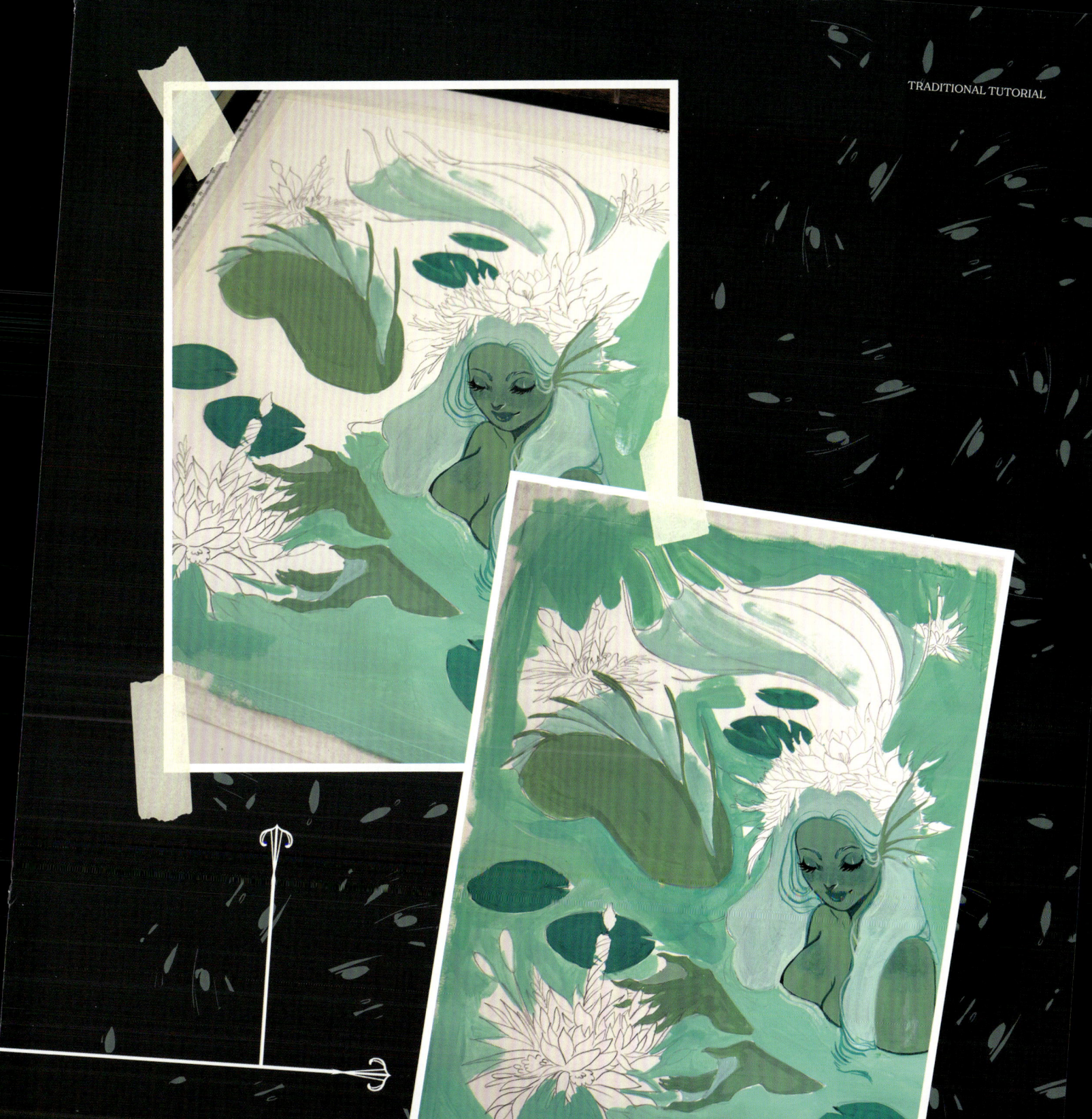

STEP 08: ADDING LINE ART

Now that the base and background colours are in place, I start adding in line art and the details above it.

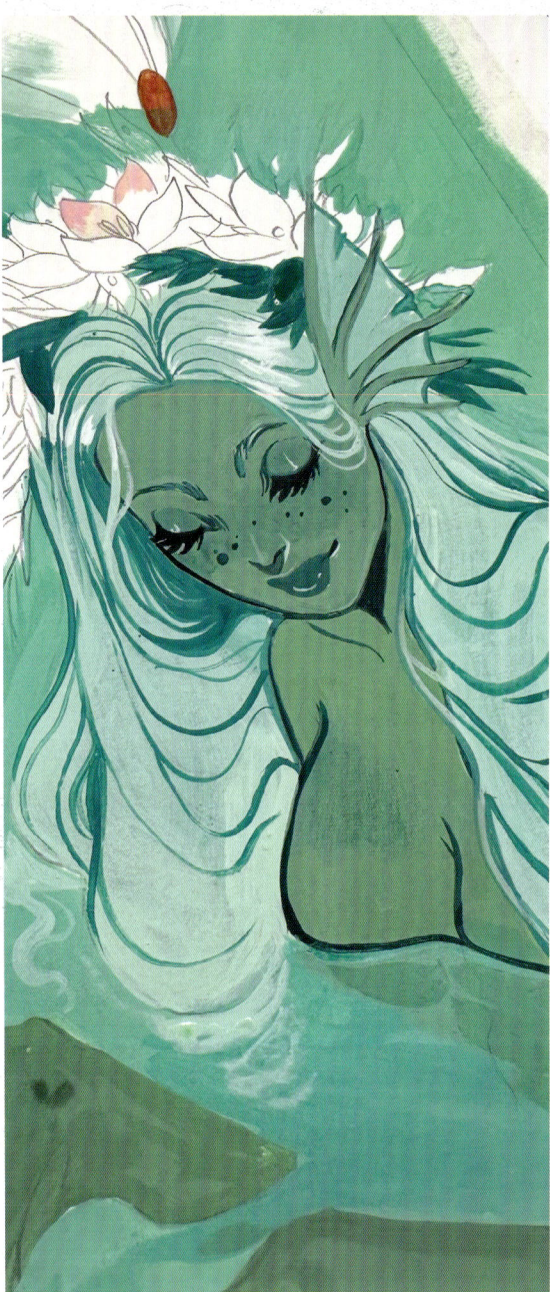

STEP 09: ADDING THE DETAILS

This right here is the real fun part – the details! I start from the face and work outwards, slowly adding more and more details and making sure to clean up the edges as I go.

DETAIL SHOT

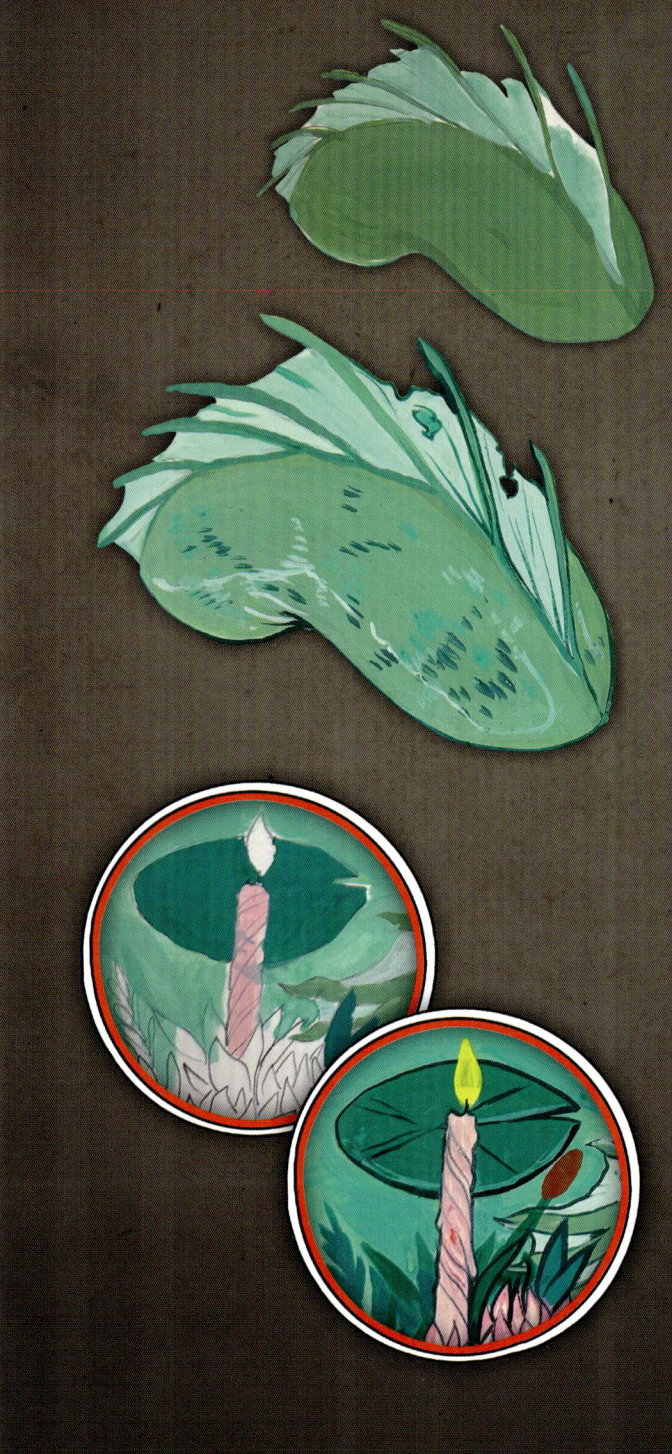

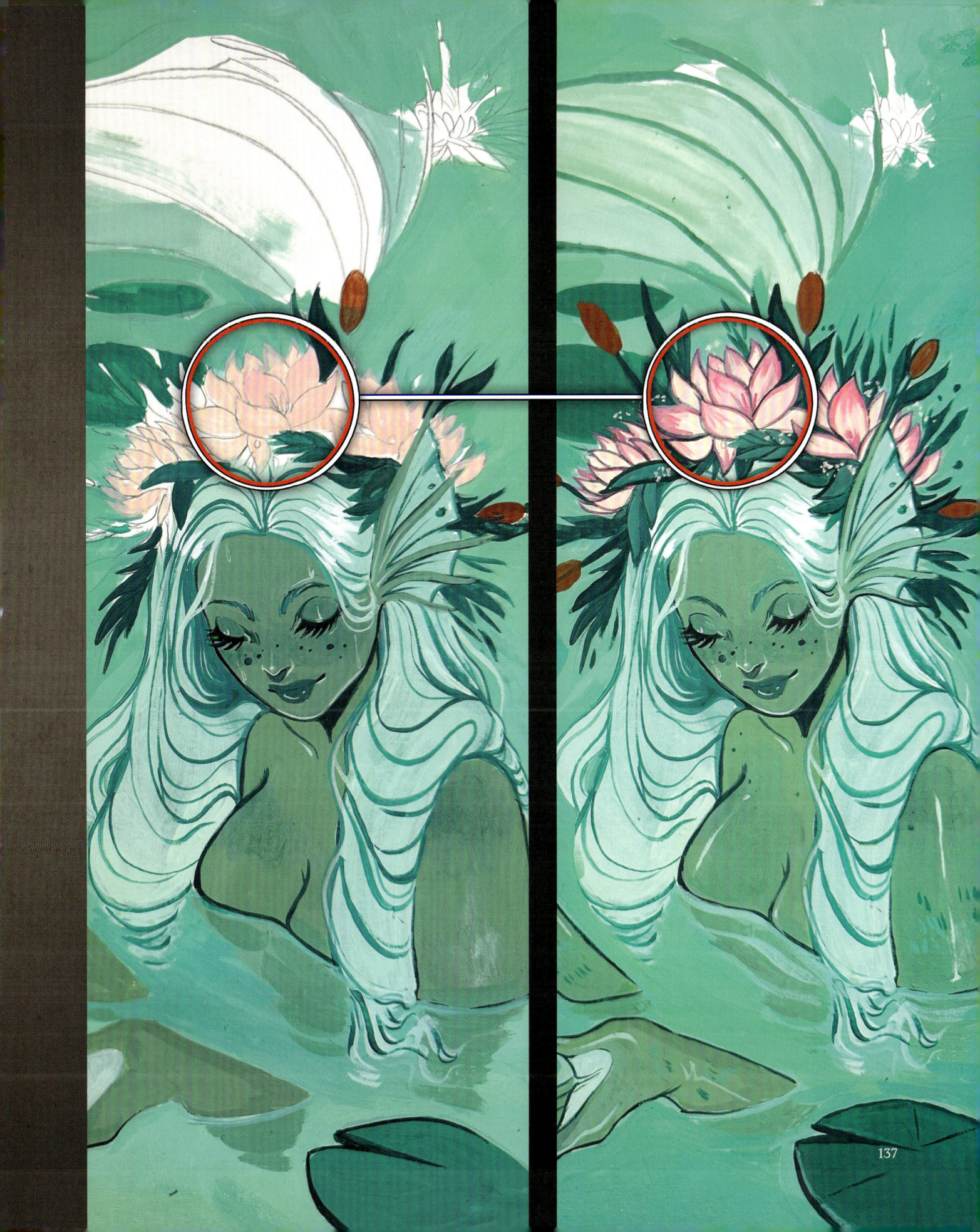

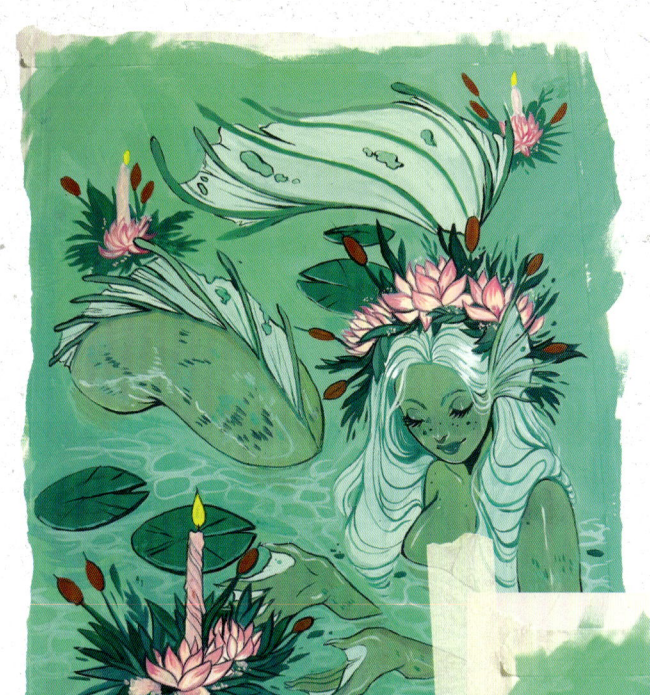

STEP 10: BACK TO THE BACKGROUND

As soon as I get all the details down on the main subject, I get to work on the background. I don't usually go too heavy on those areas to avoid attention being taken away from the subject.

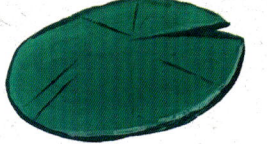

ALMOST FINISHED PAINTING!

◀

STEP 11: FINAL TOUCHES

Now all that's left to do is clean up the whole image and add little details here and there!

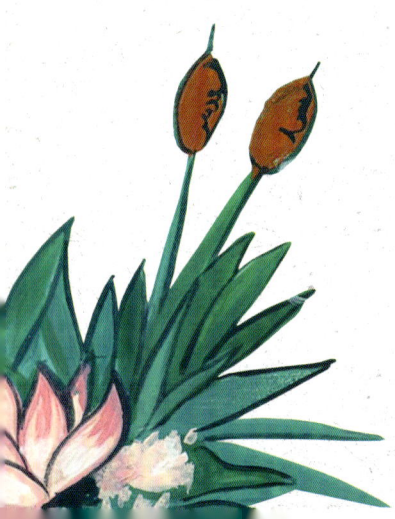

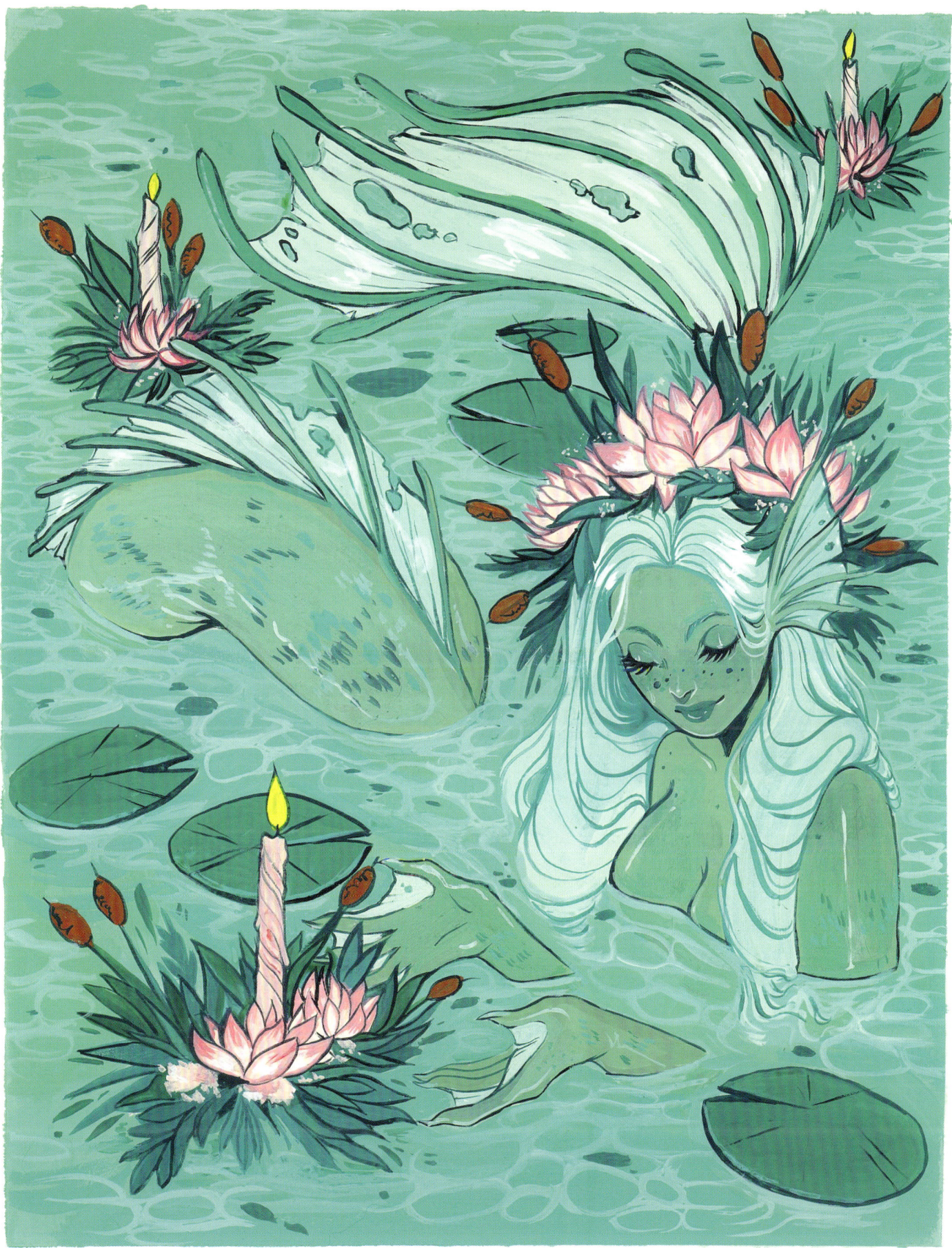

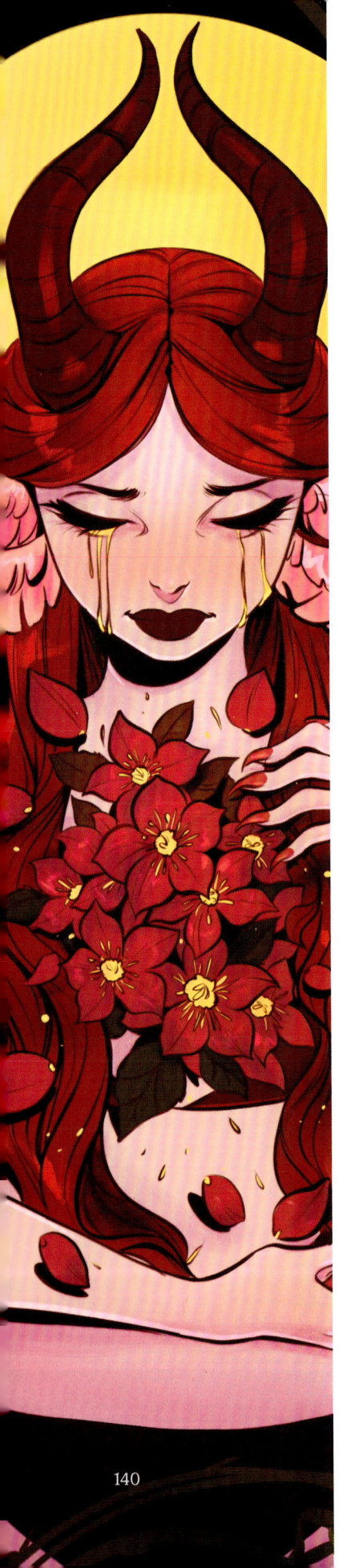

Digital tutorial

In this tutorial, I will show you my process when it comes to creating digital pieces. The reason I like working in digital so much is that it creates room for experimentation. I'm not the best at making decisions, so being able to change something mid-process is a must for me. For most of my digital pieces, I use my iPad Pro and Procreate, but as I mentioned before, I've used a tablet and Photoshop in the past, so either tools work!

I have a collection of brushes I have downloaded from other creators, but one of my favourites – and the set I'll be using for this tutorial – is Georg's Brushtober set.

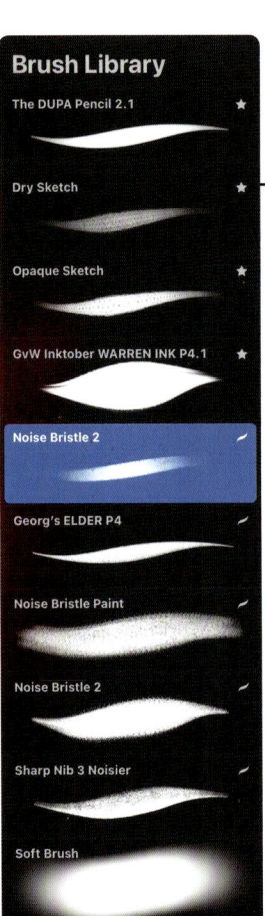

STEP 01: THUMBNAILING

This is the very beginning stage, so I'm mostly just doodling and getting lines on 'paper'. I do this multiple times until I find a thumbnail that I like. Make sure to take your time and choose one that you're happy with. The beauty of digital art is that you can always go back and make changes, so don't feel too pressured.

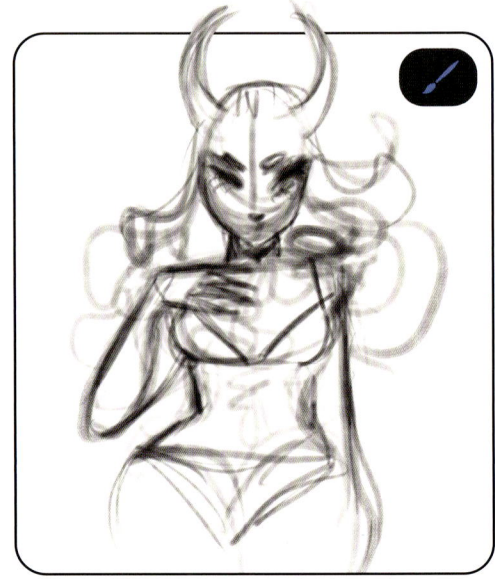

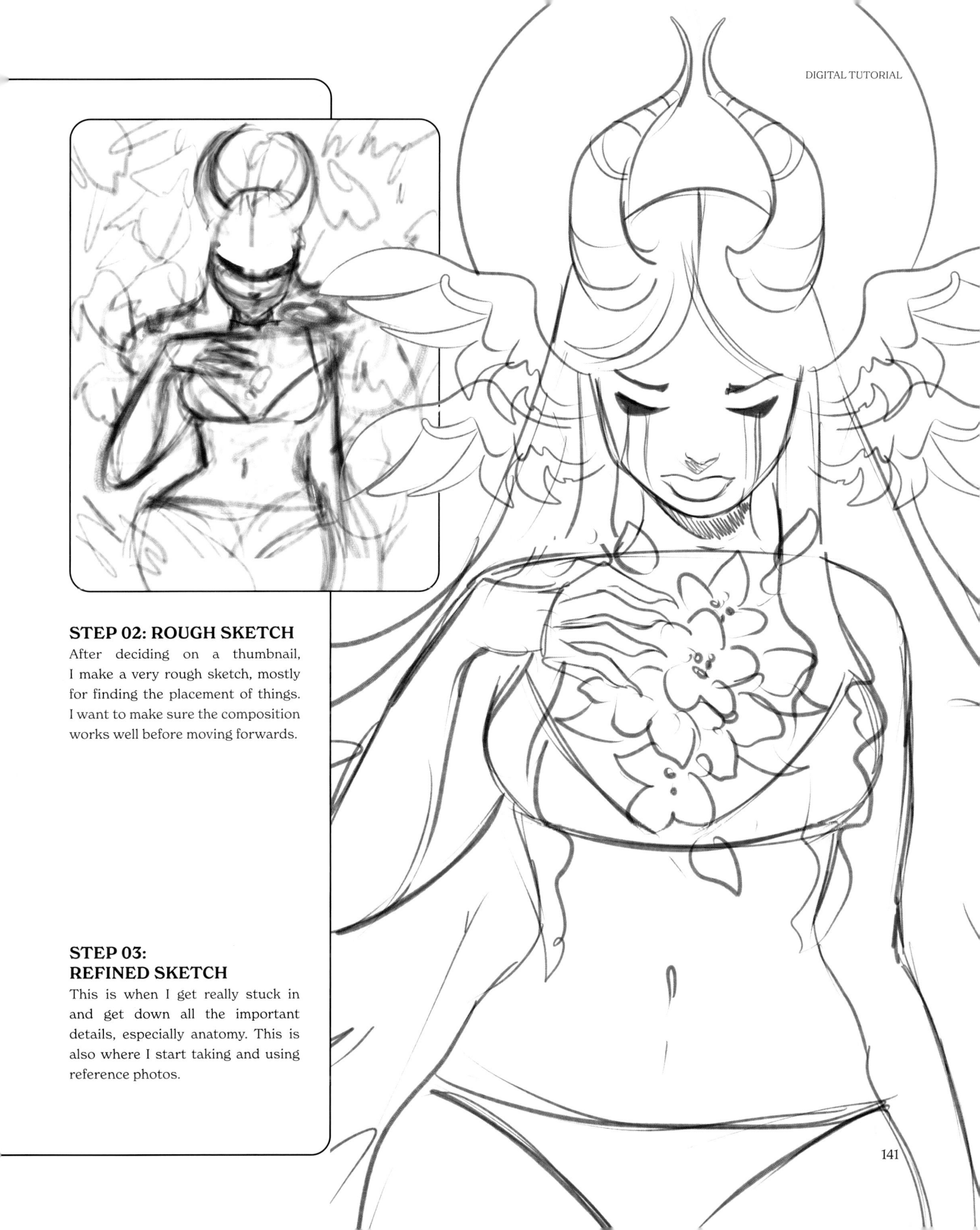

STEP 02: ROUGH SKETCH

After deciding on a thumbnail, I make a very rough sketch, mostly for finding the placement of things. I want to make sure the composition works well before moving forwards.

STEP 03: REFINED SKETCH

This is when I get really stuck in and get down all the important details, especially anatomy. This is also where I start taking and using reference photos.

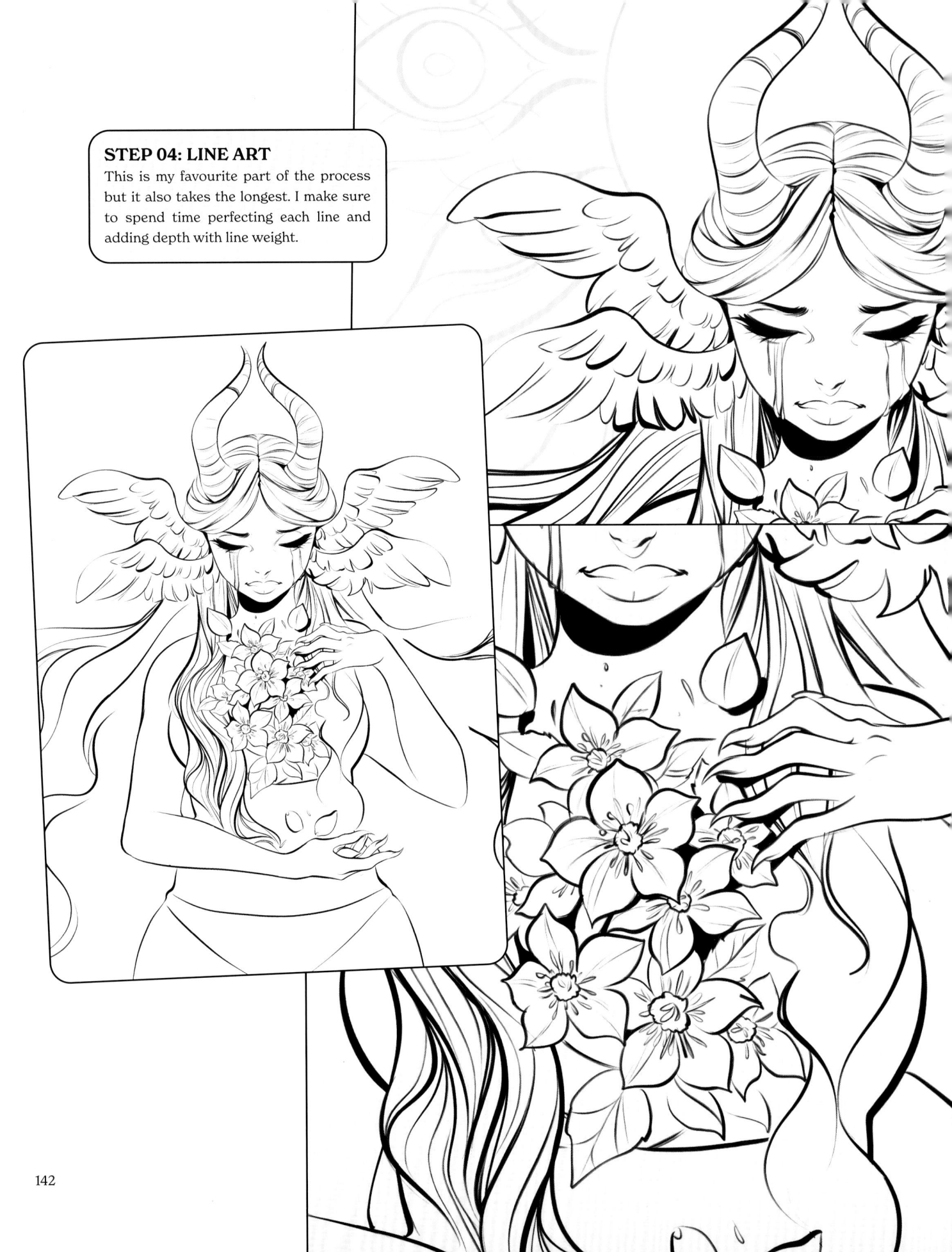

STEP 04: LINE ART

This is my favourite part of the process but it also takes the longest. I make sure to spend time perfecting each line and adding depth with line weight.

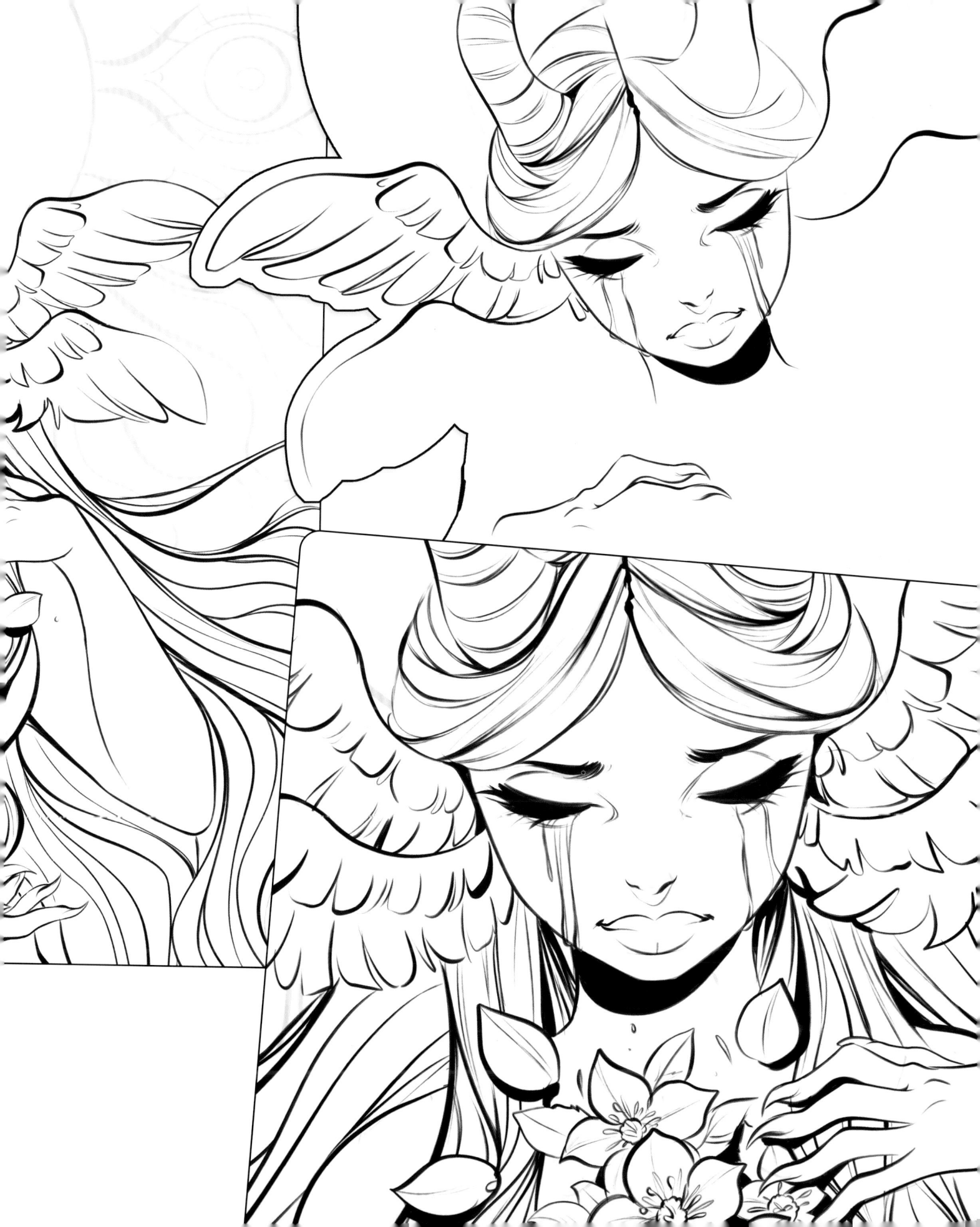

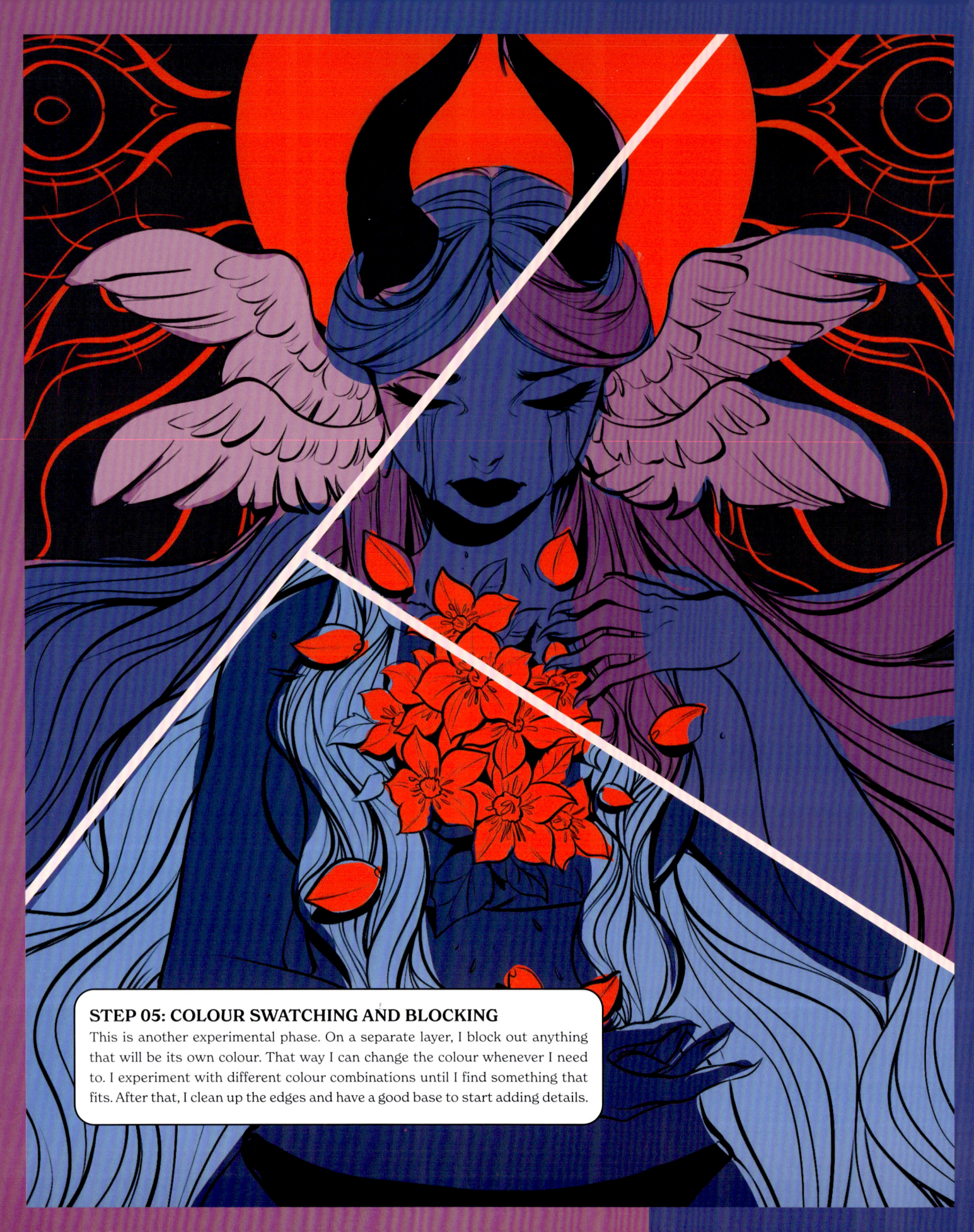

STEP 05: COLOUR SWATCHING AND BLOCKING

This is another experimental phase. On a separate layer, I block out anything that will be its own colour. That way I can change the colour whenever I need to. I experiment with different colour combinations until I find something that fits. After that, I clean up the edges and have a good base to start adding details.

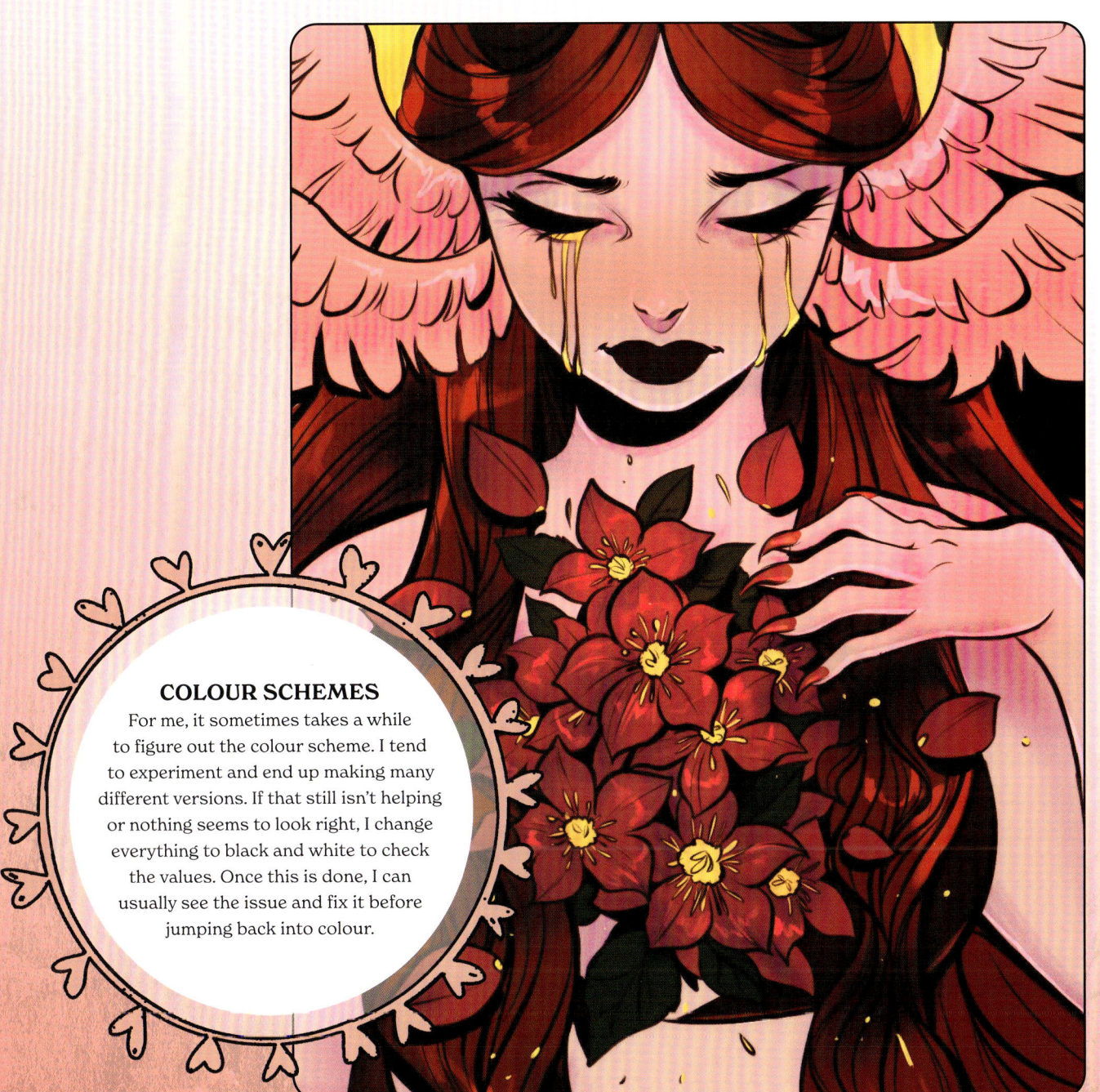

COLOUR SCHEMES

For me, it sometimes takes a while to figure out the colour scheme. I tend to experiment and end up making many different versions. If that still isn't helping or nothing seems to look right, I change everything to black and white to check the values. Once this is done, I can usually see the issue and fix it before jumping back into colour.

STEP 06: HIGHLIGHTS AND SHADOWS

Just like when I block in colour, I have a layer for highlights and a layer for shadows. That way, I can easily change the colours just in case it feels like it's not working. I usually use a sharp-edge brush for this and then smudge the harsh outlines later on.

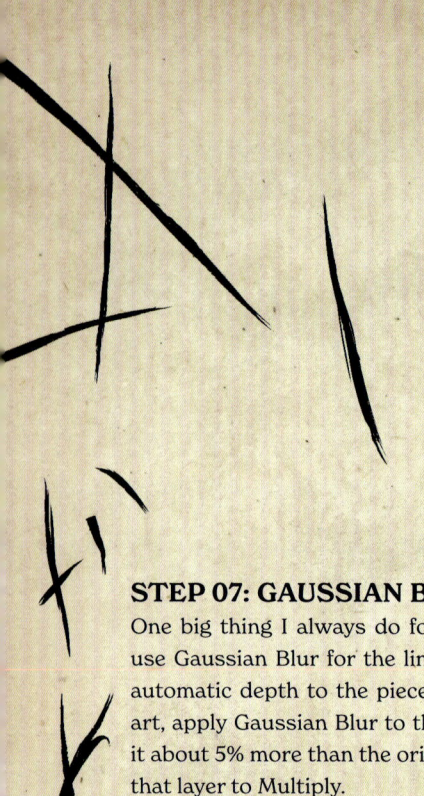

STEP 07: GAUSSIAN BLUR LINE ART

One big thing I always do for my digital work is use Gaussian Blur for the line art. It provides an automatic depth to the piece. I duplicate the line art, apply Gaussian Blur to the new layer, making it about 5% more than the original line art, and set that layer to Multiply.

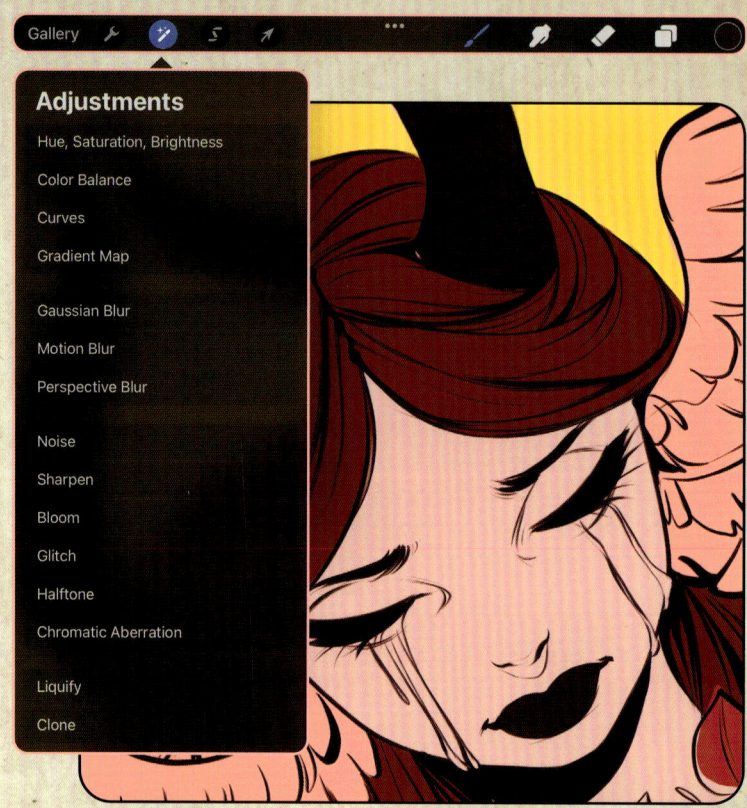

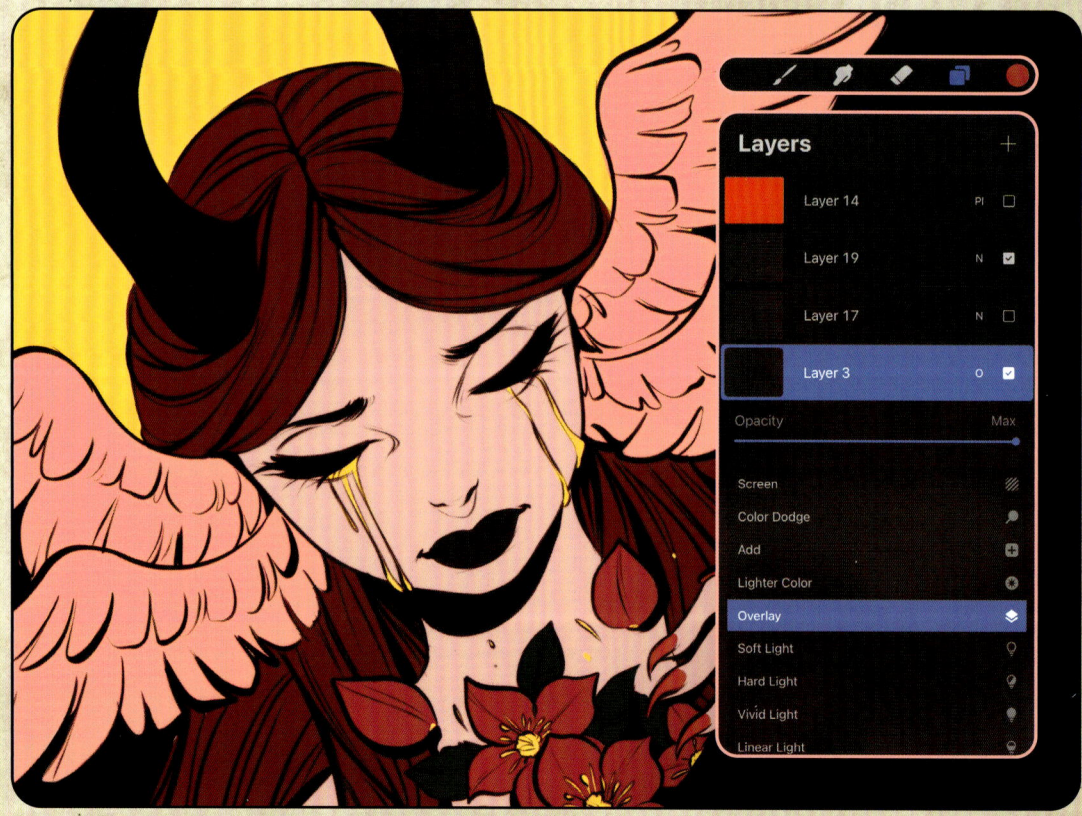

STEP 08: DETAILS

Next, I add in some small highlights and shadow details in the places that I might have missed, mostly in the background.

STEP 09: OVERLAY

To make the piece feel cohesive, I usually add an overlay of colour using Colour Dodge, but I always experiment with what looks best.

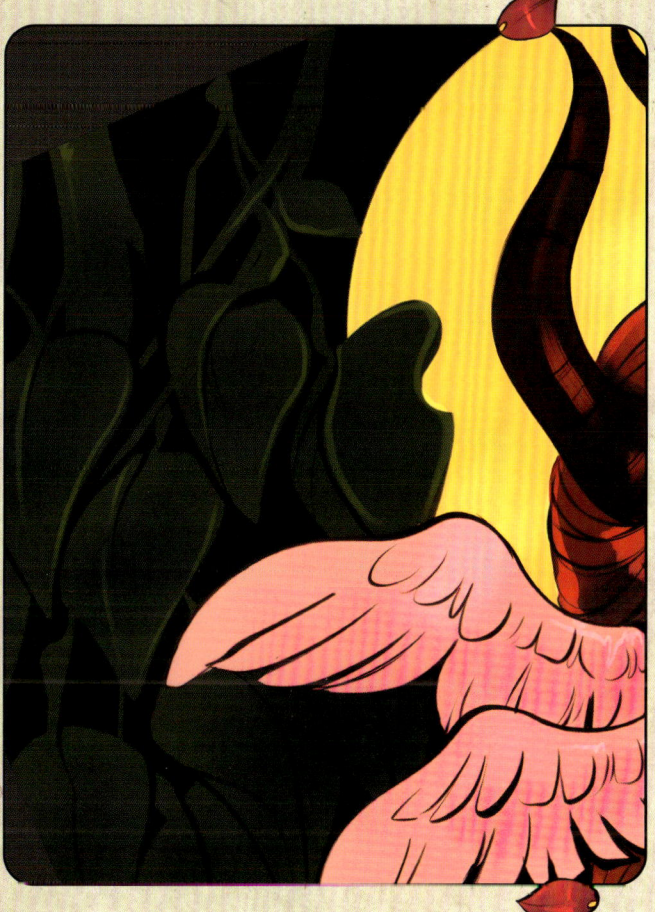

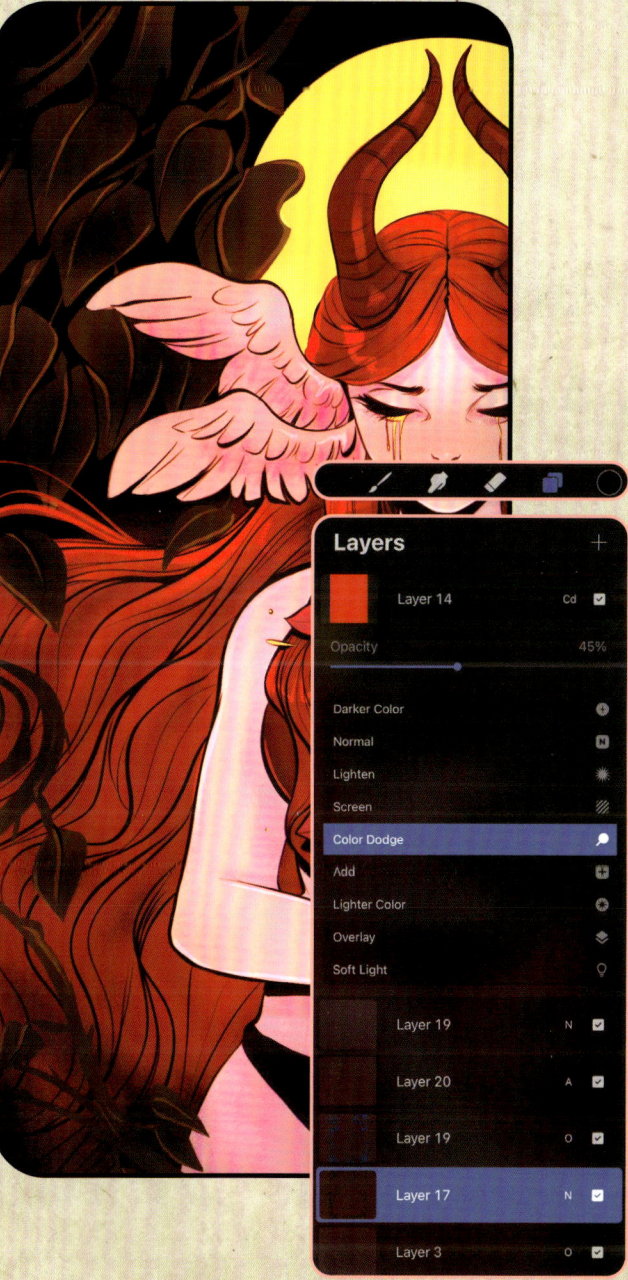

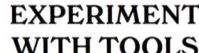

EXPERIMENT WITH TOOLS

When working digitally, there are so many tools you can use to add more to your illustration. I love using Colour Dodge to mess with lighting. I also use Add Noise to add more of an old computer-pixel type of vibe. Experiment and have fun! After all, that's the best part about painting digitally!

STEP 10: FINAL TOUCHES

At this point, the piece is pretty much done, but I do still look for any areas that might need a bit more detail or texture.

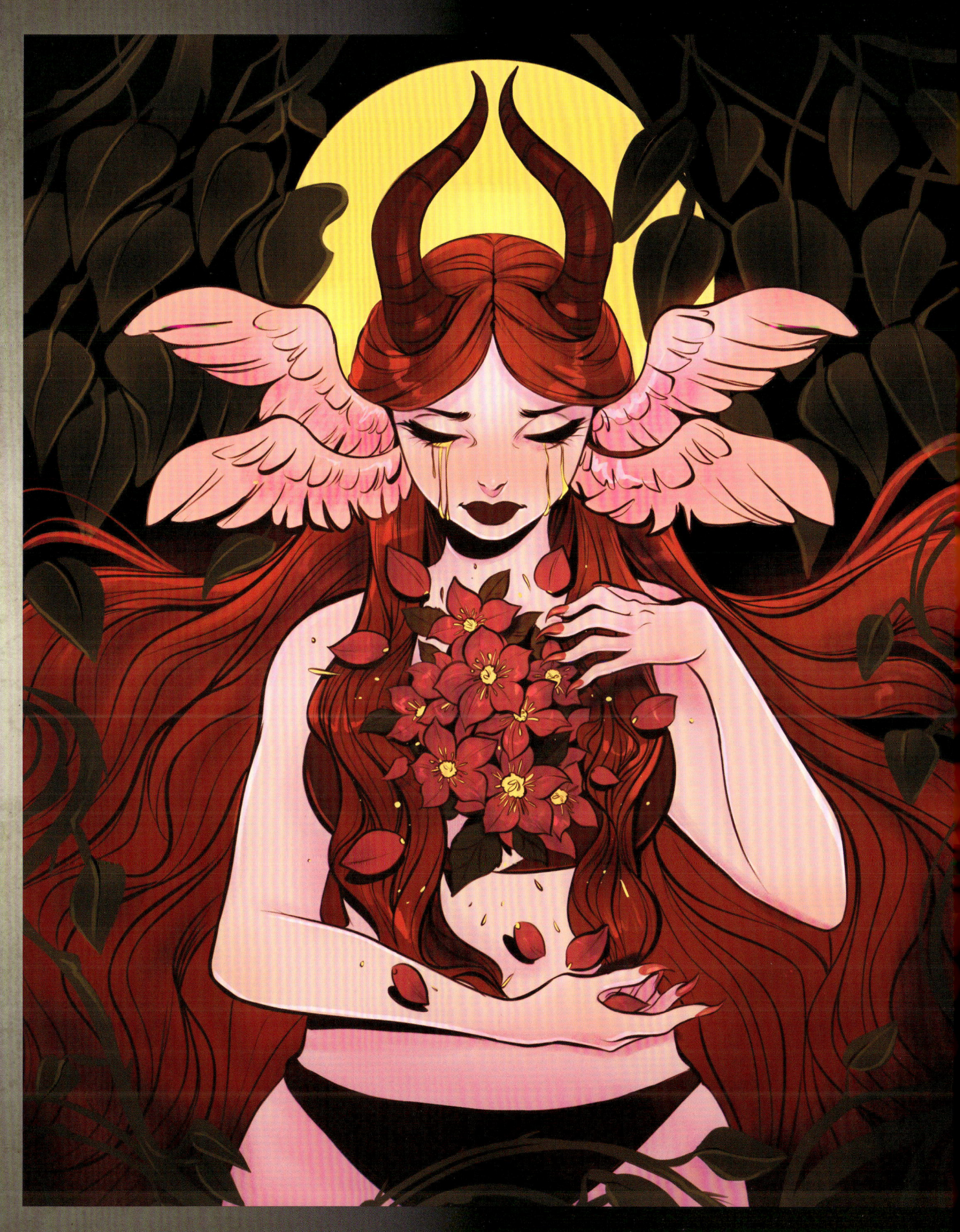

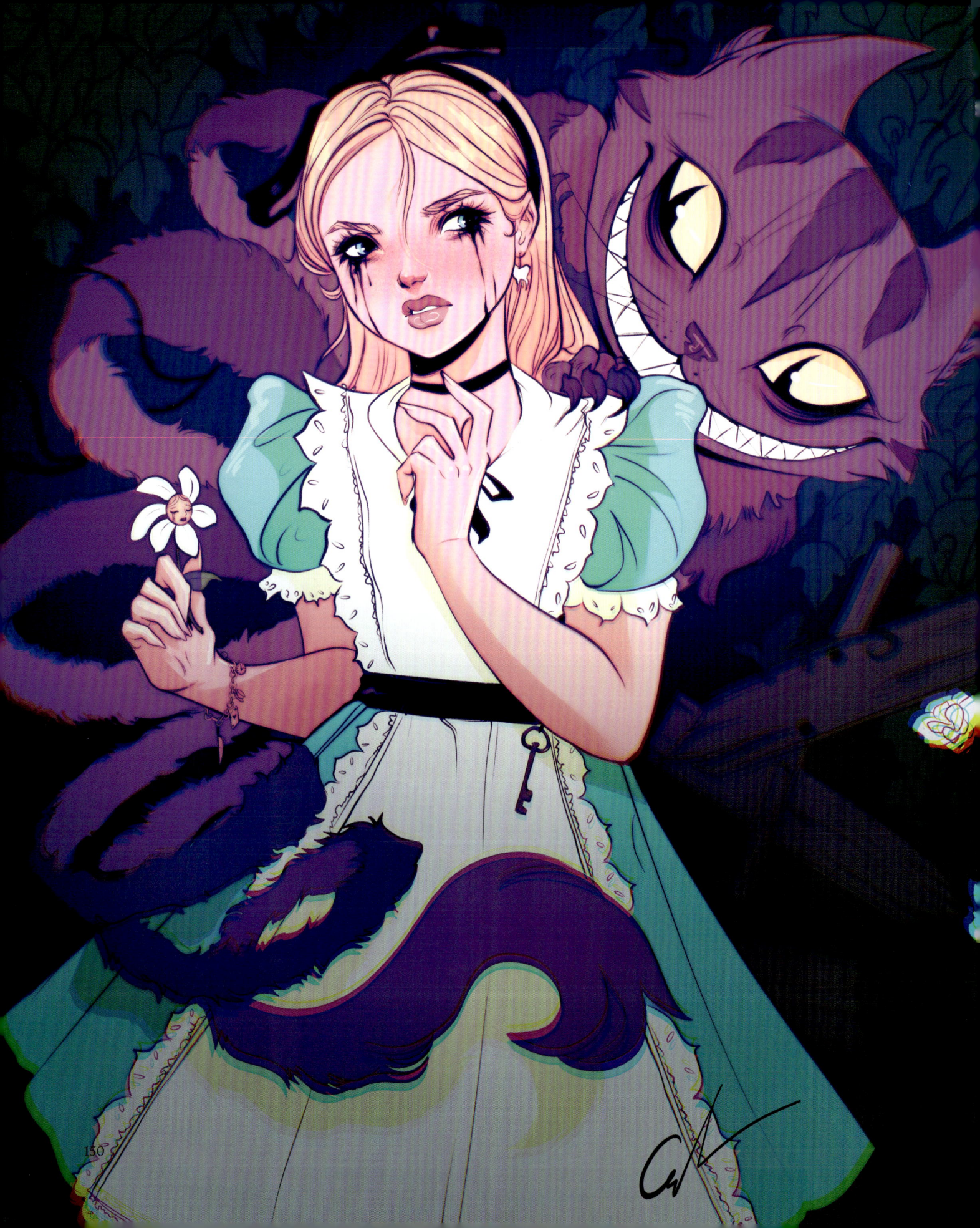

Thank you

I want to say a HUGE thank you to all of those who have supported my work in any way, big or small. I wouldn't have this book if it wasn't for the loving support of all of you out there. I'm so grateful for this opportunity. I hope it is helpful for your artistic journey in some way, or that you just had a fun time reading.

I also want to thank the team at 3dtotal for giving me this opportunity and helping me so much along the way! Thank you to Simon for putting this all together, Rhee for being with me every step of the way, Joe for the amazing layout and design work, Nicole for putting in all the hard work to make the Kickstarter happen and, of course, everyone else on the team who had a hand in making this project come to life. Thank you all so much for believing in me – I'm so honoured to have worked with all of you.

Lastly, I want to thank my friends and family: my parents for constantly helping and supporting me, my husband for being my biggest cheerleader, and my friends who have always encouraged and pushed me to be a better artist. I would not be the person I am today without the amazing support system you all have built around me.

I'm so excited to bring more art into the world and see what the future has in store!

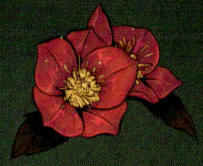

3dtotal Publishing

3dtotal Publishing is a trailblazing, creative publisher specializing in inspirational and educational resources for artists.

Our titles feature top industry professionals from around the globe who share their experience in skilfully written step-by-step tutorials and fascinating, detailed guides. Illustrated throughout with stunning artwork, these bestselling publications offer creative insight, expert advice, and essential motivation. Fans of digital art will enjoy our comprehensive volumes covering Adobe Photoshop, Procreate, and Blender, as well as our superb titles based around character design, including *Fundamentals of Character Design* and *Creating Characters for the Entertainment Industry*. The dedicated, high-quality blend of instruction and inspiration also extends to traditional art. Titles covering a range of techniques, genres, and abilities allow your creativity to flourish while building essential skills.

Well-established within the industry, we now offer over 100 titles and counting, many of which have been translated into multiple languages around the world. With something for every artist, we are proud to say that our books offer the 3dtotal package:

LEARN • CREATE • SHARE

Visit us at store.3dtotal.com

3dtotal Publishing is part of 3dtotal.com, a leading website for CG artists founded by Tom Greenway in 1999.

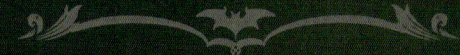

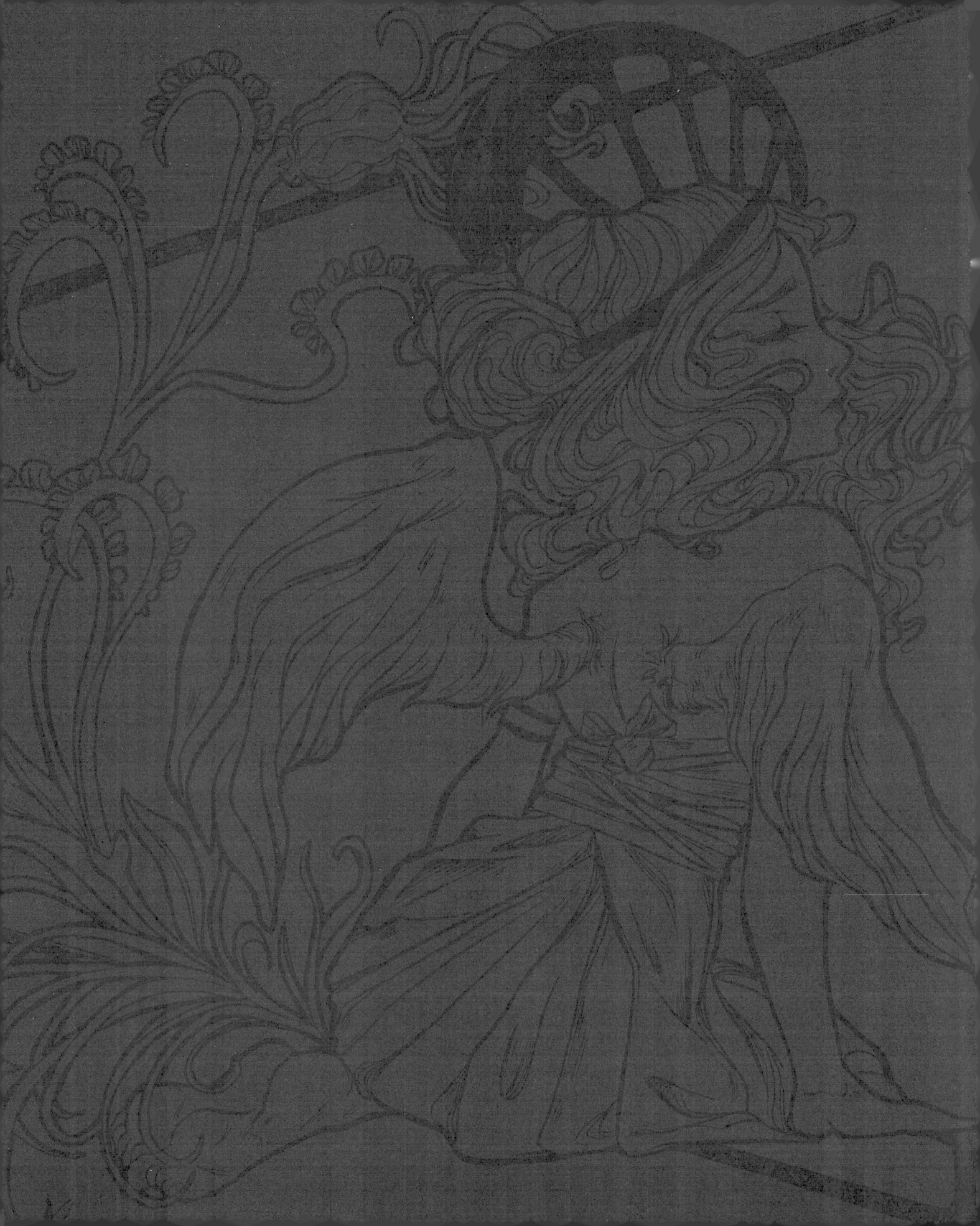